OUR BROKEN WORLD:

getting from

confrontation to cooperation

by former diplomat

John Pedler

BY THE SAME AUTHOR:

Cold war spy stories under the nom de plume Dominic Torr:-

Diplomatic Cover
The Treason Line
A Mission of Mercy
Hoodwink (in print and on Kindle, 2013)

Our Broken World: getting from confrontation to cooperation
© John Pedler, 2016

All rights reserved
The author's right to be identified as the Author of the Work is asserted under the Copyright, Designs and Patents Act 1988

Isbn: 978-0-9935018-2-1

Published by: John Pedler

Two endorsements and a review

One of Britain's outstanding diplomats and one of the world's leading proponents of 'climate change' says this about Our Broken World:

"Children like to ask their parents difficult questions. Here John Pedler takes the broadest of views, ranging from politics and science to religion and beyond, and paints a picture of the world as most of us have yet to see it. As a former diplomat there is almost nowhere he does not know; and as a writer he puts a thousand stories together, this time for grownups, and makes elegant and convincing sense of them."

     Sir Crispin Tickell, GCMG, KCVO, FZS

Leading international journalist, John Pilger, widely known for his criticism of current governmental policies worldwide says:

"In these wise reflections, John Pedler reminds us that the best diplomats are mavericks, exceptions to the rules of power. Acutely aware of history and a sense of right and wrong, Pedler exemplifies an intellectual and moral independence that's all too rare today."

Pre-publication review by Claire Coveney for Population Matters -

If, like me, you have read many books on the subject of population growth, the impact of global warming, mass consumption and globalization, and fancy something a little less 'dry' shall we say, then I thoroughly recommend this book.

Described as a 'former diplomat's weltanschauung', this book is essentially an essay that John Pedler (who is indeed a former British diplomat), now 85, describes as an effort to answer all of his children's questions about his life, his opinions, what he has learnt from his many years of service etc.

Not your average starting point for a book that covers huge subjects; a snapshot of which includes: religion, war, terrorism, science, the media, as far-reaching as World War II, to Rupert Murdoch's media empire, to the current civil war in Syria. However, the result is a captivatingly honest and emotive (without being sentimental) essay on how these factors have all collectively influenced the way in which governments and individuals consider the major issues that the world is facing today, such as populations growth and climate destabilisation.

This book is not despairing or preachy, but rather heart-felt, insightful, and at times quite funny. The over-riding sentiment I believe can be felt in these imploring words by Pedler in a section titled 'The next generation': 'A house is built of many bricks, but each one must be laid and each one plays its part however minuscule in the creation of the whole building.' A message that at times can get lost in the sea of academic documentation on the major problems that the world is currently facing, which is why 'Our Broken World' is so refreshing.

About the weltanschauung genre

This essay is an example of a new genre: the weltanschauung (world view) genre. Although it is listed under all of these, it is not history, nor foreign affairs, nor comparative religion. Nor is it autobiography or a memoir- there is only a minimum about the author, just enough to place his view of the world.

There are quite a few books in this genre, a genre which deserves to be added to the present BIC and BISAC book categories. At present this one is BIC: JPSL/geopolitics and HRAM2/ religion and politics. The BISAC is: POL011010/international relations/ diplomacy and REL017000/religion/comparative religion.

Just one other example is: 'Watching The Tree' by Adeline Yen Mah which tells us much about what it is like to be Chinese with only a minimum about herself.

Merriam-Webster definition of *WELTANSCHAUUNG* as an English word:- 'a comprehensive conception or apprehension of the world, especially from a specific standpoint'.

Origin of *WELTANSCHAUUNG:* German, from *Welt* world + *Anschauung* view. First Known Use: 1868

For my children

and, in due course, for my grandchildren

- - - - - -

Anyone who challenges the prevailing orthodoxy
finds himself silenced with surprising effectiveness

George Orwell, 1984

The owl of Athena flies only at dusk

Ancient Greek saying cited by G. W. F. Hegel

Mastering the Future Before the Future Masters Us

Subtitle of a book by Professor Leon Fuerth

With acknowledgements to Microsoft's 'Word for Mac'
without which this essay could not have been written.

Part I - The material world

Guide to contents:

- p 1   'SETTING THE STAGE'
- p 3   FROM THE BEGINNING TO THE ATOM BOMB
- p 9   EXISTENTIAL CHALLENGES: CLIMATE AND POPULATION
- p 29   GOVERNMENTS AND THESE CHALLENGES
- p 56   POLITICS, IDEOLOGIES, CAPITALISM
- p 72   OUR WORLD TODAY: HOW DID IT GET THAT WAY?
- p 81   EXTREMIST ISLAM
- p 99   MAINLY ABOUT RUSSIA & EUROPE
- p 113   HOW CONFRONTATION RETURNED
- p 119   THE UK & EUROPE: SEEN FROM A BACK SEAT
- p 133   MY OWN MINI-PARTICIPATION IN EVENTS: BOSNIA, CAMBODIA, LAOS
- p 148   THE BANKERS, LEADING ON TO ISRAEL/PALESTINE
- p 155   SOME WORDS ON DIPLOMACY
- p 166   INDOCHINA – MY TWO WARTIME VISITS
- p 175   RICH AND POOR
- p 183   SEX, PROSTITUTION, HOMOSEXUALITY, 'GAY' MARRIAGE & 'PC'
- p 195   THE MEDIA, TRADITIONAL AND ELECTRONIC SNOOPING
- p 202   GETTING OLD

Guide to contents Part II – 'THE BEYOND' - is at page 207. The POSTSCRIPT is at page 273

By way of introduction:

If humanity is to deal with the twin existential threats we all face - climate change and over-population - we'll have to exchange our present age of confrontation for an era of cooperation. This won't be easy - confrontation, whether for individuals or for nations, comes all too easily, cooperation demands far more of us.

Here I explain how, since the two World Wars, we have arrived at our present impasse of civil wars, armed interventions, gross inequality, and religious extremism (not confined to Islam). I go on to discuss how, if mankind is to survive, we'll have to rethink our present approach - among other things - to the doctrine of 'growth', gross inequality, education for women, ownership of the media, objective information for voters, control of banking, our reluctance to invest massively in the future - and our near universal worship of the golden calf. And I stress how diplomacy can be critical in overcoming the impulse to confront, and instead to cooperate - provided it is given a chance. Right now this is particularly important in the case of Europe - both the European Union in the west and Russia in the east. For Europe, as a whole, has a major part to play on the world stage, leading towards that era of cooperation. I stress how, what divides us now must and can be removed.

The December 2015 United Nations Conference on Climate Change has given some grounds for hope that that move towards cooperation has begun now that 196 or so of the world's rulers have a last recognised unanimously the existential nature of this challenge. But 55% of the countries producing 55% of greenhouse gasses have to ratify the agreement before it is binding – and, given the continued obstruction of the U.S. Republican Party which has blocked American progress on climate since the election of President G. W. Bush in 2001, the all but essential US ratification remains in doubt. Indeed, the Conference is no more than a long delayed beginning - it will take an immense effort at all levels to gather the momentum needed to make real progress towards that era of cooperation. This cannot be left to the world's politicians – as I mention, they are constrained more than the rest of us from bringing about the change of direction that our predicament requires.

Diplomats and those involved in foreign affairs, can rarely reveal what they really think about the world situation as a whole, so this book is something of an exception. Diplomats, like members of the armed forces, must follow the policies decided by Ministers otherwise their country would have neither a foreign nor a defence policy. Those in 'think tanks' often need to temper their views to accord with the outlook of their sponsors. Journalists in foreign affairs must trim their views to reflect the politics of their employer - and, increasingly nowadays, must also avoid giving offence to advertisers.

And we consultants need to confine our work to the matter at hand - for our positions on other matters could well lose us a client! But now on the brink of retirement, I can at last speak out - indeed I believe I should speak out for I find that my approach to the world today broadly reflects the outlook of many others involved with international affairs - as is suggested by the endorsements I have been so fortunate to have from Sir Crispin Tickell and John Pilger.

Anyone's 'world view' will at some point all but inevitably raise hackles or concerns such that the rest of what one says gets passed over. One such subject of contention is Russia, the leitmotif of Part I where, along with distinguished company, I part for now with the received wisdom of governments and media. And then there are those 'concerns': perhaps the easiest way to attract attention today is to find an enthusiastic 'celebrity' to support you. One I approached told me "Your book opened my eyes to the state of the world, thanks so much; but I'm afraid I can't be associated with your take on marriage".

As this is not an academic work, but a book for the general reader concerned about the way the world is going, I'm presenting it in the form of answers to the questions I'm being asked – and which are being asked increasingly by an ever wider section of the public in ever more countries. My adult children are no exceptions - so, to keep the tone informal, it is their questions that I answer: a composite of what they've asked over the years. The answers sum up the conclusions I've reached about our world as a whole – the material world (Part I) and what I have called 'the beyond' (Part II) where I consider the phenomenon of religious discord that so troubles us today.

Although I have written for the general reader, I think this essay will fill in some gaps for those diplomats, foreign affairs gurus, and the media's foreign affairs specialists. Many of us are specialists, so finding how a colleague views the overall picture can add usefully to our understanding.

I write especially for the young – the next generation worldwide who will have to deal with the daunting problems we are bequeathing them.

This book differs from many others in that I come from no ideology - for example I find the concepts of 'left' and 'right' outdated and unhelpful. I belong to no party. I have no preconceived views - it is what works, what could best solve our problems, that interests me: a non-ideological pragmatism, if you like. I have no national bias beyond that Europe is my country, East and West, and I believe that it has a major role to play if mankind is to have a better chance of surviving those looming existential threats. I am not a historian nor a theologian so I'd be grateful for corrections where I've made factual errors despite my 'googles' and several other check-ups to avoid them. I'm on: dipconsult@hotmail.com

Part I
The material world

You've been involved with foreign affairs most of your working life so we expect the state of the world will take up quite a bit of your weltanschauung. But first we'd like you to kind of 'set the stage'. How do you see the first quarter of our twenty-first century in history, meaning in the whole story of mankind?

Yes, 'setting the stage' is good idea. I'll try to do that in a moment. And yes, world affairs must make up quite a bit of what I've got to say. I've been a rather privileged observer of the international scene since 1951 when I joined the Foreign Service (now the Diplomatic Service) though I've played only a minuscule part. But just because I was never a significant actor, I've nothing to defend - no actions of mine, no ideology, no nation or political party - and so I can look back impartially and try to make some sense of what I've learned. At least that's what I'm trying to do, though I expect it will raise quite a few hackles!

I ought to warn you at the outset that I believe the world is going in an altogether wrong direction right now, and that something of a U term is required if humanity is to survive for a couple or more millennia. When I started writing this for you I wanted, in Part I, to bring out the immense importance of Europe, East and West, speaking with a single voice on the great issues and in particular on the existential challenges facing mankind in the first quarter of the 21st century. That means: 1) the UK (including Scotland!) remaining in the EU and playing a leading role in the reform of its institutions. 2) The EU and Russia cooperating to this end.

But even as I was writing the politicians, EU and Russian, through sheer ineptitude, have brought about not cooperation but confrontation between them over the Ukraine. And UK politicians have succeeded, equally ineptly, in still further alienating UK voters leading to the rise of the isolationist
United Kingdom Independence Party (UKIP) which wants the UK out of the EU. And the Scottish referendum looms right now and

the UK itself threatens to unravel! As I finalise this essay in early June 2014 I'm afraid it may be harder than ever to reverse these isolationist trends in both the UK and Russia - one at the extreme west of Europe and the other at the extreme east. These severely threaten humanity's ability to deal with the interrelated challenges of climate destabilisation and over-population. I can only hope that - as so often happens - real national interests will return to the fore before too long.

There has been some unexpected good news in the last three months - there's been an unexpected surge in worldwide government, corporation, and public awareness of climate destabilisation and the need to do something about it. This widespread perception should help end the hold 'climate change deniers' have over the Republican party in this autumn's US elections. Perhaps though, it is too much to hope that any set-back for the Republicans would suffice to end the paralysis they have brought to the US government which would free America to take a lead over climate instead of continuing to delay action by others.

That said, I believe history shows that mankind is capable of fundamental changes where survival is concerned. And we now have the technological and biological revolutions to help us end our fixation with confrontation and usher in an era of international cooperation which is absolutely essential if we want a future. The alternative is for humanity to ride to extinction through its inability to escape the evolutionary struggle which got us here, but which also pits man against man.

Our evolution has required two distinct ways of behaving: confrontation and cooperation.

To survive, we have to confront other species from mammoths to viruses, including our fellow men. But this confrontation has been accompanied by cooperation - for the tribe must act together whether to hunt or to prevail against other humans. And today that means cooperating no longer on a tribe or nation scale, but on a world scale thanks to globalisation - and thanks too, to the need for unprecedented cooperation worldwide to meet those daunting existential challenges mankind now faces.

If we continue to confront each other as we are doing now we humans will go to perdition with our wars becoming ever more vicious as the ecological net fastens around us. But if the nations can put aside strife and enter a new era of cooperation, seeking to overcome these existential challenges all of them face, then human ingenuity may well find the answers. But how long will that take - or will it be too late?

I believe diplomacy has an indispensable role to play here - provided it ceases to be the handmaid of the military, and the military instead becomes the handmaid of diplomacy.

But diplomacy, that fundamental tool of statesmanship, is not a science but an art, and like all arts there are basic rules which must be respected unless there is some truly overriding reason to break one, or even more of them. It is not only dictators who ignore this - now and again our own leaders have also failed, usually simply by ignoring common sense, or by clinging to some out-dated preconceptions.

FROM THE BEGINNING TO THE ATOM BOMB

Setting the scene

To my mind, these few years in this first half of the 21st century may well prove to be the most important in the (Stoemer/Crutzen) anthropocene period in the world's history: will it be curtains for mankind? Or are we on the cusp of a new historical period - the overlapping eras of the technological revolution that began in the 20th century and the biological revolution of our 21st century - both of which stemmed from the scientific revolution of the 16th, 17th and 18th centuries enabling the Industrial Revolution of the 19th century?

The biological revolution really began with the discovery in 1953 of the double helix form of the molecule that encodes the instructions for all forms of life. This was followed in 2003 by the success of the Human Genome Project which 'maps' our genes. Very soon after that, in 2010, the 'richest, most powerful man in biotechnology' J. Craig Venter revealed that his team had made a new self-replicating creature (Laurie Garret *Biology's Brave New World* Foreign Affairs for Nov/Dec 2013). Like nuclear research which led both to the atom bomb and to nuclear power, this 'synbio-revolution' holds grave implications for 'dual use' - for construction and for destruction (one might say 'for good and for evil'). Man now has the techniques necessary to create a virus capable of wiping out homo sapiens or at least greatly reducing its numbers. So it could be that Man himself will do nature's work in solving the overpopulation problem!

We cannot know what the nascent biological revolution holds in store. Even now concentrated thought can activate an apparatus. What about input - will it be possible electronically to insert information into a brain, for example a language? Or to know what someone is thinking? Just Science Fiction? Perhaps but there will certainly be surprises and also serious problems about 'dual use'.

There is such a huge disparity now between our amazing ability to reach conclusions and make progress with the so called 'exact sciences' based on mathematics, and our present inability to make much real progress with the social sciences where human psychology and behaviour are involved: notably economics, sociology, psychology, and - most of all - politics. Yet these four 'feeble reed' inexact sciences (which undergraduates tend to disparage as 'the easy option') are also just as essential to our understanding of the world. What I have to say is mainly about the social sciences, not the ones based on mathematics. Just as well, for I have difficulty even in counting my change!

Indeed these are the disciplines we have mainly to rely on to get the vital decisions taken for mankind's survival at this critical juncture in history. As I say, what we are still witnessing today is the primordial 'man against man' mind-set of struggle and war. The mutation from confrontation to cooperation requires nothing less than a total rethink: hard indeed, but not impossible provided the inexact sciences work in concert with the ever-growing resources of the exact sciences of the technological/biological revolution. Mankind needs to promote cooperation from being an internal matter for nation states, to becoming a worldwide imperative.

Where we are today in the story of mankind

Yes, your question does indeed bring us straight to the heart of my thinking about the material world - though of course I'll have a bit to say about the spiritual element in life in Part II. Here's the way I look at it:-

By 'the story of mankind' I expect you date that from the appearance of a sentient primate which is conscious of its own existence and is aware that it will die? And perhaps more precisely of one that has conscious awareness, however primitive, of what is, or is not, in the interests of the tribe - a nascent conscience? We are told that something like our homo sapiens has been around for around 200,000 years, but just when he became self-aware we don't know, nor when the sense of right and wrong developed. Curiously, that fits well with the Adam and Eve story where the history of Man starts with the awareness of good and evil.

Let's look a moment at the larger time-scale in which we exist and we see that the story of Man is but a tiny blip within a blip. For they now say the 'big bang' happened some 13 billion years ago, that the world was formed some 4.5 billion years ago, and that life arrived here some 3.5 billion years ago. So the appearance of homo sapiens is indeed just a tiny blip in time. Then 'history began' some 12,000 years ago with the Agricultural Revolution when land was cleared and crops grew feeding classes of people who did not grow them - and that's a blip within that blip. Take that one stage further and our lives, however long, are just a teeny blip within that little blip of 'history'.

We don't know with much precision when Man, beginning his worldwide diaspora, was the 'new thing' out of Africa ('*ex Africa aliquid semper nova*' as the Romans said). But there is much agreement that around 30,000 years ago Cro Magnon and other peoples had arrived as far north as France. Then there was that Agricultural Revolution around 10,000 years ago making what we call 'civilisation' possible, each with its class structure (e.g. kings to slaves) and its own customs, laws, and religion.

When 'history' began

The earliest writing creating 'history', in the sense of records from the past, began in Mesopotamia (cuneiform, developing from hieroglyphs), and in China (characters also developing from hieroglyphs), and ancient Egypt (hieroglyphs that we can still see today). These are all from around 5,000 years ago. Alphabetic writing (abc) and abjad (first four letters of semitic –'alphabets': e.g. Arabic and Hebrew) are both about 3,000 years old. What I find fascinating it that it seems all alphabetic writing derives from Egyptian hieroglyphs which contain phonetic elements as Jean-François Champollion discovered when he was finally able to read ancient Egyptian scripts. This was some twenty years after Napoleon's troops in Egypt found the famous Rosetta Stone with the same text in hieroglyphs, Demotic (a sort of simplified vernacular form of Eyptian hieroglyphs), and Greek.

That gives you a sense of how scarcely believably long (billions of years) it has taken to come to where we are today and how extremely short (some ten thousands of years) is the story of Man. And the history of civilisation is very much less than that. And it's now only a couple of hundred years since the Industrial Revolution began and only about three quarters of a century since the very first computer was built to break German codes in the second World War.

I have thought all this worth mentioning because it illustrates dramatically a fundamental fact we all know: the vast disparity between the time it takes to create and the mere moment it takes to destroy: 13bn years to produce humanity and the thousand or so years we need to wipe ourselves out. (I'm not challenging the 'creationists' for, allowing the existence of God, He is, as Muslims say, 'the Owner of Time'. Being outside time 13bn years isn't even a blip! He can say "let there be…" and it may take billions of years to happen!)

We live in this fascinating nano-blip in time where we can do so many things no one could do when my father was born in 1891 before motor cars, and my mother in 1901 before aeroplanes. When I was 18 what joy I felt to have been born, just late enough in history, to live the dream of Daedalus and his son Icarus, and be up in the sky with bird-like freedom flying an RAF Tiger Moth just 43 years after that first flight at Kitty Hawk! And what delight I feel today with my computer writing this and, with a couple of clicks, I'm in touch with friends pretty well anywhere in the world!

From agriculture to industry and the acceleration of scientific discoveries

Life for most people in Britain at the dawn of the 19th century was basically similar to that in societies which appeared in the wake of that Agricultural Revolution. There had of course been a great many advances since then, but they had come only slowly over the millennia. Then quite suddenly, built on those mathematical and scientific discoveries since the 16th century, there came the massive acceleration of change brought about by the Industrial Revolution. These spawned the advances we are witnessing today with new discoveries and new applications occurring ever faster with each year that passes. The law of diminishing returns suggests that this acceleration cannot last - but there is no sign of that yet.

To the atom bomb and Mutually Assured Destruction - MAD

In the 20th century what we call 'progress' was even more astonishing than in the 19th which ended with the motor car only half born and powered flight unknown. In 1899 electricity had only just begun to come to private houses and surgery under anaesthetic was still in its infancy. Nobel's high explosives also were new - enabling the Alpine railway tunnels to be bored, but enabling too, a revolution in warfare. From 1900 the necessary technology developed with surprising rapidity until we arrive less than half a century later when Man could destroy himself with the atomic bombs he had made.

Some time in 1960s, when mankind had begun to live with the hydrogen bomb, some people were wondering whether any other civilisation in the universe had broken through to the scientific age and survived. Was science and its application a gateway to a new future for intelligent life, or had it already proved catastrophically destructive on other planets? Have we arrived at the 'end times' or is this a frightening period of transition leading to a better future? This remains impossible to answer. Although listening posts were set up in an attempt to intercept meaningful radio emissions from outer space, none have yet been discovered. And although we are finding planets in our galaxy that could possibly provide conditions for life, intelligent life is quite another matter. But in the whole universe with its billions of planets it is reasonable to assume that we are not alone but just far too far away both in space and in in time, to benefit from mutual experiences.

Proliferation of thermonuclear bombs

Once made, an invention is all but impossible to suppress and very often extremely difficult to control, as it has proved with nuclear bombs and is proving with viruses. So we in the 21st century continue to live in the shadow of the 'atom bomb' developed in the mid-20th century. Attempts to prevent the proliferation of nuclear weapons consume much time that could be devoted to new at least equally important concerns. And, even so, experts warn that not nearly enough is being done to prevent catastrophic accidents given the immense quantities of nuclear materials the nuclear powers possess, and to ensure that none can be hi-jacked by terrorists. And all the while the nuclear bomb hangs over our heads along with the other challenges which are quickly becoming apparent. (See *'Command and Control, Nuclear Weapons, the Damascus Accident and the Illusion of Safety'*, Eric Schlosser). As for threats of 'first use' - remember the legal dictum: 'You use a gun if you point a gun when you rob a bank'.

EXISTENTIAL CHALLENGES: CLIMATE & POPULATION

Over-population

During the 20th century we added to the nuclear threat still further - very possibly even less easily controlled - existential threats: the 'double whammy' of over-population and climate change. Characteristically - because they point to the need for hard and unpopular decisions - politicians have still not generally accepted that both these threats result from human behaviour: entirely in the case of over-population and at least very largely in the case of 'Climate Change'.

It was my colleague in the Diplomatic Service, Sir Crispin Tickell, who fully awakened me (and far more importantly, Prime Minister Mrs Thatcher!) to the international implications of climate change - his *'Climatic Change and World Affairs'*, 1977). Following Tickell I prefer 'Climate Destabilisation' for we can't see any new more-or-less stable climate emerging, only that the climate we've known - more-or-less - since historic times is fast losing its relative stability. Extreme events are already becoming much more frequent, if not even more extreme. I write just after the publication of the latest and most disturbing UN report from the Intergovernmental Panel on Climate Change (IPCC) calling for immediate action by governments.

Malthus etc.

When I was at university in the latter 1940's there was much dispute about the Reverend Malthus' *'Essay on the Principle of Population'* (1798). There was a divide between those who argued about technicalities (for example whether Malthus was correct in observing that population increased 'geometrically' whereas food production could only be increased 'arithmetically') and those who saw the larger picture: that increases in the world's population, whatever was done about agriculture, must inevitably lead eventually to planetary over-population unless drastic steps are taken to reduce the number of births per woman.

I was soon convinced that that was the right way to look at over-population given the immense improvements in transport (limiting localised famine) hygiene and medicine (drastically reducing maternal and infantile death rates). Before the end of 19th century growth of world population had been slow largely because of maternal deaths and the death of children before the age of five. We say it is terrible to lose a child - parents should die first. But, even in the UK, it was only in the first years of the 20th century that death rates for the under fives began to drop from a historic 20%. That began with the spread of vaccinations (notably after Jenner) against smallpox and the discovery of micro-organisms (notably after Pasteur, the first really to follow up Leuvenhoek's microscopic discoveries at the end of the 17th century).

Britain's nearly thre fold increase in population (despite massive emigration) in the 19th century would have had severe consequences if the industrial revolution had not made Britain 'the workshop of the world' and had it not come to import so large a proportion of its food from abroad after the repeal of the Corn Laws in 1846.

By 1947 when I was a still a student those factors, transport, hygiene and medicine, were increasingly having their effects so that population was rising throughout the world at least as fast as it had in Britain in the 19th century. The dogmas of religion, the forces of tradition, and the need to rely on one's progeny in old age, favoured this expansion. And the effects of industrialisation and women's education were lagging so markedly in the non-industrialised world that it was clear that the progressively lower birth rates we had experienced in England thanks to rising living standards and birth control, would be long delayed for the most populated parts of the world. Thus world population would massively increase from the then 2 ½ billion which some of our teachers were suggesting was about optimal for this planet.

Some figures of population growth since 1950

In the sixty years from 1950 to 2010 world population grew from around 2.5 billion to around 7 billion - nearly threefold, like

Britain in the 19th century. And, just to take a few examples by country, in those sixty years the population increased: Nigeria from 31 to 161m - over 5 times; Iran from 16 to 77m - nearly 5 times; Brazil from 53 to 201m -nearly four times; Pakistan 40 to 184m - over 4 ½ times; China (despite the one child policy since 1979) from 562 to 1,330m - nearly 2.5 times. And likewise, India 359m to 1,210m - also nearly 2.5 times.

I find the cases of Egypt, Iraq and Syria among the most disturbing. Egypt's population grew from 21 to 80 million - nearly 4 times, Iraq had some 5.2m in 1950 and some 31.5m today - an increase of about 6 times. In Iraq the number of children per woman has fallen from no less than 7.3 to 4.8 - but improvements in hygiene and health care mean there is still a marked population increase, though this is likely to have been much reduced with the US/UK invasion and the resultant civil war. And Syria had some 3.4m in 1950 and 24m today, no less than 7 times! Here too, the on-going civil war appears to have reduced if not ended any further increase.

By contrast the population of Europe only grew from 549m to 742m - increasing by just over 1/3. Of course this low figure is partially explained by the loss of 60 million or more who died as a result of the second world war (which reduced the then world population by as much as 2.5%!) But even allowing for lower fertility as a result of this slaughter the link between living standards and population growth is clear - and one only needs to look round the world to see that overpopulation and extreme poverty are closely linked.

At present there are many demographic experts who decry the falling fertility rates in much of the world because of the burdens that will fall on the younger generation - and they will indeed be hard to mitigate. But there are many others who welcome lower fertility substantially below the 2.1 children per woman (needed to maintain a steady population) because of the vital need to reduce the pressure of over-population on the planet. These are the neo-Malthusians and I believe that quite clearly they are right. We certainly don't want nature to resolve the over-population problem with its ruthless ways!

Over-population - economics and politics

Right now there's a lot about the turmoil in Egypt. Few point out that the fourfold increase in population in a country with exceptionally little agricultural land has led to Egypt being unable even to finance its food imports. The result - as food prices rise - is increased poverty and unemployment, street protests and violence. No matter who rules Egypt over-population is the country's fundamental problem. Today's solution is a huge subsidy from Saudi Arabia - but this comes at a price: any Egyptian government must bend to the wishes of the donors.

Look around the Middle East and its civil wars or uprisings, look too at Syria's sixfold and Iraq's sevenfold increase of population - only the ruthless Saddam Hussein, and Assad father and son, were able for a while to cow their subjects into submission. The population problems of so many Muslim countries lie behind the simmering discontent. Indeed recent research has shown that over-population and related unemployment, results in poverty, not religion, being the primary motive for young men from 'third world' countries joining terrorist groupings. Over-population has many unexpected side-effects!

'Green Revolution' a one time fix?

During the period of the 'green revolution', from around 1950 to the end of the '70s, grain production increased so dramatically with new varieties, improved fertilizers and insecticides that 'neo-Malthusians' like Paul Ehrlich *('The population Bomb'*, 1968) were dismissed for unfounded pessimism when their forecasts of demographic disaster failed to materialise. But few took into account how far the 'green revolution' had succeeded in producing more crops only because of the huge increase in inputs needed to achieve such striking results: notably fertiliser, fuel, insecticides and water - each with its disadvantages, environmental costs, and shortages.

Because of this the 'green revolution' was far from the definitive agricultural answer to Malthus that it appeared to be. Still, it was an agricultural 'fix' which successfully matched food production to increased population for a decade and more. But it was a one time 'fix'. The next time population demands greatly increased food production human ingenuity will have to devise some other solution necessarily with less damaging side effects - but right now there is no sign that this will prove possible.

<u>Some further effects of over-population</u>

Now though, we are beginning, far too late, to realise that over-population is not only a matter of whether we can feed some 10 billion people on the planet (the number now predicted for 2050 unless some sociological change takes place or major international action is taken in time) but what are the other implications if we do reach such a figure, or even if we begin a slow decline. Will there be water enough for people as well as the increased demand for irrigation (for agriculture given the 'green revolution') and for industry (few of us realise how much water is needed for industrial production)? Will there be 'lebensraum' even with the growing concentration of population in cities? How many others will live below even the harshest poverty line? What habitat will be left for nature? As man increasingly impinges, will the world's rain forests, already decimated, still exist as an effective 'carbon sink'? Will the increasing number of the comparatively rich, with their demand for bovine meat, force much needed grain and much needed land to be devoted to animal consumption?

The interconnection between over-population and climate is particularly well illustrated by the Amazon rain forest. That four times increase in Brazil's population has led to massive deforestation which is now threatening the very existence of this immense 'sink' absorbing a large proportion of the carbon generated by burning oil and coal. Largely, this is to provide land for the production of beef for the increasing numbers of the more affluent. It is beef farming that uses the most area of any form of agriculture.

Indeed, will the rapidly growing 'middle class' throughout the world with their demand for 'stuff' as their income rises, do immeasurable harm to the environment (and climate) at the expense of the even more rapidly increasing numbers of the poor and the desperately poor?

As the answer to all these questions is 'very probably not' neo-Malthusian thinking is back in vogue in some influential scientific circles. Even in 1947 it was possible to forecast with some certainty that, failing a world campaign to lower the birth rate in the un-industrialised countries (it was already tapering off in industrialised Europe, even in Italy where over-population only a short while earlier had led to massive emigration) that a Malthusian scenario was bound to occur, possibly even within the lifetime of us students.

So over-population has been at the centre of my political and international thinking all my working life. To summarise, what we foresaw was immense pressure to increase acreage for agriculture which would lead to the reduction of the world's forests and their wild life; a huge increase in demand for water for both agriculture and industry, as well as for population, which would prove difficult or impossible to meet; a huge increase in demand for all manner of commodities from coal and oil to minerals required to meet vastly increased demand for the products we in the West have long enjoyed. And perhaps worst, the inability to meet just the basic human needs of the majority of a newly swollen humanity. In other words, while eliminating the world's worst poverty was perfectly possible with a population of 2–3 billion, soon into the second millennia, without massive action, it would become impossible to curb scarcely endurable poverty - even unendurable poverty - and so the premature death of many millions. Since that is the way nature solves over-population, we humans should surely find a better way?

What can we do about over-population?

Of course world population is something we can do something

about if there is the will, for example through the education of women and directly through birth control of one kind or another. Unfortunately there is the opposition, in particular, of Islam and the Catholic Church. Much of Islam believes that God will provide for population increase, and the Qu'ran enjoins 'procreate and abound in number'. The Old Testament likewise enjoins 'be fruitful and multiply'.

The Catholic Church (notably the encyclical Humanae Vitae of Pope Paul VI in 1968) forbids artificial birth control. But there is also the Catholic teaching that one must not go against one's conscience if properly informed (and anyway birth control is classed as a minor sin). This is invoked by Xanana Gusmão, the first president of East Timor - for though a Catholic, he knows well that without population control East Timor will fail as a state.

Although ambiguous, the teachings of the two major monotheistic religions have greatly impeded the spread of birth control particularly in 'third world' countries that need it most. It is to me strange that their God can only speak once. Genesis is said to have been written in the 15th century CE - three and a half thousand years ago when world population is assessed at around 50 million. In the 7th century CE, at the time of Mohammed, the population of the Arabian peninsula then could be measured in tens of thousands, and total world population was about 200 million. Were Allah to speak today with 7 billion people on the planet is it not reasonable to suppose He might well say something very different?

Problems of a diminishing population and immigration

Of course the reduction of world population brings its own problems (we see them already, particularly in the European countries) of an ageing population at a time when life expectancy is increasing. If work is found for the elderly to help them pay their disproportionate health cost, that must not lead to unemployment among the young people who have the burden of supporting the elderly who cannot work. At the same time pension arrangements have to be made for those same young people.

Possibly the biggest problem - already evident - will be immigration. The pressure to emigrate will inevitably increase given population pressures in the 'third world'. Immigration in the short term provides the labour needed to make up for a shrinking population and, through taxation, funds with which to support the aged. But then the immigrants, in turn reducing their fertility, will themselves become another generation of aged needing support. We cannot foresee how these problems will be resolved, nor how immigration can be limited in the face of pressures from emigrants seeking to escape the misery caused by over-population in their own countries.

Nevertheless as I say, given the will, humanity can do a lot to resolve world over-population. The trouble is that over-population is inextricably linked to that other existential challenge - climate destabilisation.

Facing up to both over-population and climate destabilisation

I have mentioned the Amazon rain forest as an example of how overpopulation and climate destabilisation are linked - how over-population is only one strand of a 'double helix' of a twofold existential challenge facing mankind. Like most of us, I was unaware of the important scientific work on climate in the 1950s. Indeed it wasn't until the early 1970s that I became aware of Paul Ehrlich's linking of climate change with over-population in his 1968 book. Only after that did I see Crispin Tickell's '*Climate Change and World Affairs*' (1977) and was fully awakened to the link between climate destabilisation and over-population.

In my own papers about the world's international problems, I took to ending them by remarking that such and such a situation was diverting political attention from the overarching challenge of climate destabilisation. One example: in 2002, six months before the invasion of Iraq in March 2003, it figured, last but very much not least, as No.
8 in my list of reasons - all of which have proved correct - why

the United States and the United Kingdom should not invade Iraq: namely that it would distract attention from dealing with the climate crisis.

As I told you I was awake to over-population long before I understood anything about climate destabilisation. But the world has been awakening to climate destabilisation first largely because of the taboos of racism and religion surrounding the question of population. Now that all, except the extreme right climate change deniers, are awakening very fast to climate destabilisation and the need to do something about it, a great deal more needs to be done to being home to governments, the media, and the world's public opinion the vital need to take urgent action on population. It is certainly not just 'something the Chinese worry about'! (see 'Population Matters', to which I belong)

Population/climate linked to many other problems

So, when we speak of the existential challenges to the future of humanity in the opening years of the 21st century, we don't just recognise the nuclear threat which burst into our lives in 1945 with Hiroshima and Nagasaki, we now face the intimately linked threats of climate change and overpopulation. But that is not all. Largely as a result of existing climate destabilisation coupled with the tripling of the world's population since my birth in 1928 we have generated further existential threats. That population/climate 'double helix' has links to a host of other phenomena - like the linking of over-population to terrorism which I've mentioned. In fact this double helix is linked with a vast number of our contemporary problems.

In the financial world, for example, insurance companies, were and still are, among the first to wake up to climate destabilisation: as one remarked: "extreme events which used to happen every century or so are now happening every two or three years. Premiums must rise drastically to cover the risks and the less well off may not be able to pay for them. Our business model is itself at risk". This is a problem already on the Connecticut coast following typhoon Sandy in 2012. Remarkably the people of

Connecticut were among the most generous in aiding the Philippines after it was struck by Typhoon Haiyan - the worst ever to hit the Philippines (i.e. a more than a 'once a century disaster': a 'first' for climate destabilisation). There is another 'first': the rise in sea levels in the Pacific putting islands under water and now threatening the existence of entire countries.

Then there are those who never had insurance - the victims of years of drought. Desertification is increasing, driving them elsewhere where they make over-population worse particularly in cities: and they still have to be fed from the remaining land. And the rise in poverty leads to ever more would be migrants to more advanced countries, particularly Europe. At the same time drought and desertification has an effect on climate destabilisation because clouds reflect the sun's rays back into space countering global warming. The direct political effects of prolonged drought can already be seen in Syria - this lies behind the impoverishment of many and the cry for reform that, unanswered, led to the civil war. An enduring and worsening problem for whoever governs Syria after that war!

The great corporations are awakening at last

Now Coca Cola - the gargantuan provider of sweet fizzy drinks - has joined the insurance industry making an important contribution to this awakening by drawing attention to climate change at this year's 'top people' meeting at Davos. They drew attention to the resultant diminution in available water on which their industry depends. The famous 1%, who have been among the most resistant to the premise that man is in any way responsible for climate, are beginning to conclude that their own interests are at stake.

The pharmaceutical industry is another involved: for example it may benefit considerably by the demand for vaccines. The possibility of global pandemics has already greatly increased with the present increase of population (global crowding in cities makes epidemics far more difficult to control) and the advent of air travel has immensely speeded their potential spread. We have already seen instances of a disease being spread across the world in a few days by a single air traveller. Indeed there are those who suggest that it will be through the spread of some virus that nature will reduce global population to a more sustainable level. In fact only the scale would be changed: great plagues have periodically roughly halved populations in the nascent civilisations of the past - of course the one we in Europe mostly remember is the Black Death in the 14th century.

As I've said, there is no reason to suppose that nature will not act with the same ruthlessness in the future. As I write there are three alerts. First, efforts are being made to control an outbreak of Ebola (EHF) fever in Guinea and its neighbours: it is highly contagious, there is no known cure, no vaccine, and the death rate is around 90%. Control requires specialist medical staff with special protective clothing, so if politicians do not quickly wake and act decisively, the shortage of both in West Africa could quickly make Ebola a global threat via air travellers. The second is Middle East Respiratory Syndrome Coronavirus (MERS-Cov), hitherto confined to Middle East countries but now carried by (mostly air) travellers to several western countries. The third is antibiotic resistant tuberculosis now causing increasing concern. (I suppose the best fiction about epidemics is Albert Camus' *'La Peste'* - *'The Plague'* - which deals with the psychological, existential, and allegoric aspects, as well as the reality of an epidemic).

Overpopulation has already led to warnings about the strain all this already puts on over-stretched medical resources. On present trends cancers are expected to increase by 75% primarily because there will be more people and more of them elderly. Already in the less advanced countries there are seriously inadequate resources - more doctors, nurses and medical technicians need to be trained urgently to meet both present needs and to provide for the future: but funding is already overstretched. R & D (Research and Development) is needed now to find ways to reduce the 40% or so of cancers that are avoidable.

But with the tobacco firms pushing the consumption of today's even more carcinogenic cigarettes in the less developed countries, we are not reducing but increasing the cancers that kill around half of smokers. Also, although we are on the way to understanding the causes of that peculiar epidemic of our prosperous times, obesity, politicians are reluctant to intervene, for example with supermarkets, 'fast food' chains, and Coca Cola and other suppliers of sugary fizzy drinks. Opposing giant enterprises leaves politicians open to be derided as creators of a 'nanny state' - a powerful pejorative catchword used by vested interests whose products are under criticism for causing illness or death. (Why not 'healthy state' in place of 'nanny state'?)

The "sovereignty" of Trade Agreements

There's cause for much concern about Trade Agreements for they override countries' own laws and can seriously damage efforts to improve health. So a country may not be able to ban the import, for example, of cigarettes. As science progresses more and more of what we consume is found to be damaging public health. There are already many experts who urge banning those fast food chains and sugared fizzy drinks - and several other forms of marketing, notably supermarket chains. So Trade Agreements need to contain a clause permitting member countries to ban the import of any item or any business on health grounds. Indeed few realise how far seemingly innocuous Trade Agreements, both existing and now proposed, are or would, gravely restrict sovereignty in matters of major importance including health.

It is very difficult to know what is being considered - the proposed Transatlantic Trade and Investment Partnership (TTIP) is being negotiated in secret. Like every international treaty, Trade Agreements involve restrictions of sovereignty. But most treaties do not directly concern how we shop, how we live, and our nation's ability to guard our health. These ones do, yet we have little or no democratic control over what is agreed - it is well-heeled laissez-faire lobbyists who influence such negotiations in the perceived interests of their clients.

A shining example of international cooperation though, is the work of the world's health professionals under the UN's World

Health Organisation and the United Nations Foundation. Their successes in eradicating small-pox, and almost eradicating polio are just two. This international research has been essential in understanding AIDS and SARS. Recently, when a new version of avian 'flu emerged in China, H7N9, with world scientific cooperation it was only a few days before the genetic makeup of the virus was known. So long as politicians were kept out of their work on small-pox all went well. But politicians leapt in and demanded that the remaining US and Russian samples of smallpox be destroyed. Fortunately the scientists involved did not obey thus enabling valuable lessons to be learned from studies of this complex virus of immense importance the studies of other viruses.

With the vigilance of virologists the world has some chance of avoiding another epidemic, like the 'Spanish 'flu' in 1918, which, it is claimed, infected some 500m people killing some 50m to 100m - deaths in Europe far exceeded the total of those killed in World War I. Interestingly politics had a hand in this too - for all the belligerents instructed their censors to play down its incidence, but the papers were free to report on the incidence of the epidemic in Spain. So it became known as the 'Spanish 'flu!

Extinctions and eco-systems

Yet another consequence of the over-population/climate 'double helix' is extinctions. Already it is calculated there are at least a hundred times as many extinctions per year as in pre-industrial times. A growing number of scientists believe that a very considerable diversity of species is needed for our ecosystems to survive and that with the current rate of extinctions it cannot be more than a few hundred years (or even less) before we experience general ecological collapse. The argument is that forms of life are so interdependent, like the feeding chain, that the loss in some cases of a single species can cause the collapse of an entire ecological unit. Just one example is the vulture - in India and Africa the poisoning of just one species, vultures, which consume all but the bones of dead animals, is leading to a gap in the ecological system in both places: fewer vultures, not enough to eat the carrion, so for instance feral dogs substitute with the potential for a major increase in the incidence of rabies.

The oceans

Of particular concern are the seas: a member of the Center for Marine Biodiversity puts it - "Over the last several decades human activities have so altered the basic chemistry of the seas that they are now experiencing evolution in reverse: a return to the barren primeval waters of hundreds of millions of years ago." Overfishing to feed the demand of ever-growing populations has led to indiscriminate 'hoovering' of the world's deep oceans with massive waste of unwanted species. There are now gaps in the ecosystems from plankton to whales which threaten total collapse.

In addition the seas are polluted with huge spills from oil drilling. Plastic bags and other floating waste fill an immense patch in the Pacific. Run-offs of chemicals - both industrial and fertilizers - bring another form of land based pollution. But, as in the case of CFCs, a lot could be done by governments to save the oceans - indeed some over-fishing is being controlled thanks to international action. Fortunately it does seem that governments will quite soon wake up to the threat to mankind from human destruction of the marine environment and will take the drastic actions required. Unlike other threats from over-population/climate destabilisation, the threat to the seas would be comparatively easy for mankind to counter.

A last word on climate destabilisation: it is the poor who are already suffering the most, also those who are closest to nature (like American Indians and jungle tribes). After typhoon Haiyan in the Philippines there was talk of suing the countries of the developed world for the increased CO_2 in the atmosphere and other anomalies. The small 'disappearing' countries supported this suggestion before it petered out. But in future such an initiative, if supported by organisations concerned with climate destabilisation, could
perhaps do much to draw attention to this existential challenge.

As I write the extreme climatic events in North America and Europe during the winter of 2013/2014 has brought climate change into the news such that few climate change deniers are still getting their message through as effectively as in the past. But from talking to people and by 'googling' I find more and more fear the future for their children but feel impotent to do anything because only the politicians can act and their interest is in fashionable but far less important things which grab their attention. And their positions are so much conditioned by the wishes of the 1%, their lobbyists and their control of the media worldwide. 'Politicians are part of the problem, not part of the solution' is a phrase that keeps getting quoted back at me.

Is there still time to act decisively?

There are of course other existential threats that, at least in the present state of our knowledge, we can do nothing about. Mega-volcanic eruptions even greater and far more threatening than Karakatoa in 1883 are always possible, so are astral collisions and outsize meteors much bigger than the one that recently struck Russia. But climate destabilisation, over-population and the security of nuclear materials all clearly demand far more of our attention than they currently receive. And that has to be followed by huge and decisive international action.

So I would say of this period in history - the first quarter of the 21st century - that it could well prove to be the last in which there was still time for the world fully to awaken to the climate/population threat and its offshoots before it became too late. My hope is that those scientists (e.g. Steven Emmott, *'10 Billion'*- a 'must read') who believe that nothing will be done to prevent this world becoming uninhabitable are wrong, and that there is still enough time for human behaviour to undergo the sea change required for a sustainable future (as, for example, distinguished climatologist Alan Robock cautiously believes - he is one of the lead authors of the Panel on Climate Change for that just published IPCC report).

But the doom-sayers could well be right in pointing out that the rise in planetary temperatures take about half a century to become apparent - so what we think to be a rise of about 0.8C of a degree from pre-industrial times could actually already be about 2 degrees and what we are doing now could translate to the limit of over 3 degrees somewhere around 2065.

So you do fear that the world might not awaken in time to prevent the worst consequences of the climate/population threat?

That could be the case for number of reasons. Psychologically humans do not like being obliged to contemplate grave danger. Consequently it is often only when such danger can no longer be denied that a society will rise to taking the action needed to survive. We saw this in 1930s Britain as Germany morphed in less than a decade from a 'basket case' into an all-but unbeatable opponent under the Nazis. There were those who saw the danger coming and worked together to be ready to confront it despite the head-in-the-sand 'peacenik' behaviour of government and media alike. It was fortunate indeed that Winston Churchill, then something of an outcast from the political world, was one of those who did. Luckily there was, for example, powerful backing for the development of radar and of Reginald Mitchell's Spitfire with all haste to be ready for the coming war. Still it wasn't until ten minutes to midnight when Hitler was on the other side of the channel that Britain was fully awake.

Today though, the existential threat is approaching at lightening speed in geological terms, but slowly in terms of human perceptions. That makes it very difficult for the media to keep it in mind - it happens too slowly so it isn't news except when some climate change denier makes some highly controversial statement or some extreme event claims attention. Although it has long been established that emissions such as CO_2, methane, and chlorofluorocarbons (CFCs) do have a major effect on climate, the world's politicians (whatever their personal beliefs) have been hamstrung in taking measures anywhere proportional to the size of the threat. Under the G.W. Bush Presidency the United States refused to ratify the 1997 Kyoto Protocol to the UN Framework

Convention on Climate Change. But the failure of the US (and Canada) to take a full part in emissions limitations is only a partial reason for the failure of the Convention to make truly significant changes. For both the developed and undeveloped countries have what are claimed to be 'over-riding' needs for energy which at present can only be met from coal and oil.

The hopeful CFC precedent

There is, though, the hopeful precedent of emissions of CFCs where strict application of the 1989 Montreal Protocol has led, or is leading to, their substantial elimination in favour of alternatives particularly for refrigerents. I say a 'hopeful precedent' because here is a case where overwhelming scientific advice persuaded the world's politicians that something had to be done quickly or the ozone hole over the Antarctic would widen disastrously. Not only did they act within a very few years, but realising they had not done enough in Montreal given that CFCs not only destroy the ozone layer but also act as a super greenhouse house gas, they strengthened the ban in London a year later. It is likely that HFCs - hydrofluorocarbons - will also be banned (as fortunately there are now alternatives).

This was also a commercial precedent - for DuPont Chemicals, which owned the main patents, itself took action against those who denied that CFCs were harmful. And DuPont was the leader in warning the world that world-wide action to ban them was essential. It is not necessarily the case that companies that make most from some noxious product will not work in the public interest when the evidence is overwhelming. And it is not necessarily the case that politicians will fail until it is too late to take drastic action when convinced of the need to do so. But the CFC (and HFC) case does suggest that there must be a viable option when something is to be banned or severely limited.

Without political interference, scientists can work well together worldwide

So capitalism does not always have that 'unacceptable face' that

Tory Prime Minister Edward Heath complained of. And, when we get away from the world of politicians and big business, worldwide cooperation is, as I say, often excellent. There are now very few cases of poliomyelitis which used to be such a scourge (a childhood friend of mine died of it in the US Midwest in 1944, and another friend lost much of the use of his arm) - except notably in Pakistan where the Taliban do all they can to prevent health workers administering the vaccine - a rather different type of political interference in health matters!

In 2013, once again it was scientists working together worldwide without business competition or political intervention who in a matter of days identified the virus causing a 'bird flu' which appeared to be transmittable human to human. Health authorities took prompt action to get worldwide assistance, and for the moment this type of 'bird flu' has been contained. Let us hope that the same international scientific cooperation will contain Ebola fever, MERS, drug resistant T.B., and Bubonic plague (which also still exists). The problem is while political interference must be avoided, nothing much can be done without political backing, at least tacit. As I write there is no emergency funding for resources to contain the present outbreak of Ebola fever. The world's 'political community' have yet to awake to the need to stop the outbreak before it spreads beyond its present focus.

International scientific cooperation also extends to astronomy and physics despite some hefty political opposition. Somehow the scientists succeeded in getting mammoth funding for a new generation of telescopes to peer back to the origins of the universe, and the European Council for Nuclear Research (CERN) got the €7.5 billion funding for its Large Hadron Collider near Geneva - which 'found' the famous 'Higgs Bosun'.

Alternative energy

In 2006 *New Scientist* carried an article warning: "global warming requires nothing less than a reorganisation of society and technology that will leave most remaining fossil fuels safely underground." This may well be true but it will be a long time before this is acted upon!

So, to my mind, one 'existential' question is - can an alternative be found to the use of coal and oil, or at least to their atmospheric emissions? A great deal of work is being done worldwide on the capture, storage, or decomposition of CO_2 produced by the coal fired generation of electricity. A breakthrough would make possible the use of coal to create electricity which could then power transport - cars, buses and lorries - in the same way that electricity is used to power railways. That could leave just aircraft and shipping to rely on oil for motive power.

Many say we should turn to nuclear power to generate electricity and that it is now very safe if you don't have out-of-date nuclear reactors and don't misplace them - like the Japanese did in Fukushima on their tsunami prone Pacific coast. But uranium mining (as the hapless Tuaregs have found in what was 'their' Sahara) is environmentally very unfriendly. And anyway, unless massive new deposits are found, there would not be enough to rely on for a major worldwide shift to nuclear electricity generation. And, of course, already there is the massive and growing problem of disposing of their nuclear waste.

The planet has one inextinguishable source of abundant energy: the sun which shines down 24 hours a day. So it is perfectly possible that fairly soon - given the speed of technological innovation - the difficulties of exploiting the sun's heat to provide all the energy the world needs will be resolved. There are problems in getting 24 hour supplies from it, of storing and transmitting the heat captured which appear insolvable today. We only have roof panels! There have been ideas for been capturing the sun's heat in space and beaming it down to earth, or making the Sahara, the Gobi, and Australia the receptor points for transmission elsewhere. That sounds impossible: but who in the 19th or even the mid 20th century foresaw where technology would lead us in the 21st century?

There is much interest too, in geothermal energy following the Croation scientist Mohorovičić's discovery in 1909 of the discontinuity between the world's rocky mantle and the intensely hot molten centre of the earth. Theoretically the heat of the earth could indefinitely supply all the world's energy needs through geothermal power. This is already providing power in many parts of the world though drilling and pumping water through one hole and recovering super heated water or steam to drive turbines through another. Many problems remain - e.g. the separation CO_2 and other pollutants and return them underground.

The uncertain time factor

The time factor is, as I've pointed out, the great unknown. Even with luck in finding a CO_2 solution, or resolving the problems of geothermal energy in say a decade or two, will there be time to adopt those before the effects of climate destabilisation have reached the point of no return? With the acceleration of scientific discoveries there is a real hope that what seems so unlikely now will prove entirely do-able in the near future. No one remotely foresaw the advances in the 19th Century that resulted from the scientific discoveries of the 18th century. And even 20th Century science fiction writers have been able to foresee no more than a tithe of the ever accelerating flood of inventions of our 21st century. It would be folly entirely to dismiss the capability of technology to resolve the most daunting problems - especially when faced with global catastrophe.

GOVERNMENTS AND THESE EXISTENTIAL CHALLENGES

You remark that humanity doesn't like hearing bad news. Can democracies ever be in the lead in taking the severe and unpopular actions needed to counter the climate change/over-population threat?

The word 'democracy' is all the fashion these days and gets twisted in a number of ways - one of the worst is the claim 'we are bringing democracy' when invading a country or interfering with the CIA or other 'special services'. Everyone knows Churchill's famed remark that "democracy is the worst form of government except for all the others that have been tried…" But who is studying impartially and scientifically how a better form of democracy might look, let alone seeking the outlines of what might prove a better form of government altogether? We aren't even considering substantial reforms to our present democracies.

In the UK there is a scheme to 'reform' the House of Lords to make it more 'democratic' but this is based more on political ideology than on rigorous scientific sociological study of government. And making the House of Lords 'more democratic' in the manner some propose could well make it even less able to steer the government to take vitally needed but unpopular actions. In the US there's a similar shortfall of what many would call 'democracy', for no fewer that 8 of the 44 presidents of the US were sitting Vice-Presidents, chosen by a President in his belief that they would help his ticket.

All forms of democracy rely on the electorate, which cannot be expected properly to understand the issues because of their complexity, choosing as their representatives individuals who are far better informed to act for them and so vote for the policy most likely to accord with their country's best interests. Even to do this, the voters have largely to rely on receiving accurate information from the media on the issues of the day. But that's often not the case because so much of the media is biased by the owners' personal opinions, usually those of the political 'right' and/or those of the 'politically correct' - that fashionable 'modern way of thinking'.

Then there is the psychological peculiarity, not confined to democracy, of 'time for a change'. A government in power for some time, may be doing reasonably well, but the voters think they will be better off with the opposition because 'it's time for a change'. But as we have often seen, this can be 'out of the frying pan into the fire'. Even democracies can lead to extremes. For all these reasons and more, you can see the truth in Churchill's remark.

Democracies – presidential and parliamentary: presidential

There are now just two main types of democracy: the first is the presidential form where one person is elected president. This all too frequently leads to dictatorship because ambition is so great and power so hard to abandon. There is though, the American form whereby important powers (like taxation and the ratification of treaties) are denied the president but held in one or more elected chambers, and perhaps in a supreme court. In the US, even more effective in preventing *'The Coming Caesars'* (the title of Amaury de Riencourt's 1957 book) is the constitutional convention that a president's term of office is for only 4 years and, if re-elected, can only serve one more term. This convention has only been broken once - when Franklin Roosevelt was elected for a third term during World War II, pleading 'don't change horses in mid-stream'.

Some critics say that convention, begun when the first president, George Washington refused a third term, has stopped a 'Caesar' from arising, but that since the fall of the Soviet Union that has not stopped a succession of temporary 'Caesars' from attempting to create a unipolar worldwide US hegemony. There may be some truth in this, but the election of Barack Obama may, from necessity, be the beginning of the end to American pretensions to a unipolar world. All the same, the US will for long remain the *primus inter pares* in the multipolar world which is emerging. It is ironic that Russia, which is the most vocal critic of American 'unipolarism', is itself producing a 'Caesar' once again!

In the presidential form where presidents are not dictators, they can be hobbled in both their foreign and domestic policies by opposition from an elected chamber. That can happen even when the president's party has a majority. Usually this occurs when the opposition party has control of at least one of two Houses. One need only think back to the 1920s of the catastrophic results this had when mid-term elections gave a majority to the Republican party in the Senate, which meant that the Democrat President Wilson could not get ratified the United States' membership of the League of Nations. The resultant withdrawal of an isolationist United States from the League proved a major, and likely the defining, factor in Hitler's ability to wreck the League's ability to ensure peace. Had the United States ratified, the global catastrophe of World War II might well have been avoided. The disastrous fallout from that war is, of course, with us today.

'Right wing' ideology

Today as I write a similar situation has arisen since the mid-term elections of 2010 - President Obama, at an equally critical period in world history, is all but unable to act decisively either in foreign or domestic policy, let alone on the existential challenges, for the Supreme Court and the House of Representatives have Republican majorities. As in the 1920s (and in the 1930s when President Roosevelt was denied the powers needed to oppose Japanese [1933] and later Nazi aggression [the 'Neutrality Acts']), the Republicans are driven by an ideology which trumps pragmatism.

This time it is not that of 'isolationism', but the ideology of 'small government' and zero tax increases for the rich. This ideology calls for counter-productive, across the board (say 10%) 'austerity' cuts at a complex economic and international juncture which, to the contrary, needs the government to take the lead towards a quite different future. For that, there has to be an actual <u>increase</u> in both government and private investment in order to promote the quite new directions now essential, plus a <u>reform of taxation</u> to reduce crippling inequality which not only works against democracy but also against the economy (e.g. see Thomas Picketty: *'Capital in the 21st Century'* - now the butt of right wing anger). But, of course there do need to be <u>carefully selected cuts</u> to end glaring waste.

In all countries at all times many traditional items of expenditure were or have become unnecessary and need to be supressed altogether. Other items need drastic slimming of unnecessary 'pork' and other waste. Some financially insignificant items like libraries and cultural subventions need to be continued at least on their existing budgets or actually increased. Some budgets need some increase now to prevent future expenditure becoming unmanageable - for example steps to reverse obesity and smoking to cut the great expense of treating these conditions. Then there are other programmes which not only must not be cut, but actually very substantially increased to meet R & D and other government investment to get the economy on the right track to meet the future.

Given the Republican ideology with its insistence on budget balance, indiscriminate retrenchment, and a taxation code favouring the very rich, a Republican majority in the House of Representatives has made US government grind almost to a halt. In the eyes of the world and of many of its citizens, the most important power in the world has become all but ungovernable. (Of course it is just possible that the midterm elections this autumn could rectify this). American style presidential government can only face up to our existential challenges if there is a true awakening by politicians shaken by the realisation of impending doom. And still they have to carry the media and their voters with them. Strangely, the best hope may be popular pressure from the bottom up. Indeed President Obama has said that only with popular support can he act on the most important issues.

On wealth and poverty, waste and insecurity, Tu Fu, the great Tang Dynasty poet in the 8th century, observed:

> Behind red painted doors wine and meat are stinking:
> On the wild roads lie corpses of people frozen to death.
> A hair breadth divides wealth and utter poverty.
> This strange contrast fills me with unappeasable anguish.

I think it is imperative that the Republican Party return to being a reasonable and acceptable alternative government for the United States. As things stand, with its indifference to the ever widening gulf between the extremely rich and the middle class let alone the poor, and its strange refusal to admit the human contribution to climate change, and other untenable positions - even paralysing the US government, it strikes fear into well-wishers of the United States in many countries. Governments, especially the closest allies of the US, cannot express publically their dismay at the prospect of an eventual Republican total control of the US congress, let alone the presidency, for that would be seen as 'interference in US internal affairs' and counter-productive. And that certainly would not help America's friends and allies for they would be obliged to work as best they could with a victorious Republican administration.

Race still an albatross

Many observers point out that Barack Obama never got the overwhelming vote a 'white' person would have got after the 8 disastrous years of President G. W. Bush. A recent poll in the southern states revealed a very high percentage of voters who said that under no circumstances would they vote for a 'black'. Another survey showed that among working class white voters there was a marked reluctance to do so. Add to this the subliminal racism in the United States, which is practised by such 'right' wing organisations as Mr Rupert Murdoch's Fox News and its chain of radio stations.

So it seems quite clear that in both presidential elections racism denied Obama the overwhelming vote he required to bring about the changes America needed. Both this open and concealed racism undoubtedly helped the Republican Party take over the House of Representatives in the mid-term Congressional elections in 2012. The Republicans are now able to criticise Obama for the defects in his health care Act and other measures he managed to get through Congress - although many of these defects were caused by their opposition and the amendments they forced! It is most unfortunate that at such a critical moment in its history, this exceptionally able man bears the Albatross of race round his neck. And to compensate for this drawback he, alas, has not got President Johnson's gift for working the 'polling-ticians'.

Obama was left an appalling legacy by Bush - both financial and international - far beyond any president's ability to overcome in two terms. He managed skilfully to carry the generals with him in what he was perhaps primarily elected to do: end the wars in Iraq and Afghanistan and not get into another. His former Defense

Secretary, Robert Gates, in his memoirs tells of how Obama was highly sceptical of the Afghanistan surge. It could well be that, by giving in to what the military demanded, he let generals themselves come to see that the Iraq war was lost, and that the situation in Afghanistan was little if any better. And he has until now deftly avoided getting dragged into another war, whether in Syria or Iran, or indeed in Libya. Even his controversial 'drone' programme, inherited from Bush, killing its hundreds, is at least an improvement on the wars that have killed hundreds of thousands in Iraq, Afghanistan and Vietnam.

But war is war as Tu Fu's famous six characters so pithily remind us:

> Blue smoke war
> White bones men

The neo-conservatives' come-back and the American legacy

Although the neo-conservatives led by G. W. Bush's Vice President Cheney were obliged to lie low during Obama's first term, many of those whom Dick Cheney & co. placed within the G. W. Bush Administration have now been able to re-create a demand for confrontation in foreign affairs. This will be hard to resist although the 21st century is crying out for 20th century confrontation to be replaced with an era of cooperation. The American presidential system is so far proving all but incapable of leading this vital turn around.

Perhaps what's most worrying about America since the end of the Cold War is the precedent it has set for the contenders for future supremacy - for example: its failure to substitute cooperation for confrontation; its 'hyper use of military power' that Russia's President Putin complained of in his speech in Munich in 2007; its readiness to override the United Nations; its disregard for the lives of non-US civilians (e.g those massive civilian deaths and injuries in its wars); its use of arbitrary assassination (often by drones); its incarceration of such a high proportion of its population (it is said: 5% of world population but 25% of those in prison); its widespread use of torture and failure to respect 'human rights' (e.g. Abu Ghraib, Guantanamo, 'Extraordinary Rendition' etc. Currently the CIA is still delaying publication of the 2012 Senate Intelligence Committee report on detention and enhanced interrogation); its pervasive (often 'subliminal') racism; its inability to accept even well-intentioned criticisms about its capitalist system; its ever-widening gulf between rich and poor; its widespread use of drugs (both legal and illegal); its gun toting citizenry; and its subservience of politics, economics and even foreign policy to multi-billionaires, huge corporations, and press barons even to the extent of being unable to lead in meeting the challenge of climate destabilisation, let alone over-population. What is perhaps most damaging to the US and the world is the lack of political control over what is sometimes called 'the Fourth Branch of Government': the 'National Security community' numbering 17 agencies. Here lie many of the proponents of an American 'unipolar' world seeking that elusive New American Century of the now resurgent neo-conservatives. After the wreckage left by their military interventions, they now claim that President Obama's attempts to disengage from their adventures with least damage to Western interests, has proved so unrewarding that only another dose of US force will restore America's supremacy. A Siren call which now has echoes in the State Department and even in some Democrat circles - including that of supposed 'president in waiting', Madame Clinton.

Imagine if China one day becomes the dominant superpower replacing America and it behaves in the same high-handed way America has done ever since the end of the Cold War in 1990! A check to America now would greatly help in checking China then.

At present, because of its pre-eminence in so many fields and because of so much that is good about the US, much of the world tends to follow its lead uncritically. But I believe the time has come for Europe in particular to look again at that inevitable and welcome dependence on America which followed World War II and continues today a quarter of a century after the Cold War ended. I'll have much to say about how a united Europe, east and west, offers the best hope for ushering in an era of cooperation in place of today's confrontation that the world so desperately needs.

We need the closest possible relations with the US, of course, but its governance is dysfunctional and its foreign policy equivocal and often dangerously misconceived. So Europe needs to re-assess its national interests and promote them independently of the US.

That said, Europe's need for close military cooperation with the US remains essential. The prevention of genocide and mass slaughter can demand joint armed intervention for instance. But each use of armed force should be steps towards international policing of the world - actions undertaken by the UN or at least with very general international consent. Here again, of course, Russian cooperation is key. Regional alliances like NATO need to be carefully monitored. NATO remains important where it is truly defensive - but we are seeing over the Ukraine and Georgia just how destabilising its 'mission creep' can be.

Europe could even help the US to overcome its present political paralysis. Just one example: given Congressional inability to take a lead due to Republican climate-change deniers, President Obama has had to use what presidential powers he has in an attempt to counter US pollution, but this is no substitute for US world leadership. Here far more pressure from a truly united Europe could tip the balance changing the whole world's response.

Parliamentary Democracy

The second type of democracy is British style parliamentary government where the Head of State has little more than a formal role. (In the UK the Queen's prerogative includes the right to 'advise, encourage, and warn' the Prime Minister - though only in private). Here the Prime Minister has all but supreme power as long as he can retain the support of a majority in the House of Commons. But here too, ideology in the form of currently fashionable opinions too often determines party sentiment.

Sometimes deference to a major statesman carries the day without proper consideration - as when Sir Anthony Eden, Churchill's foreign minister during World War II, quite wrongly saw Egypt's President Nasser, dictator though he was, as another Hitler. So Eden overrode all opposition, and insisted on invading Suez in 1956 with the disastrous consequences we all know. (Who learns? As I write it's fashionable to denigrate Russia's would be autocrat President Putin - even the Prince of Wales appears, most unwisely, to have likewise compared him to Hitler).

Or, when the Commons should have been considering the wisdom of joining an invasion of Iraq in 2003, valuable time was taken up debating a ban on fox hunting. This took MPs attention away from foreign affairs and the consequences of an invasion of Iraq were not properly examined. This diversion may well have enabled Premier Blair, pleading urgency, to get his vote to invade with the near catastrophic results for Western - indeed world - interests that we are witnessing today. However much one may value the lives of a few hundred foxes it is strange that the lives of our soldiers then in Afghanistan and of those it was intended to send to Iraq did not count for a great deal more - let alone the lives of a million or so Iraqis! In the 'developed world' where there is such emphasis on 'equal rights for all', 'Vietnam' and 'Iraq' have shown that 'all' does not include those of the civilians whose countries we in 'the West' choose to invade!

Democracy and the problem of minorities

In the case of both forms of democracy there is the fundamental problem of majority rule. What happens for the minority? In the case of the UK the opposition party forms 'Her Majesty's Loyal Opposition' - an alternative government in being, meanwhile usefully demanding attention to minority interests. In the US and in many other presidential systems another government has to be formed and 'learn on the job'. But there are countries, whether supposedly presidential or parliamentary, where a few hundred votes can bring about a dictatorship by the majority with no concern for the minority. These are often countries with tribal or other groupings where there has to be give and take between the factions or a strong man has to take over to enforce peace or to support one side or the other - possibly the minority faction. (The newly recognised South Sudan is a case in point).

Iraq is the classic example: Saddam Hussein ruled using the minority Sunnis at the expense of the substantial Shi'ite majority. His successor, Nouri Al Malaki, now favours the majority Shi'ites at the expense of the large Sunni minority. As the Americans, with their belief in majority rule, gave the country to the majority Shi'ites, civil war was inevitable - particularly when America's ally, Saudi Arabia (a theocracy with an extremist Wahabist version of Sunni Islam) is a supporter of the Sunnis. The United States' insistence on installing 'democracy' more or less *à l'américaine* as the thing to do after an occupation has been a major cause of the disaster in Iraq and the threatened disaster in Afghanistan.

In Iraq, surely, what was needed immediately was a 'Viceroy' to rule until a suitable form of government could be imposed. The G. W. Bush administration seems to have understood this with the appointment of Lt. General Jay Garner, but US insistence on swiftly setting up an Iraqi government, coupled with Garner's failure quickly to handle the extremely difficult constitutional problems to be resolved to ensure minority rights (Sunni, Shia, Kurd etc) led his early dismissal.

In the growing chaos Bush personally (it is said) appointed Lewis Paul Bremer III with the powers of a real Viceroy. He was even less successful. Where Garner had favoured keeping much of the largely Sunni civil service as the least disruptive way of ensuring effective government, Bremer favoured the Shia majority. He took the disastrous decision to disband the (largely Sunni) Iraqi army so creating an armed and embittered professional force with Sunni sympathies. Bremer then handed back 'qualified' sovereignty to Iraq - in effect to the Shias - before he too was dismissed. An Iraqi civil war had begun which would boil over into Assad's Syria. That soon led to the return of Iraq to the sphere of influence of the Shia theocratic Islamic Republic of Iran (which considers the US to be 'the Great Satan'). So the 2003 Anglo/American invasion failed to install a neutral arbiter. The invaders instead favoured the Shias, so exacerbating the sectarian divisions, and bringing the Sunni theocracy, Saudi Arabia, America's ally, into the equation, both in Iraq and in Syria. Saudi Arabia's harsh Wahabism opened the door to Wahabism's ultra extremist Al Qaeda and its even more dangerous 'clones'.

The harsh lesson of 'Iraq' should have taught the US (and other countries too) that for democracy to succeed it must not be 'majority takes all'. There must be respect for minorities and minority parties - but it seems this lesson has still not yet been learnt in that citadel of democracy, the US Congress.

Rulers, democrats or dictators, must be ready to allow reforms as soon as there is a widespread demand for them - that's if they wish to avoid relying on repression and encountering armed resistance. Syria is the prime example: the Syrian civil war and the destruction of that country started with a demand for limited reform which was crushed mercilessly. As Confucius has it: 'knowing where to stop the ruler becomes immortal'.

<u>There is also the validity of elections.</u>

Must the results of elections always be considered somehow 'hallowed'? Too often an opposition party wins simply because the electorate deems it 'time for a change' even though the government in power is doing fairly well. As I write we are waiting for the results of India's election which could put the Hindu religious party (the BJP) in power endangering religious toleration - in particular toleration of 70 or so million Muslims. This is because the Congress party has been in power since independence and has many faults – one being corrosive corruption. For a number of reasons no other party has arisen which would provide an alternative secular government. But it is not only democracies that can suffer from 'time for a change': many are the Iranians who, when young, helped topple the Shah believing it to be 'time for a change' and have since gone into exile rather than live under the theocratic dictatorship they helped install. It remains to be seen whether any of the 2012 'Arab Spring' countries will find their new regimes any more tolerable than those which were overthrown with such enthusiasm.

The most cataclysmic 'elections' were of course the German elections that brought Hitler to power. But the existing Weimar government was weak and crippled by the huge demands for reparations that Germany had to pay under the treaty of Versailles. That had led to hyper-inflation and the near ruin of the middle class. The communists were offering Stalin's Soviet utopia - few outside Russia then knew the murderous truth about that. Yet many feared a communist takeover and, for a lot of them, the choice was between communism or the Nazis.

Hitler was already suppressing any politicians with any signs of competence - Germany's thousands of unsung martyrs. And no one knows how many failed to vote for fear of Hitler's Brown Shirts outside the voting booths. Yet such is the mystique of elections that a number of history books still proclaim that 'the Germans' freely elected Hitler.

There are of course 99%-ers and 100%-ers who do without even the pretence of universal suffrage - Mao Tse Tung was an example. The degree to which subjects of draconian regimes can be terrified or brain-washed came home to me in Canton during the Cultural Revolution. Like other foreigners at the Canton Trade Fair I was required to attend a political indoctrination lecture. We were being informed of the heresies of Liu Shao Chi, the recently deposed President of the People's Republic of China who had imprudently criticised Mao's disastrous 'Great Leap Forward'. Being bored I copied rather badly the three quite easy characters of his name (刘 少 奇) into my notebook. Suddenly the lady sitting next to me grabbed it and wrote 'down with' (da dao, 打倒) in front: either from fear or from brain-washing she could not let the former President's name stand without 'down with' preceding it!

Many a dictator pays lip service to democracy with 99% results for himself. In 2002 the Iraqi President, Saddam Hussein, created enough fear to get every single voter to vote for him - 100%. The dear leader in North Korea is another ninety-nine percenter. It is not always so unanimous as that - the recent Crimean referendum only just got 95.7% though there was no real alternative on the ballot; 'strong dissuasion'; and because of boycotts (notably by the 200,000 odd Tatars whose history under Stalin's Russia was about as terrible as the history of the Chechens). Although 'Russians' amount to a bare majority (maybe 54%) in Crimea even some Western 'progressives' are accepting that the referendum was fair!

A majority of the 'Western' media opined that President Morsi of Egypt was a democratically elected leader and that any attempt to overthrow him amounted to an unacceptable coup d'etat. But the only political party that was half-tolerated by President Mubarak was the Muslim Brotherhood, so after his ouster it was the only party ready to face elections. These were called so quickly that all the other parties were disorganised and had had no time to coalesce and challenge the Brotherhood. Yet, had they had time enough it is unlikely the Brotherhood would have been able to form a government. Can you call that a 'fair' election? But many 'Western' governments did, and took the position that the overthrow of Morsi, as the elected President, was an illegitimate coup d'état.

In March, General Sisi, Egypt's army commander, said he would run for Egypt's presidency. He may well prove another 90 percenter and these same governments will no doubt hasten to recognise him. Like the Iranians, the Egyptians who overthrew one dictator seem likely to have to live under another.

Often it is not at all clear that the winner of a genuinely free election is really the choice even of the electorate who actually voted. Those who did often only amount to about a third - for throughout the world many are disillusioned with politics and politicians and don't think their vote will help improve anything. Indeed, quite often there is the risk of supposedly 'free' (or even truly free) elections proving to be 'one man, one vote, one time' - as with Hitler. That is still the aim of dictators and it is also the aim of some Muslim extremist religious parties.

Another grave problem preventing democracies from reflecting the will of the people is the extraordinary difficulty for third parties to replace one of two leading parties. American voters are well aware that, though often fed up with both Democrat and Republican, a vote for a third party is a wasted, even a dangerous, vote for it might lead to the defeat of what they perceive to be the least bad of the two. In the UK only one party has replaced one of the two parties of government in the last century - the Labour party which replaced the Liberals.

In the UK today, the voter must decide which is the worse of the two leading parties and whether his vote for the 'LibDems' or UKIP in his constituency will be a wasted vote, or a dangerous vote which will enable the candidate for the 'worst' of the two to win. In Scotland a vote for independence is due. The decision will have long-lasting consequences though the vote is likely to be determined by short term considerations without all the citizens of the UK first being asked: 'do you wish the Union to continue?'

So the most effective way to force change could be a 'box' on ballot papers for 'None of the above'! Surely elections should not always be 'king' and trump all else - even if they truly are 'free and fair'. And a rush to legitimise a government is not always appropriate, and generally not if foreign armed forces are on the soil as in the Crimea a few weeks ago, or as in Iraq after the US/UK invasion. (One notable exception: the highly successful Federal Republic of Germany had a large number of Allied forces still on the ground when the first elections were held in 1949).

Recruiting honest and able politicians and providing an alternative government

One major problem for democracy is how to encourage truly able people to become politicians. There are in the UK, the US, and other countries 'safe seats' where a politician has a reasonable chance of a more or less guaranteed career. But for the majority of Members there is uncertainty, often extreme uncertainty, about keeping one's seat at the next election. Many who would make very able politicians are put off by this. They choose a career with steady rewards in line with their considerable abilities. Others form close relations with businesses, trade unions or other entities, providing alternative careers in the case of need, thus giving these entities some extra influence in parliament or Congress.

And the party in government must constantly bear in mind whether its policies, vitally necessary though they may be, will cause a revolt in the party or harm prospects for winning the next election. This means that far too many politicians are 'polling-ticians', always with an eye on Gallup, Pew, etc. and not on what needs to be done! Yet the leaders that we need are those that are able to push through policies which are what are needed - not which are popular. Politics may be the 'art of the possible' but a true statesman has to make possible what many regard as impossible.

While the UK system of parliamentary democracy leaves the door open for leaders from many different professions (perhaps too often the law), presidents of the US come from a very limited group. Only 4 presidents out of the 44 have not been state governors, US senators and congressmen, or top US military. And today, as the right wing Supreme Court is removing restrictions on political donations, that 1/10 of the 1% (the billionaires and immense corporations) has exceptional power to influence the outcome, naturally in favour of its interests. Today the US Supreme Court, its majority appointed under Republican presidents years before, can largely determine the outcome of US politics under a president elected precisely to prevent power syphoning off to corporations and the mega-rich. The most disastrous Supreme Court decision - perhaps ever - was to award the Presidency to George W. Bush in 2000.

<u>Politicians: can they be part of the solution, and less part of the problem?</u>

Politicians are indeed very often not the solution but a major part of the problem in a large number of today's challenges which, without their interference, could otherwise be resolved. Indeed this is such a truism that I hesitate to make the point! Technical 'czars', as the UK press calls them, are occasionally appointed to advise and take charge of some problems. But something far more advanced is needed to ensure that politicians, even candidates for election, are properly briefed on the effects of the policies they are thinking of proposing or of reforms they are considering.

Ensuring that would-be candidates are outstanding and well-informed is, in the UK, supposedly the job of the local party. Maybe choices could be improved by bringing technicians into the selection process to show up candidates who clearly know little of the problems they will have to face. Scientific Advisers (probably with much expanded staff), need to be closer to those they should advise: not just the leaders, but also members of the Houses of Commons and Lords, and of the House of Representatives and the Senate in the US.

Equally, all politicians need qualified advisers - in particular in economics and foreign affairs - who are professionals above party politics of 'left' and right' and the ideological baggage of both. At present there are too many political advisers with some axe to grind. A tall order, I agree, but specialist advisers with common sense and pragmatism could go a long way to improving political competence.

Excessive drinking of spirits and habitual use of foul language (often fuelled by the drinking) by senior politicians and even leaders is particularly disturbing. Hard drinking is well known to affect judgment - driving a country 'under the influence' can have far more serious consequences than driving a car! And the use of obscenities suggests the dominance of emotion rather than reason - the reverse of what politics and foreign policy require. In the 'West' it is typically whiskey, in Russia -vodka, and in China - Maotai.

A few more words on democracies

Maintaining an alternative government may be viable for larger countries, but to keep the truly able in place to form a government after the defeat of an outgoing government can be impossibly hard in some smaller countries - there just are not sufficient would-be politicians of real ability, ready to face so uncertain a career.

With the presidential form there is near impossibility for even the most able elected politicians to take executive power - unless they stand for the presidency. A serious discouragement for the truly able. For it is the president who chooses the key officers of state who generally are not among the country's elected representatives. As the presidency is open to anyone who can conquer it (typically a senator or governor) there is the risk of a president coming to power without the requisite experience be it in domestic, or in international affairs (as was the case with G. W. Bush). Indeed typically a US president has himself to learn on the job. That can be the case even with members of his cabinet.

Under the parliamentary system in contrast, the leader of the opposition and his 'shadow ministers' are handling both internal and international affairs on a daily basis with access to most of the information available to the Prime Minister. He or she is thus more able to step straight into the prime minister's shoes when the opposition comes to power.

Another point I think worth making: in the event of a major error by the head of government, a prime minister can be voted out in a single day - as happened to the hapless Neville Chamberlain in 1940. Whereas under the presidential system the unseating of a disastrous president means waiting until the end of his current term or resorting to impeachment - which at best takes time. Meanwhile, as it was for President Clinton, it is nearly impossible for a president to 'run the world' while at the same time fighting impeachment.

There is one other reason why democracies may not be able to act quickly, decisively and effectively to deal with climate change/over-population. Politicians commonly have close relationships with the business/financial and the military/industrial complexes. Their interests - even though properly declared - can have a restraining effect on taking expensive and unpopular action which affects those circles of power. So, because many politicians have such 'dual loyalties', even a president in his final permitted term, like President Obama now, may not be able even to begin to take the actions he deems essential to counter those existential threats. Indeed it is hard for a president to exploit those final years of comparative freedom and avoid being written off as a 'lame duck'.

The 1/10th of the 1%: individuals and corporations

And behind all lesser mortals are that famous one tenth of the one percent and the huge international corporations which together form an immensely powerful, but non-governing, worldwide oligarchy seeking ever greater wealth and dominance. They don't want the fundamentals to change - among them are the great deniers that human activities (largely theirs) are responsible for climate destabilisation. Some pay huge sums to set up think tanks for paid-for scientists to pooh-pooh existential threats and to denigrate those scientists who are trying to wake up the world to the danger. The support of the Koch brothers (the coal magnates), and of Exxon Mobil and other oil companies for the 'Energy and Environmental Legal Institute' is just one current example.

There is, though, a hopeful development. Since Bill (and his wife Melinda) Gates, the billionaire IT tycoon, and the financial tycoon, Warren Buffet, gave a large proportion of their fortunes to charity, it is said that around a fifth of America's 500 or so billionaires worth some $250bn, have undertaken to donate much of their wealth to charity. The results are already becoming apparent in subventions to science. There is a downside - for the choice of what to support is theirs and is tending to be the more glamorous subjects. Nevertheless it frees a lot of government money for R & D to be devoted to the fundamental work that the billionaires are not funding. This does not apply to the Gates Foundation which puts over-population at the top of its agenda. It appears to be doing more about that than any other NGO or government.

It is good to know that today's top class, the money rich, are developing a social conscience which, at its best, characterised the old aristocracy, at least in the UK. But that though does not answer the deeper question that the French economist Thomas Picketty tries to answer in his *'Capital in the 21st Century'*: what can be done to lessen the extreme disparity of wealth in today's world, both in democracies and in dictatorships and oligarchies? This disparity stifles the 'American dream' (the idea that everyone has a chance to get to the top by hard work and enterprise) and the very harmful social, economic, and political results which occur when there is too great a gulf between rich and poor. Progressive taxation and anti-corruption measures can help, but more fundamental changes are needed. This is the more difficult because governments want to attract the very richest to invest in their countries.

The 'West Virginia voting pattern' where one of the poorest states, formerly a Democrat stonghold, went for the Republicans, is far from unique. (The Republican Mitt Romney won over 62% of the vote there). In democracies many none-too-rich people vote against their financial interests. Sometimes this makes sense - in England many poorly paid farm workers historically voted for the landowner Conservative party and not for the Labour Party which stood for the working class. But there was a reason behind this - the landowners also stood for rural England and its way of life.

Psephologists suggest that, right across the 'pink' Republican central states, there's a traditional voting pattern greatly increased by humble people whose mind-set is 'respect for authority, religiousness, and conservatism' without regard to their personal financial interests.

This rather confirms my own observations on my last visit to the Mid-West where the universities are oases of the cosmopolitan. Just one example, a supermarket check out girl, she could hardly have been 25, told me she voted Republican to try to preserve the old moral values of the US she had been brought up in by her family and church - these, she believed the Democrats were jettisoning. Like many in the Mid-West she knew next to nothing about foreign affairs or indeed of the world outside the US. She had little or no idea of other Republican policies damaging to her financial interests. There are of course many reasons why those in the 'pink' states vote Republican but, like the English farm workers, readiness to try to preserve one's way of life is a powerful one.

Widespread 'pink state' ignorance and lack of even minimal interest in the world beyond the US has, as I've pointed out, led to military disasters and still makes possible Republican control of Congess, and even another Republican president.

A third form of government - the top down

Apart from dictatorships and democracies there is another form of government to consider. That is the top down form of government where the power elite takes the decisions. The Vatican is one such (with the pope, cardinals and a bureaucracy ruling - this one has lasted some fifteen hundred years) and communist China is another. There are also many hybrids - nominal democracies where a ruler effectively dictates (today's Russia and Sisi's Egypt are examples). Unlike the international non-governing oligarchy, China's, like the Vatican's, is a governing oligarchy. When the governing oligarchy - or a substantial part of it - is convinced change is essential, it can take drastic and hopefully effective action. (Pope Francis' Vatican is an example and President Xi Jinping's State Council could still prove to be another).

After the despotic rule of Mao Tse Tung the Communist Party of China took the extraordinary decision to adopt the capitalist system - albeit under their oligarchic control. This resembles the state capitalism (or corporatism) of fascism: of Hitler's Germany and Mussolini's Italy where capitalism does what the state wants. And when convinced that China risked disaster from over-population, the oligarchy decreed the 'one child' policy which was ruthlessly enforced - and is today with some modifications. Even in so personal a matter, popular opposition was crushed. Under President Xi, China is currently attempting to wipe out corruption - seen as essential both for China and the Communist Party. This is being pursued against the wishes of many of the most influential people and a great host of lesser ones.

So you could say that the Chinese oligarchic government has the credentials to take unpopular world-shaking decisions. China just could be the world leader in taking the even more drastic policies required to try to counter the climate/population threat. So far China has, to the contrary become the world's second largest polluter building coal fired power stations by the hundred. But, even as I write, the oligarchy is awakening to the appalling pollution their industrialisation policy has caused.

You cannot live in Beijing the country's capital without risking severe damage to your health. When there is a high pollution alert the authorities tell you to stay indoors. Foreign embassies are alarmed for their citizens' health, several advise embassy staff and business representatives not to bring their children with them. Foreign countries are protesting - Seoul and even the West coast of America are sometimes getting Chinese smog. So this year, 2014, could see the Chinese governing oligarchy taking a much needed lead. If it fully awakens in time it is just possible that China takes major initiatives that the democracies find so difficult, so pushing the rest of the world towards effective action.

Corruption – the cancer of government

Inhibiting such action not just in China but in many other countries is the sclerotic effect of mammoth corruption on which 'top down' power elites thrive. Indeed corruption has also been described as the 'cancer of democracy' - but it is, of course, the cancer of all forms of government. Much work has been done in a number of countries on how to reduce corruption in both local and central government. There are techniques now (in auditing for example) which can greatly reduce this scourge. But to beat corruption you first need honest expert cadres, especially incorruptible auditors whose figures actually get published!

Perhaps the most expensive corruption from the point of view of the taxpayer is in the 'defence' industry. In almost all countries the sale and purchase of military equipment is a state secret so no figures get published. Occasionally some item comes up which cannot easily be hidden - like the payment of bribes to the rulers of Saudi Arabia by those seeking billion dollar contracts for the supply of military aircraft (Britain recently got caught out). Such bribes can be two-way - for purchasers want their purchases to go through and the provision of arms has defence implications for the sellers who fear that the arms they supply will end up in the hands of enemies or potential enemies. So 'greasing the paws' of high ranking civil servants, even politicians, may help in okaying a contract.

Exposures have shown that bribery is a way of life for '*marchands de canons*' inseparable from their business -such costs get added on, and it is the taxpayer who ultimately pays. According to the Stockholm International Peace Research Institute (who try to keep track of this opaque business) the world arms industry amounted to $1,747 trillion in 2013 and arms amount to 2.3% of UK GDP and no less than 9.3% of Saudi Arabia's. So the scope for corruption is huge. (It's curious that mankind spends such a high proportion of its wealth on killing itself! But profit is profit wherever there's a chink in regulation).

Not so long ago it was the fashion to argue that corruption actually oiled the wheels of many economies and contributed to efficiency, but today, as its extent, ubiquity and destructive effects have become more evident, the many forms of corruption have been identified and studied. These range from petty corruption (a dollar or two to individual policemen, a small present here and there) to systemic corruption at the highest levels of government. Extortion is yet another form of corruption which is becoming increasingly disruptive as secret societies like the Italian and Russian Mafias proliferate, using violence and fear to enforce payment of their percentages. Bribery is another - particularly threats to expose matters political and business celebrities wish to hide.

The theory that decentralisation can reduce corruption is also being studied - for example whether corruption can most easily be reduced at state, provincial, or at national level. In Nigeria the results at municipal level seem ambivalent. Some report that properly audited and published municipal accounts are putting pressure on the central government to do likewise, others claim that this has often funded 'the proliferation of Nigerian godfathers to succeed individually while co-existing with one another'.

There is some agreement that the degree of corruption is closely linked to whether there is competition or monopoly; the discretion allowed to those who take decisions; transparent auditing which is published; and the moral environment: where factors such as local customs, adequate payment of officials, the poverty of the society must be taken into account. (IMF Working Paper – *Corruption, Growth, and Public Finances,* Tanz, Davood).

This mammoth worldwide phenomenon must be fought and minimised if the kind of pragmatic decisions we need are to be adopted. Such a high level of corruption distorts political decision-taking.

To summarise - a shock will be needed before much is done

Taking all this into account, my answer has to be that, in neither form of democracy, nor in a governing oligarchy, is it likely that the drastic action will be taken to face our existential threats **unless** in some way the imminence of the threat becomes overwhelmingly apparent to business (especially to the world's non-governing oligarchy); to military and security circles, to the greater part of the media, as well as to politicians and scientists - not to mention to the 'man in the street'. This is not impossible as the threat of climate destabilisation becomes ever more widely and ever more rapidly accepted.

The 2014 report of the Intergovernmental Panel on Climate Change (IPCC) published just a couple of weeks ago as I write, is based on the work of 1,250 climate experts and is approved by 194 governments. It declares that climate change is 'unequivocally caused by humans' - an important blow to deniers that human activity is in any way responsible for climate change. Its findings, though dire, are softened by the need to assure governments that the measures that should be taken will not involve any great cost. No doubt this assurance was needed to get at least some of those 194 governments to approve the report.

Much expert opinion suggests though, that what is required to have any hope of limiting the rise of temperature will involve a huge redirection of resources at unprecedented cost. But the cost of redirecting resources means investing in other ways, putting money into new technologies which will often be provided by the same corporations and work force. So the real cost would indeed be far less).

Now the US Global Change Research Program too, has just published its 3rd National Climate Assessment containing, I gather, very similar dire predictions.

Equally as convincing as those two reports is the NASA/University of California report, also published only days ago, warning that the melting of the Antarctic glaciers is now unstoppable and that this will inevitably cause dramatic rises in sea levels threatening seaside cities and farming land. That has started a big debate about how much and when.

Perhaps even more importantly Americans, formerly noted for their 'climate change deniers', have been impressed by the number of 'extreme events' in the US in the past year. These, perhaps even more than the three recent scientific reports, have led Americans to believe that climate change has already arrived. So they are at last fast catching up with much of the rest of the world.

A 'wakey wakey' moment

I think that a 'Hitler on the other side of the channel' moment, when everyone accepts that drastic action cannot be delayed, could now occur much earlier than expected. And, if the democratic countries fail even now to act decisively it might just - as I've suggested - be China's governing oligarchy, supported by many smaller countries concerned for their own survival, who will oblige effective action by the 'developed' world. The question is - will that happen too late to do anything effective? Will at least one tipping point have already been reached, like the Arctic feedback loop when there is too little ice and the sun's heat is no longer sufficiently reflected, causing more heating of the sea and even less ice and so on progressively? Or will that 'unstoppable' melting of glaciers, leading to maybe 20 metres rise in sea levels over the next centuries, so reduce available land, destroying cities and agriculture, thus forcing a revolution in human life as we know it?

Despite this welcome awakening, unless something terrifyingly dramatic happens very soon, I do not see the present generation of leaders managing to organise any effective action to counter either climate destabilisation, or over-population. The fashionable worship of the 'Golden Calf'; the fixation on growth; the still almost blind belief in 'the market'; the obsession with terrorism (both terrorists and victims); and the consequent failure to prepare for the future - are all too widely held as ultimate truths for this generation to abandon them and think 'out of the box' as our predicament requires. But the young, the teenagers and the 'twenty somethings', even children, are beginning to question all these supposed 'givens', and for the first time are starting to look at the world and its people as a whole, and not simply at their own country and its people.

The next generation

In particular I am encouraged to find that economics students worldwide are complaining that their teachers have betrayed them with their mathematical approach to economics and finance with its blind belief in 'market forces' to solve all mankind's problems. They drop Milton Friedman and his 'monetarism' in favour of John Maynard Keynes' proposition that economics is not an exact science but a social science where the unpredictable human factor has to be taken into account - something the recently fashionable mathematical formulae for economics cannot do. That's a point Georges Soros the billionaire philanthropist keeps making - and he has proved its validity by making the odd billion by factoring in the human factor when making his investments.

No one is taking all these climate warnings more seriously than young people. Currently teenagers in California are suing the US

Government (Environment Protection Agency and five Departments) because 'failure to rapidly reduce CO2 emissions and protect and restore the balance of the atmosphere is a violation of youth's constitutionally protected rights and is redressable by the Courts'. Perhaps predictably the US National Association of Manufacturers is supporting the government's defence. Coal and Oil interests are reported to reckon that for every dollar spent on lobbying and campaign contributions to political candidates they get back $59 in subsidies. Win or lose this law suit is attracting world attention. So it is youth against the non-governing oligarchy, timid politicians, and ostrich-like governments! To his great credit President Obama is refusing to delay his action plan to combat climate change although many Democratic candidates from coal and oil states want him to desist until after this autumn's elections. Obama is thus setting a much needed precedent for other heads of governments. But he can only do so much using Executive Authority. Real progress needs Congressional backing - and that requires the Republicans to cease paralysing the US government.

My hope is that it is not too late - that the legacy of my generation, those who missed serving in World War II and came of age to enjoy an era of waste and profligacy, has not already destroyed the future for our children and grandchildren. We, the culprit generation, should do all we can to prepare the world's youth to shoulder the heavy task we have left for them. I hope that this essay may help in however limited a way. A house is built of many bricks, but each one must be laid and each one plays its part however minuscule in the creation of the whole building.

POLITICS, IDEOLOGIES, CAPITALISM

You suggest that our more-or-less laissez faire capitalism and our emphasis on growth are concepts we must discard? Doesn't that suggest that in politics you're even further to the left than the far left?

I believe the concepts of 'left' and 'right' have become unhelpful. The 'right' defending the property of, and forwarding the aspirations of, the wealthy classes, while the 'left', in the interest of the poorer classes, seeks social control of 'the means of production, distribution and exchange'. Variations of this confrontation enable both sides to appeal to the growing wealth of a majority of voters in 'developed' countries (leading to today's 'centre left' and 'centre right'). This left/right distinction leads to ideology - a whole way of thinking where being 'left' or being 'right' carries with it a long traditional list of things 'your' party supports, although many of these sacred cows may actually impede reform or scupper the adoption of some much needed policy. The Labour Party's Clause Four seeking nationalisation whether appropriate or not, was an example. In 1995, when Labour was in opposition, its leader Tony Blair did the party a long overdue service when he got this clause abolished: an outdated nostrum that had become an inhibiting ideology.

Political correctness, ideologies

One of today's leading ideologies is 'political correctness' which now, in large measure, crosses party lines. The term seems to have originated as a right wing smear on left wing 'new-speak' particularly about gender (the use of chair-person etc. in place of terms which may seem to exclude women). It regards itself as 'the modern way of thinking'. PC has always used emotional, not rational discourse. But now it has become a term for disparaging, even punishing, dissent and 'stigmatising social heresy' - i.e. any departure from the views which are currently the fashion in 'thinking circles' (the new intelligentsia, the successor to what used to be 'the establishment'). Examples range from not smacking children to a distorted interpretation of 'equal rights' (leading, inter alia, to an almost obsessional concern with homosexuality and 'gay' marriage).

PC involves ignoring traditional morality and religion, which 'has no place in politics'. Even at Hyde Park Corner, that once internationally famous venue for free speech, you risk arrest if what you say is not PC - as happened to a man who quoted the bible! No wonder the actor Charlton Heston is said to have remarked "Political Correctness is a tyranny with manners"!

Indeed PC is behind much of the self-censorship which is so prevalent today (see for instance Nick Cohen's *'You Can't Read This Book'*). There's a new reluctance to permit criticism which might offend - including unearthing the mistakes of one's own side (partly because many of those responsible for blatant errors are still prominent in those 'thinking circles'). As I have found, right now the media largely avoids criticism of the 'West' over the Ukraine - for fear of being dubbed 'pro-Putin'. Indeed if you want to put forward serious criticism, you have increasingly to turn to the internet where a whole parallel media exists (the problem there is its 'ideology' trashing everything in the conventional media!) PC requires for example, exaggerated deference to Muslims and Freemasons (who might strike back, the former with bombs, the latter with litigation). And it's not PC to argue against 'gay marriage': if you do, you risk sanctions even the loss of your job.

PC presents an ideological rather than a pragmatic approach to resolving political concerns and often thwarts the true interests of the state. PC is often held with such conviction that unintended consequences ensue. Not the least of which is the waste of parliamentary time on PC concerns by elected representatives. PC also demands a great deal of media space to air its preconceptions, swallowing non-PC views on the real issues of the day.

If humanity is to meet the immense challenges it faces the traditional ideologies of 'left' and 'right' and the new constraints of PC will need to be abandoned in favour of pragmatism: irrespective of the old assumptions about politics, what works - or what is most likely to work - must be the policy adopted. There is a lot of ideological baggage, including PC, that all parties will have to drop.

Capitalism

As for capitalism, it has long proven an extremely good servant but an ultimately disastrous master. Unless it is directed, it follows the 'invisible hand' - that is, it leads to wherever the market believes there is a profit to be made no matter whether that is useful or harmful to society. It has no moral concerns, it does not take the environment into account - not just the physical environment but the historical and political environment. By itself it will neither prepare for war, nor for peace - that will depend on whether there is profit to be made. That 'invisible hand' will certainly not forge policies to overcome our existential challenges. Capitalism in the 18th and 19th centuries lay behind many of the great discoveries in engineering and science and their application. But left to itself it also brought negro slavery and appalling conditions for the working class - squeezing slaves and workers for increased profit. Fortunately governments were obliged to intervene and we got, just one example, the Acts limiting the hours of work.

Today's right wing simplistic 'capitalism good, regulations bad' has led to private ownership being extended to institutions for which it is inherently unsuitable. One example is the mushrooming privatisation of prisons where the 'customers', the prisoners, cannot effectively make complaints against the short cuts to increase profits inherent in unregulated capitalism. Yet customer dissatisfaction is what limits malpractice - along with strictly enforced regulations. Without these, corners will be cut in search of greater profit and capitalism becomes an affliction. That said, regulations must constantly be reviewed: some are out-dated, others unnecessary, and some may indeed be genuinely 'in restraint of trade'.

Capitalism became increasingly humanised as the 19th century progressed partly because people like Robert Owen showed other mill operators (and parliament) that humane treatment of workers actually brought greater profits, and partly because there was some considerable moral sentiment in British society (successfully appealed to by such as Lord Shaftesbury) largely deriving from Christianity. Indeed it was moral outrage that e72nabled people like Zachary Macaulay and William Wilberforce to abolish the slave trade. So it was an increasingly humane form of capitalism that Britain exported to the world in the later 19th century because a whole nexus of laws and regulations were enforced to limit exploitation, deceit, dangerous practices, etc. But it was, all the same, a capitalism based on 'the invisible hand' of the market and profit expectations.

Although capitalism had suffered cyclical slumps due to a faulty banking system, it was not until the collapse of the US stock exchange in 1929 that the capitalist system itself was seriously questioned by those with economic and political expertise in the advanced countries (the rulers of the new communist Soviet Union opposed it absolutely). Two strains of non-communist thought emerged. There were those, like John Maynard Keynes, who pressed for far greater government control over the conditions in which capitalism operated (in other words a much more controlled but not directed capitalism). The alternative for getting out of the Great Depression was the 'corporatism' I've mentioned of Mussolini and then Hitler - directed capitalism but controlled by Fascist states preparing for aggressive war (like Hitler), or actually waging one (like Mussolini in Ethiopia).

As I have said, I believe capitalism to be an excellent servant but a bad master - so I believe an enlightened form of <u>directed</u> capitalism is the only way forward. That means making profitable the direction in which society needs to go, both for the country concerned and for the world of the future. In most countries it is a requirement that a publicly owned company must seek maximum profit for its shareholders in accordance with the law. Beyond that it is, as I say, morally and socially blind. If society cares about something it either wants or regards as harmful it must act by taxation policy, subsidies, or legislation, to achieve its aims.

All these tools and more will be needed if capitalism is to be rendered both less destructive and more capable of playing its vital role in meeting the challenges the world is facing. Perhaps one of the most important right now is the need to end the obsession of businesses with the present instant's values of their shares. Companies are obliged to seek the most profit for their shareholders but it is counter-productive to define 'shareholder value' as short term returns: a company must obviously work to the future and make investments and other arrangements to ensure or increase profitability even some years away.

CEO's must not stand in fear of being sued by shareholders (who now typically only hold their shares for a few months instead of the traditional 5-10 years) for missing a few pennies on quarterly earnings. At present many companies are now actually self-destructing by artificially boosting their share prices - often to counter hostile takeovers which can lead to the destruction of socially valuable companies. Indeed massive takeovers by huge companies are making Marx's prophesy come true - capitalists swallowing capitalists until only a few monopolies remain.

One particularly hopeful development is the Benefit Corporation where a company is not obliged to maximise profit in every way legal but, in its search for profit must also seek to benefit society and the environment. Maryland pioneered with the necessary legislation in 2010 since when many other states have adopted or are considering legislation for B Corporations. This immensely important development bridges the gap between well meaning but often inefficient NGOs and the social and environmental damage caused by traditional capitalism where even environmentally conscious CEOs are legally obliged to maximise profit regardless.

The 'unacceptable face of capitalism' (Prime Minister Edward Heath)

As it is, it is not only the oil and coal industries that are environmentally reckless. The cigarette industry is equally reckless in its search for ever greater profits at the expense of human life. A great many people knew by the end of World War II that 'cigarettes kill'. In 1946 a doctor in his thirties, who was dying, told me he knew it was cigarette smoking that had caused his lung cancer. He had then only just got married to a close friend of my family. He died just after he had held his baby son in his arms. By the time of King George VI's death in 1951 most people knew that the king had died of lung cancer due to cigarette smoking. But such was the tobacco industry's denial that smoking caused any diseases that it was not until a report by the UK's Royal College of Physicians led to the US Surgeon General's

1964 report nearly a quarter of a century later, which established this connection as officially accepted by the US government.

Nevertheless the tobacco industry to this day continues its attempts to deny the truth and to fight against all attempts to reduce cigarette smoking. And now, when smoking has been significantly reduced in the advanced countries, the response of these powerful companies, and of their shareholders, is a campaign to maximise cigarette smoking in poor countries with little or no anti-smoking legislation and no adequate medical resources to at least palliate the sufferings of their victims. Their lobbying is so effective that even governments in the advanced countries have difficulty in taking measures to reduce smoking - the British government recently felt it had to capitulate, abandoning a requirement that cigarette packets be made less attractive.

The power of great international corporations to pursue anti-social, even immoral actions, illustrates the way laissez-faire capitalism can often only be controlled by governments acting with the same determination to enforce their will as did the fascists of Italy and Germany. Directed capitalism can only succeed where harmful lobbying and misleading advertising can be resisted.

Of course capitalism today is in fact already very largely directed by government: one only needs to look at the huge contracts the military/industrial complex enjoys. This can be pernicious. Both Presidents Lincoln and Eisenhower, a century apart, warned against the power of corporations and in particular the 'military industrial complex'. In letter dated November 24th 1864 Lincoln presciently wrote "As a result of war, corporations have been enthroned, and an era of corruption in high places will follow, and the money power of the country will endeavor to prolong its reign by working upon the prejudices of the people until all the wealth is aggregated in a few hands and the republic is destroyed". In his farewell speech on January 1961 Eisenhower famously warned: "In the councils of government, we must guard against the acquisition of unwarranted influence, whether sought or unsought, by the military-industrial complex. The potential for the disastrous rise of misplaced power exists, and will persist."

There are a great many other ways, often beneficent, that capitalism is controlled - by minimum wages, by building regulations and a host of other such regulatory requirements. And of course there is the criminal law prohibiting business in addictive drugs, limiting gambling and many other lucrative but anti-social activities. Meeting today's security requirements is another large area.

But there is very little overall direction aimed at preparing society for the future. At present this is limited to important subsidies for research and development, for education, and items like electric cars in a nod to the environment. The major financial crisis in 2007/8 was a wake up call to end the era of waste we have been living in since soon after the second World War. 'Right wing' politicians are correct in calling for retrenchment - government and domestic borrowing has grown to unsustainable levels since resources are being wasted on an enormous scale (for example according to one survey 40% of all food produced in the US is wasted - a loss of $165bn. One reckoning has it that half of all food produced worldwide is wasted for a wide variety of reasons).

'External costs'

Because so called 'external costs', like harmful emissions, do not enter into accounting calculations it is the environment that is left to bear them. One example is the way immense damage to the environment is caused by aviation and transport by road and sea - companies pay for the fuel, but not for the damage done to the environment. The worldwide mushrooming of supermarkets and hypermarkets would hardly be feasible if they had to pay all their external costs, so much do they rely on transporting products not just around countries but around the world. If damage to the environment were paid, this reliance on transport would, in a great many cases, not be profitable. Surely we should instead be supporting local produce so eliminating such external costs. That would also be far better for our health, consuming as we do so much processed food.

We should as far as possible also be buying items made in our country (or the EU in the case of Europe) rather than abroad. But we are going in the wrong direction and need to make that U turn we should anyway be making for so many other reasons. There are many ways some of these environmental costs could be collected, one is by charging, in addition to any tariff, an amount representing the cost of transport.

Coal burning is of course the prime example of huge 'external costs' not only because of the CO2 it generates but because of air pollution. That is happening worldwide, notably making not only many Chinese cities but many others in the world all but uninhabitable.

Our era of waste and our reliance on GDP, and 'growth'

But the problem of 'external costs' goes far beyond such emissions. It goes to the very heart of our present era-of-waste economic model. Continuous 'growth' as measured by Gross Domestic Product (GDP) is regarded as essential for all societies 'to raise the standard of living' and 'provide full employment'. But GDP, arrived at by recondite and dubious statistics, is in fact a very blunt tool for it too, pays no attention to whether this 'growth' is wasteful or even actually harmful for the society concerned (see e.g Diane Coyle's wittily informative '*GDP*').

So success as measured by GDP, the present near universal measure, is no real measure of an economy's 'fitness for purpose'. According to the doctrine of 'growth at all costs', the production of consumer goods is the very purpose of economic activity - 'stuff' which the populace must buy, whether meeting real demand or not. A huge advertising industry in the traditional media and on line makes sure that it is bought - and then, as it meets no real purpose, much gets thrown away barely used. Consumption is forced on us through the constant assault of advertisements - just like the goose gets force-fed for foie gras. Worse, this system, through the ever-repeated psychological appeal to 'keep up with the Jones', deliberately encourages consumers to take on debt they cannot afford, so increasing the profits of banks.

For any society to live within its means (and this applies to the world society too), it must discourage this endless production of unnecessary and half consumed 'stuff', wasting resources and placing an unsustainable burden on the environment. With the growing world population the substantial minority with 'middle class' incomes is already putting ever increasing demand on non-renewable resources (e.g. rare earths and suchlike, not just oil) and on what were renewable resources but are no longer (e.g. land and food for beef, as already mentioned). This clearly has to stop. That can only happen under directed capitalism, which as I say, is something close to that 'corporatism' of Mussolini - but this time making capitalism the servant not just of one country but of the world as a whole.

Not only directed capitalism but also limiting births

But if directed capitalism is to prepare for the future it is obviously important to decide what precisely is required, beyond suppressing waste, to meet that necessarily ill defined future with that daunting 'double helix' - climate/ overpopulation. As this is a race against time and we don't know how much time we have, the first priority must be to muster all the scientific expertise there is to meet the climate challenge with the same energy, resources, and priorities, that the US used with the Manhattan Project to get the atom bomb before Hitler did (actually he had got nowhere). Where government investment is made, private investment follows.

But equally the same determination must be shown in reducing the world's population. Here it is not only the scientific elite we need to recruit. Major investment needs to be made worldwide in education in general - and in particular the education of women, as the best way to limit births. There has to be a changed mind-set: worldwide we need to promote the idea that you can be better off with two or three children both now and in the future, for several impoverished grown up children can do less for you than just one or two who are well-educated and have good jobs. If that population curve flattens and descends as many demographers say is possible with wise intervention, then combatting both the existential challenges will be helped immensely.

This is a delicate matter, for when the 'developed countries' (mostly 'white') press the third world, which most needs birth limitation, to have fewer children this leads to charges of racism or of intolerance of Islam and Catholicism. The best the 'West' can do is to provide the money (or rather the necessary means) as tactfully as possible, via neutral organisations such as the UN, so enabling cadres trained in-country to promote and provide birth control, while at the same time giving the medical aid needed to reduce perinatal deaths. This is not a contradiction: if life expectancy for children increases then so does the need to have children decrease.

Bill and Melinda Gates with their Gates Foundation were among the first to see the connection between over-population and climate destabilisation. They have spent hundreds of millions to educate not just women but the world as whole to accept that population control is a *sine qua non* for humanity's future. For this they have received much criticism - particularly Melinda Gates, who is a Catholic in the line of the pro-contraceptive Xenanu Guzmão of East Timor whom I mentioned.

Advertising

To end the era of waste there is another truly daunting problem - advertising, one of the biggest big businesses. All day long we are assaulted by ads - in newspapers and magazines, on tv and radio, and even more intrusively on line (where we get free e-mail, 'googles', social media and much else because we are subjected to it). All of this is designed to get us to buy something. Yet what the world needs is to stop those of us who have some money from demanding 'stuff' we don't really need in favour of producing truly needed 'stuff' for those now living on say, a dollar a day as they become a wee bit more rich.

I remember during World War II the great amount of advertising put out by the government encouraging people to get by with less, how not to waste. That sort of counter-advertising is what we need today to cut down our demands on the environment. But this asking for an advertising revolution! Think Google, think Facebook, think Twitter - their book value is dependent on the amount of advertising, and hence sales, that is the by-product of their services.

Employment and the 'work ethic'

We should not be lauding the 'work ethic': 'work as near 24/7 as you can then you can buy more and the economy will be humming and unemployment reduced'. But where does that get you? I live in a country, France, often looked down upon by the 'work ethic countries' because so many of the French 'don't live to work, they work to live' and get some enjoyment and satisfaction out of life. More than many of us, they tailor their demands for 'stuff' to leave a budget and time for living life.

After all, most of our forebears had to work very long hours to get the minimum needed to survive. The Industrial Revolution as it progressed meant that not only the rich, but almost everyone, could have all the items we now consider basic. Now that we in the 'developed world' have much more than that, mankind's dreams have been fulfilled. So why can't we sit back and enjoy life, working fewer hours and taking a lot of strain off the environment? Why can't we increase those arrangements where two people take on a job once done with just one? There's a dividend too: more people can be employed to do the same job!

Indeed, unemployment is another daunting problem. As textile work became increasingly industrialised in the 19th century, the Luddites arose and smashed machinery in order to prevent it replacing traditional jobs. But, of course, as the industrial revolution progressed it created new crafts, new professions earning far more than traditional tasks could earn, so creating a middle technological class and at the same time pulling many out of poverty. But Luddite thinking is back with us now as computers and robots are coming to do the work not only of the 'working class' but of highly trained technicians. Luddite thinking, but not Luddite sabotage because the advance of technology is seen to be unstoppable. The question now is can humans keep ahead of computer technology as it brings us machines that can 'think' and do many intellectual tasks better than humans, and can also perform robotic tasks more effectively than humans? (Charlie Chaplin in *Modern Times,* 1938, comes to mind).

Already we are seeing well paid jobs disappearing (and not only because so much is now outsourced to China, India and many of the smaller countries in the East). Unemployment is now far more of a problem than it has been in the last 70 years and re-training can solve only a small part of the overall problem. What are people to do when they become even more numerous? It's nice to be French and enjoy less work and more life unlike the 'work ethic' countries, but we are threatened with mass idleness of a completely different order, especially if we are at last cutting down on 'stuff' in an attempt to save the planet for humans. How will people occupy themselves? Certainly bread and circuses will not be enough. That is something we need to think about but this seems to be receiving little thought. Of course there is always plenty to be done to relieve poverty, illness and the other afflictions of Mankind, but means will have to be found to finance these 'good works'.

The challenge of ageing populations

Yet another demographic problem is rushing in on us: the problem of ageing populations. In many societies, ranging from Europe to China, the percentage of people over 70, the traditional life span of 'three score years and ten', is rising alarmingly. Encouraging people to work as long as possible often means a longer wait for those who will replace them or, even if the elderly seek less demanding work, actually taking jobs away from those who need a job most. As illnesses like cancer and dementia are far more common in the elderly, the strain on the medical sector is set to cause not only grave financial problems for health services, but a need for a far larger medical sector. In these circumstances there are already moves to legalise assisted suicide and these could mount irresistibly.

In sum, it will be difficult indeed to wean the advanced countries from the 'work ethic'; advertising; the concept of 'growth;' and of measuring economic success by GDP - while yet at the same time allowing those in the less developed countries to obtain a minimum of the truly useful 'stuff' we already enjoy. Economists should be doing far more work on all this than they do now - my own thinking on 'growth' and GDP derives from those that are.

How are these immense changes in the world economy to be coordinated even if the world does wake up to the need to make them?

Before that 'Hitler across the channel moment', a few steps will certainly be taken as the situation becomes more obvious not just to politicians and the media, but perhaps even more quickly to the world's population. But I don't see anything effective happening until those steps have quite evidently proved too few and ineffective and there is no way even the non-governing oligarchy can refuse to recognise that fact.

As I have pointed out, dealing with the challenge of climate/population requires a multi-disciplinary approach by both the physical sciences and the social sciences. For the cutting edge of physics and the other 'exact' sciences and their applications will surely point to possible actions in the physical sphere (I have mentioned carbon capture). And the social sciences (economics and sociology in particular) will recommend ways that humanity can be got to contribute to meeting that double helix challenge.

If it were practicable, the obvious way to coordinate world measures to combat the existential threats would be (as I have suggested for birth limitation) to set up a United Nations organisation to this end. And I suppose that futurology should be the discipline for coordinating the work both of the 'exact' and the 'inexact' sciences and their applications. But futurology right now seems to me far too recent and unstructured even to be called a 'discipline'. James Lovelock's best selling *'The Revenge of Gaia'*, 2006, draws stark attention to the existential crisis but there has been no coordinated follow up, perhaps because so many 'experts' were 'in denial' and the general public didn't want to believe so bleak a picture as he draws.

But over the last decade I find that, in Europe at least, a large part of the general public has become increasingly worried, even alarmed, at the outlook for their children and grandchildren not only by climate destabilisation, but by over-population (there is universal anxiety about immigration which is exploited by the extreme right. This indirectly increases awareness of over-population). But despite this general awakening, right now most see little prospect of their, or the world's, politicians doing enough about either climate or population.

Yet if this concern about both issues becomes the norm it could do much to add popular pressure to the pressure scientists are putting on politicians worldwide. The media today puts a brake on such popular concern either because it considers it has to give equal time and attention to the nay-sayers (many of whom are handsomely funded directly or indirectly by the world's non-governing oligarchy), or because much of the media is itself owned by that same $1/10^{th}$ of the 1%.

If, as I have suggested, the Chinese governing oligarchy does indeed become more and more alarmed by pollution and thus climate, it could just be that it will be China that makes a true discipline out of futurology!

What's your real fear with these existential challenges - just that the world won't wake up in time?

No, for there's also the great danger that these primordial perils won't be solved by diplomacy and by worldwide cooperation, but by force leading to insurrections and a series of wars, small at first but becoming worldwide and uncontrollable. This is already recognised by the US military who attend climate change conferences. Jim Yong Kim, Head of the World Bank, also warns of battles over food and water. Indeed threats to water supplies are already causing conflict or threats of military action. Just to take the Nile, the Euphates, the Ganges, and the Mekong - all pass through two or more countries. Failing agreements, hard to reach, downstream countries can claim a 'casus belli'. Melting snows in the Himalayas threaten severely to reduce the flow of water in the latter two - with appalling results.

There are many other rare resources, mineral and other, where tensions, already high (as in the case of 'rare earths') could lead to conflict. But, most worrying of all, is the possibility of major war if one 'bloc' concludes that the other is acting so recklessly as to cause irremediable damage to the environment and so to mankind's ability to resolve these existential challenges. This need not be about climate, it could be to do with over-population - or both.

We are already seeing great pressure on Europe from economic migrants and refugees from our wars. There is already the likelihood that, in parts of Africa in particular, climate destabilisation will lead to such distress that pressure to emigrate will become impossible to stem. The US is learning from massive illegal immigration across the Mexican border that pressure to immigrate can only be reduced by improving conditions in the countries where the emigrants originate - in those cases remedying the political conditions where insecurity and the survival of dictatorships from Cold War days linger on. But this applies equally to emigrants fleeing climate change/overpopulation - which has already started with 'economic migrants'. To save themselves from immigration the wealthier countries must take on the immense task of alleviating the effects of these existential challenges where they are causing such hardship as to make emigration inevitable. It is indeed one world - we are all in the same boat.

The absolute imperative to win

There's another unpleasant possibility - unless efforts to reverse over-population prove successful, and, even if it is but no way is found to relieve younger generations from an unmanageable burden providing for old people, then pressure to remove certain groups could become irresistible. As I've said, there's already pressure to make assisted suicide easier to arrange. This can make the elderly feel they should make way for others. If overpopulation continues relentlessly threatening the very existence of mankind it is far from impossible that the world will return to a Hitlerian annihilation of certain categories - like the deformed and the mentally ill, and in this case, the elderly. We could see a return to nature's ruthless 'survival of the fittest' - the cull being carried out by Man himself.

When the existence of a country is threatened and it goes to war, that is something it must win and it will resort to any means, however horrible, to ensure that it does. The Geneva Conventions are scrapped if they get in the way. I have already mentioned 'MAD'. The Cuba missile crisis in 1962 brought the US and Russia to the brink of nuclear war. We have learned throughout history that in war, nothing is 'off the table'. So, if an existential challenge to the very survival of mankind is not dealt with early on and adequately, we can expect the unthinkable to become reality – the extermination of whole populations on a scale dwarfing even Hitler's 'final solution'; the Khmer Rouge's 'auto-genocide'; and what happened in Ruanda in 1994.

OUR WORLD TODAY: HOW DID IT GET THAT WAY?

Let's move on from existential challenges and tell us how you see the international scene today?

At the beginning of Part I mentioned how I deplored the set-backs to international cooperation, particularly between the EU and Russia, that have come to a head in the last three months since I started writing this. And, just as regrettable, the resurgence of isolationism both in the UK and in Russia. I said I would have more to say about both in this section.

I think we must start by looking first of all at the past for I don't think the futurologists can help much. I suppose their lead book is

George Friedman's *'The Next Hundred Years'* which is all about how today's nation states are likely to behave and the wars they are likely to wage. He has next to nothing to say about the existential challenges and how that may affect foreign and military policy. He confines himself to considering how the developed countries' low birth rates may oblige them to accept very substantial immigration: a valid point as indeed are several others that he makes. But the book is dominated by national interests as we consider those to be today: in other words it is a study in the likely future workings of today's 'real politik'.

From comparative peace to a world of violence

I've mentioned that the world I was born into in 1928, a decade after the 'Great War' ended, was remarkably peaceful compared with our world today. The European empires together ruled a huge portion of that world. Japan too, had its empire, and the United States ruled the Philippines, virtually ruled Cuba, and had the rest of Latin America firmly in its sphere of interest under the Munroe Doctrine (parts of Central America were all but controlled by the American United Fruit Company). The old Russian Empire, after 1917 the Soviet Union, included the Ukraine and everything else to the east of (newly independent) Poland plus immense territories in the Caucasus and Central Asia. Newly formed Yugoslavia and a clutch of small European countries, with Ethiopia and Siam (today's Thailand) are among the few independent countries that come to mind.

In the aftermath of the Great War there were widespread moves to hasten the time when the indigenous peoples of the European empires could be trained to make a greater contribution to governing their own countries (so, inter alia, reducing the costs of empire - a principal reason for Britain's national debt). Indeed many observers believe that had Britain not been obliged precipitously to retreat from empire after World War II, there would have been steady progress towards self-government. Even in the Belgian Congo (Conrad's 'Heart of Darkness') there were signs of progress after its brutal exploitation as the personal fief of King Leopold II.

As regards India, the 'jewel in the Empire's crown', which the British were so loathe to leave, I was old enough in the late thirties to understand that a move had to be made to satisfy self-government for India demanded by such as Nehru and Ghandi. Had there been no World War II it is quite possible that, with wise governance of the Raj, India as a single unit (religious tensions between Hindu and Muslim were then far less marked) should not, in at most a couple of decades, also have become another Dominion in the footsteps of the 'white' Dominions of Canada, Australia and New Zealand.

As I said, just one year later this remarkably peaceful world, superficially at least, with its prospects for a peaceful evolution, began to morph into the world we know today with its rash of wars, civil wars, religious confrontation, internal struggles and instabilities. For the crash of the American stock exchange in 1929 and the Great Depression that followed caused such social disruption that it paved the way for the rise of the Axis powers and World War II. Extremism flourished: Fascism or Communism seemed to provide the answers for many, even of the most intelligent - think Donald Maclean and 'Kim' Philby.

The speed with which the British Empire was dismantled post war gave no time to resolve the fundamental problem of colonies with sizeable minorities: how to devise constitutions and other measures to ensure that the departure of the colonial power, which had forcibly ensured peace or practised 'divide and rule'; did not lead to strife between factions seeking to fill the power vacuum. The most appalling example was the genocidal clashes between Muslims and Hindus during the division of India and the creation of Pakistan once it was clear the British, weakened by World War II, were obliged to end their rule in chaos. But this struggle to usurp the power of vanishing empire, or prevent repression by the faction that did, has been a common denominator in the hasty European retreat from Empire and has led, and still does, to much of our world's conflicts and instabilities. (Niall Ferguson's *'Empire'* on Britain's empire and its decline is a 'must').

OK, but our world today isn't only shaped by too hasty decolonisation. What about the 'cold war'?

Of course not. But decolonisation is closely connected to the 'cold war' - and indeed to the 'hot' parts of the 'cold war' - Korea and Indochina. The withdrawal of Japan from Korea with the collapse of the Japanese Empire, prompted the Soviet Union, studiously avoiding conflict itself, to use North Korea in an attempt to take over the whole peninsula for communism (in the South it was the Americans who had taken the Japanese surrender). Terrible though that war was, it served to convince the Soviet Union that its attempt to expand its version of communism would be met by force. Unfortunately the war cemented the communist China/Soviet relationship creating the 'Communist bloc' largely as a result of General MacArthur's glaring mistake of attempting to reach the Chinese frontier despite India's warning (good on that is *'Mao'* by Jung Chang - a gripping biography). That led to what was effectively a second Korean war after America and its allies had virtually defeated North Korea.

And after a half victory in Korea how did 'the West' get into war in Vietnam?

After Korea, Stalin's Soviet Union wanted to exploit the situation in Indochina, again avoiding committing its own troops, but using as proxies (like the Koreans before) the Vietnamese rebels struggling against the return of France to its Indochina possessions.

The Chinese had taken the Japanese surrender in the north of Vietnam and the British General Gracey had taken the Japanese surrender in the south of Vietnam and so controlled that as well as Cambodia and all but two provinces of Laos which had been taken over by the North Vietnamese or their supporters. After World War II French Indochina therefore became divided similarly to Austria and Korea.

The *paix manquée* – Vietnam's lost peace

What happened to Vietnam at the end of World War II was a heart-rending tragedy. For Jean Sainteny, the French officer parachuted into Hanoi by France in 1945, found Ho Chi Minh and his colleagues - French speakers and steeped in French culture - ready to accept a self-governing relationship within the French Union (largely as a counter to China - Vietnam's historic enemy). Sainteny successfully negotiated with Ho Chi Minh a self-governing solution for Vietnam within the French Union: the Agreement of 6 March 1946 (*'Histoire d'une Paix Manquée', 'The History of a Lost Peace'* – Jean Sainteny).

But General de Gaulle refused to meet Ho Chi Minh when he went to France to formalise this arrangement. The situation then deteriorated and war broke out after Admiral Thierry d'Argenlieu (ironically, he had been Sainteny's boss) bombarded Haiphong, the port for Hanoi. The Viet Minh (Free Vietnam) withdrew into the countryside. The United States - which had cooperated with Ho Chi Minh during World War II - was by then in 'Cold War mode' and abandoned the Viet Minh to favour France. But the French were defeated at Dien Bien Phu in 1954 and the Geneva accords that year arranged for the North to be governed by the communists and the South to be 'independent'.

So the French war with Ho Chi Minh's Viet Minh could readily have been avoided a) if it had not been for France's understandable desire to recover its colonies in Indochina after the humiliation of its defeat in 1940, b) if the West had understood that the Vietnamese (who had been pushed out of part of what is now south China by the encroaching Han race) had around a millennia of enmity with successive Chinese dynasties. That made Vietnam a natural partner in countering Chinese expansion in South East Asia, and certainly not a partner in the spread of communism to Australia as the so called 'domino theory' had it.

The opportunity for the US too, to avoid a war

After De Gaulle's France had lost its war with Ho's Viet Minh and withdrawn from Indochina after the Geneva Conference in 1954, there was another chance for negotiations with the new

North Vietnam. While any arrangement for Vietnam to remain in the French Union was no longer possible, Ho Chi Minh and his closest colleagues - including General Giap (the mastermind behind the American defeat but who was another French speaking Francophile) - were seeking true independence, not subservience to Russia, let alone China. The Vietnamese leaders had no desire to fight the Americans as Sino/Soviet stooges. And their idea of communism, deeply influenced by French-style Marxism, was far different from Stalin's or Mao's. There was real space for negotiation.

But the very word 'communism', (even 'socialism') was by that time taboo in the US. This ideological McCarthyite hang-up was disastrous because Stalin had just died (1953) and it was not clear how Soviet policy would change under Nikita Khruschev. Indeed, just a year after the French withdrawal from Indochina, Khruschev made his 1956 'secret speech' denouncing Stalin (which was known immediately to Western intelligence and very soon to the world) and from then on Sino-Soviet relations deteriorated. This led Mao to denounce Khruschev in 1961. In a word, hardly was the French withdrawal complete than Western intelligence was aware that the Communist China/USSR 'bloc' was far from monolithic.

The American war

The French defeat and the aftermath of the 1954 Geneva Conference should have caused the United States to consider its options very carefully and at least find out if there was any desire on Ho Chi Minh's part for a negotiation. There is nearly always basis for negotiation if both states share the same enemy - in this case, China. There was plenty of time to look into that before concluding that there was no option except to found a separate state of South Vietnam recreating the division between north and south that had resulted from the Japanese surrender being taken by China in the north and by Britain in the south.

But following a hasty American-organised referendum in 1955, South Vietnam did become a separate state - though crucially not in the eyes of the North. And the US backed for the presidency Ngo Dinh Diem, an extreme anti-communist Catholic who had spent much time as an émigré in the US. So the scene was set for conflict.

In October/November 1963 President Kennedy was considering the withdrawal of American Military assistance to South Vietnam because of rising resistance to the misrule of Ngo Dinh Diem. Then Diem was assassinated on 2 November with CIA connivance and Kennedy himself was assassinated on 22 November. There followed the Tonkin Bay Incidents on 2 and 4 April 1964, the second of which never took place, and President Johnson, badly advised by the 'Cold Warriors', opted for massive military involvement in the South and war with the North. (I was Foreign Office desk officer for Taiwan when Johnson, as Vice President, visited Taipeh. Our Consul General there reported that Johnson had showed himself to be a foreign policy ignoramus, brilliant though he certainly was about America's internal politics which was why Kennedy had chosen him).

The war went badly for the US from the outset. The US response took violence to an all but unprecedented extreme involving mass killings of civilians not only in Vietnam but in Laos and Cambodia. I was in Vietnam twice during the American war and was nearly killed myself. I was appalled by the total disregard for human life. Success was measured by body counts - the more killed, the better the US was doing! Everyone knows the Americans lost some 60,000 combatants, few bother about Vietnamese losses both civilian and military. The total dead appear to have been of the order of 2.5 million out of a population of 27m – nearly one in ten, without counting wounded.

The US bombed Cambodia with nearly 3m tons of bombs - more than it dropped in the whole of World War II. Little Cambodia is the most heavily bombed country in the world. This massive bombing created equally massive unreasoning hatred which effectively brought the Khmer Rouge to power with their even less regard for human life. The resultant Khmer Rouge 'autogenocide' killed, it is estimated, around 2m Cambodians out of a then population (1970) of 7 million. I served in Cambodia for two years before the American war. Just two of my many friends and official contacts survived, and they were both in France at the time.

As everyone knows, after 12 years North Vietnam, with the massive indirect support of both China and the Soviet Union, defeated the Americans. Saigon fell in 1975 in humiliating conditions for the US.

This defeat led to the so-called 'Vietnam syndrome' inhibiting further military intervention anywhere in the world by the United States. So heavy did the memory of Vietnam weigh that in 1991 President George H. W. Bush only obtained Senate approval by a vote of 52 to 47 to end Iraq's aggressive occupation of Kuwait.

Then the Soviet Union suffered its defeat in Afghanistan?

The Soviet Union did not learn the lesson of 'Vietnam' - that even a super-power can be defeated where indigenous people are fighting for their independence and for their way of life. In 1979, barely four years after the fall of Saigon, the Soviets invaded Afghanistan after a 'Cold War' attempt to bring communism to this obscurantist Muslim country. The Soviets too, had a disregard for their opponents' lives similar to the US: there were around a million Afghan casualties. America supported the largely Muslim resistance, famously aiding Osama Bin Laden. The Soviet Union, defeated, withdrew from Afghanistan ten years later in 1989. Where the US had only suffered 'the Vietnam syndrome', the defeat and humiliation in Afghanistan set in train the events which led to the collapse of the Soviet Union so ending the 'Cold War'.

Some consequences of the Cold War

The apparent victor was the United States. But the extremes to which both sides had gone in the 'Cold War' to forward their interests or to prevent the other from gaining advantage have led to much that we have to live with today. We are further than ever from the, at least superficially, peaceful world pre-1929 let alone pre-1914. Europe's 'double suicide' (the two World Wars), has unleashed a chain of violence that has left practically nowhere untouched.

Take Latin America - the United States sphere of influence. The conflict with the Soviet Union's extreme form of 'communism' and communism, even socialism elsewhere, resulted in an equally extreme reaction typified by McCarthyism. Fearing pro-Soviet take-overs the US came to rely on neo-fascist dictators throughout Latin America. (In Chile President Nixon used the CIA to overthrow Marxist socialist but anti-communist President Salvador Allende in 1973: the resultant heartless dictatorship of neo-fascist General Pinochet lasted until 1990.

In many places calls for much needed reform were repressed as being dangerously left wing, so great was the fear that they might provide an opening for Soviet style Communism to infiltrate. Take Korea and Taiwan, and Thailand and the Philippines - it was many years before their anti-communist dictators gave way to more democratic governments. Take the Middle East - here there was a struggle between the Soviets and the West to influence dictatorial rulers which Egypt's President Nasser exploited - for example turning to the USSR to subsidise the Aswan Dam so provoking the Americans to join in a kind of 'Cold War' auction as the US and the USSR bid for influence. Western reliance on these same rulers continued after the collapse of the Soviet Union until the recent so-called 'Arab Spring'. As in Latin America this Western support for far right rulers led to mounting unrest and to deep anti-Western feeling, partly accounting for the 'terrorism' poisoning our world today.

This Cold War mind-set persists today, particularly in the US where 'socialism' is still a 'dirty word' used to denigrate anyone considered 'leftie', even supporters of a European style 'welfare state'. The laissez-faire capitalism upheld as the US's political ideal during the conflict with the Soviet Union lives on, inhibiting efforts to reduce the widening gap between rich and poor so necessary today. 'Cold War' confrontation remains the knee-jerk reaction of the US to any opposition making negotiations in the search for cooperation all the more difficult. After keeping their heads down during President Obama's first term the CIA and the neo-conservatives are now back in 'Cold War' mode!

EXTREMIST ISLAM

And after the Cold War ended how was it we got to the present worldwide strife?

It was the Soviet withdrawal from Afghanistan which was to lead to consequences that turned the struggle against Soviet communism into another far from cold 'cold war' - this time against extreme interpretations of Islam.

Following the success of America's (and Britain's) support for the mixed bag of Afghan rebels against the Soviet occupation, the Americans lost interest in Afghanistan which was left to its own devices. The outcome of the complex struggle for power in the resultant civil war in Afghanistan brought the Taliban, a Muslim extremist movement backed by Pakistan, to power. It permitted Osama Bin Laden, America's erstwhile ally, to base his extreme Wahabist Al Qaeda (Arabic al-qā'idah = the base) in Afghanistan. And that enabled Al Qaeda to organise perhaps the most daring and successful piece of 'special political action' ever mounted - the hi-jacked aircraft attacks on the US of 11 September 2001 ('9/11').

Al Qaeda and 'why do they hate us so? A little history:

Al Qaeda was a reaction to colonialism. We first came across it as a reaction to the Soviet Union's communist neo-colonialism, but it has deeper roots as a reaction also to the West's (and Russia's) intervention in the Muslim countries in the Middle East, North Africa and the Caucasus. For the end of the Turkish Empire after the first World War led to the French and British Empires filling the void in the form of League of Nations Mandates - the French in Syria and the Lebanon, and the British in Palestine and Iraq. The present frontiers of all three countries were drawn by Britain and France (notably by the Sykes-Picot Agreement signed as early as 1916 even before the defeat of Turkey).

Egypt and the Sudan

France as well as Britain had a hand in Egypt going back to Napoleon's campaign there from 1798 to 1801. The Suez canal, which opened in 1869, was a French venture, though in 1875 Disraeli purchased the shares of the Egyptian Khedive Ismail Pasha (The Magnificent) whose reforms and modernisation of Egypt had got him into debt. The purchase not only ensured swift communications with India but gave Britain a major say in Egypt's politics. Britain and France supported Ismail until they removed him in 1879 due to international concerns over Egypt's finances and ability to pay the interest on its sovereign debt. His eldest son, Tewfik Pasha, succeeded him, inheriting also the financial and other problems his father had bequeathed. When Tewfik lost control of the army the British stepped in and bombarded the forts at Alexandria nominally restoring Tewfik's authority but the British were now in virtual control of Egypt with its Turkish/Egyptian claim to the immense territory of the Sudan.

Just two years later, in 1881, a tribal chief in the Sudan, Muhammad Ahmad, claimed to be the Mahdi - the predicted 'redeemer of the Islamic faith', whose followers, the Mahdiyya, were to prepare for the return of Isa (Jesus) before the 'end times'. This put him in conflict with Egypt and its new hegemon, Britain. That led to the fall of Khartoum in 1885 and the death of Britain's iconic General, Charles Gordon. That in turn led to the battle of Omdurman in 1898 which Winston Churchill attended. And the Sudan became the Anglo-Egyptian Sudan.

What is particularly interesting is that, like the Chechen rebels in the Caucasus, these Sudanese rebels were strongly influenced by Wahabism, the extremely puritanical and intolerant version of Islam that the House of Saud adopted in the 18th century. And, as

I mention later, Wahabism is only one step away from the extremist Islam of Al Quaeda, its worldwide associates and successors. In the Caucasus and in the Sudan, Europe had its first brush with what we call 'jihadist Islam'.

The Sudan Political Service

The British set up the elite Sudan Political Service – the 'jewel in the crown' of Britain's colonial presence in Africa. Entry was difficult. When I passed the examinations for the Foreign Service in 1951, I was told I could instead opt for the Sudan Service which was considered the best of the UK's overseas services - it was bringing the most enlightened administration to this key African territory. But it was dissolved in 1956 when Egypt under Nasser granted independence to the Sudan bringing an end to the Anglo-Egyptian Sudan. The remarkable work it had done was largely lost. Indeed - as the British had added the very different (what is now) South Sudan to the Muslim north they left a time bomb when the North sought to impose Sharia law on the largely non-Muslim south. It was also the British who officially added Darfur to the Sudan. Civil wars or near anarchy, have dogged both these territories since Sudan's independence nearly six decades ago.

For once a colonial power, with the very best of intentions, inadvertently brought appalling suffering to those it was genuinely trying to help. Instead of incorporating the southern part of Sudan into the Anglo-Egyptian Sudan - ethnically and culturally entirely different from the Muslim north, it should have created a separate unit of South Sudan. I suppose that was precluded by the need to maintain good relations with Egypt.

Resentment and Islam

Add to this list of European colonialism and political and armed interventions, the French, Italian and Spanish occupations of North Africa (Morocco, Algeria, Tunisia, and Libya) and the Russian occupation of the Caucasus and much of Central Asia, and it is not surprising that there was strong, particularly Arab, resentment, and that that resentment would make use of the common denominator in all these cases, Islam. Yet, In the colonial period Sunni Muslims had generally had good relations with imperial Britain and few had religion-based political ambitions involving the imposition of some version of Sharia law.

Wahabism and the House of Saud

But ever since 1744 the house of Saud, which eventually came to rule the whole of what is today Saudi Arabia, adopted the extreme form of the salafist interpretation of Islam of Muhammed Ibn 'Abd Al Wahab (salafis: those who wish Islam to return to what they consider were the practices of the first three generations of Muslims). Al Wahab's 'puritanism' went beyond that of those salafists who originally arose in reaction to Muslims who adopted much of Greek philosophy (which the Arabs had re-discovered after overrunning Egypt and territories formerly under the Byzantine Empire in the 6th and 7th centuries).
That questioning way of thinking had led to the great days of Islam when Muslim scholars (and Jewish associates) led the world in philosophical and scientific thought (indeed Europe came to owe its own rediscovery of ancient Greece to such open-minded Muslim scholars). But the salafists rejected any theological discussion of Islam as heretical except for seeking the supposed original practices of the Prophet and those around him - for them Islam remains what they believe it was and must not be studied objectively as are Judaism, Christianity, Buddhism and other beliefs.

Salafism, Wahabism, al Qaeda, ISIS, Boku Haram: 'jihad' taken to include terrorism

Wahabism, more salafist than today's Salafist parties (notably in Egypt), has been spread worldwide in schools (madrassas) set up by Saudi Arabia, mega-rich with the profits from its oil bought by the US and much of the rest of the world. So it is mainly the 'West' that has paid for these schools and the spread of Wahabism among previously 'moderate Muslims' - an adjective that can seem somehow less than devout but most Christians could also be described as 'moderate Christians' without suggesting that they are in anyway less devoutly Christian).

Al Qaeda has taken Wahabism, and reinterpreted the injunction to spread Islam, to include indiscriminate terrorism in 'jihad' = Arabic for 'struggle' (the struggle 'moderate' Muslims often regard as the internal effort to live a moral life, but it is also associated with something close to the Christian concept of the 'just war').

In 2006 Al Qaeda in turn gave birth to an even more extremist movement 'The Islamic State of Iraq' - a terrorist organisation with, for the first time, a territorial presence: an unrecognised state. This exploited the hatred generated by the US/UK occupation installing a Shia government in Baghdad so fuelling the Shia/Sunni divide in Islam. By 2013 it was taking part in Syria's civil war, and renamed itself as the 'Islamic State of Iraq and the Levant' (ISIL, now often termed ISIS). Originally part of the Al Qaeda group, it broke with Al Qaeda refusing to obey instructions and rein in its gross intolerance and atrocious brutality which had become too much even for its violent parent. As I write ISIS behaviour in Syria has led Washington to re-think its support for the opposition to President Assad. Ironically it is captured American weapons as well as deft military strategy that account for its present rapid territorial gains.

(This provokes the thought: what if the Saudi monarchy, already fragile not only because so out of tune with today's world, but also because plagued with corruption, religious division, and extreme disparity of wealth, were to collapse and Al Qaeda, ISIS or some other group of Islamic extremists were to seize power and deploy the vast arsenal of the latest weaponry that the US, the UK, and other 'Western' countries have sold it - paid for with the proceeds from the sale of oil? The present growing threat from ISIS's expanding 'state' would be dwarfed by the huge threat to the world from an Arabia no longer governed by the House of Saud).

So, thanks to the Anglo/American invasion of Iraq and the West's (and Russia's) refusal effectively to resolve the 'Palestine problem', Al Qaeda has succeeded in rallying a motley collection of 'jihadists' (the major elements now totally out of its control) to its terrorist precepts when its 9/11 attack failed to do so. When four American contractors were murdered the grossly disproportionate US relatiatory siege and partial destruction of the Sunni majority city of Fallujah in 2004 did as much as anything to generate Sunni hatred and breed extremism not only in Iraq but in neighbouring Syria. We in the West have quite a track record for creating our enemies going back well beyond Iraq and Ukraine – see for example Philippe Bourdrel's *'Nous Avons Fait Adolph Hitler'* detailing how the European democracies created Hitler.

Extremist Islam has played on this long and often bloody history of Western and Russian intervention in Muslim countries, to persuade Muslims in the UK and elsewhere in Europe that Western 'persecution of Islam' demands and justifies a violent response. 'Moderate' Muslims who were in the great majority, and remain so are, as I've said, as yet, justifiably afraid openly to challenge this 'jihadist' movement for to do so invites violent reprisal: being denounced for apostasy (which can carry the death penalty) and for 'siding with the unbelievers'.

At the same time not only Muslim theologians, but Western governments and media, are extremely cautious about making any statements about Islam that might possibly be considered 'blasphemous'. And understandably so after what happened to Salmon Rushdie and the Danish cartoonists. (After publishing his novel *The Satanic Verses* in 1988 Rushdie was forced into hiding when the Iran's first Supreme Leader, Ayatollah Khomeini, issued a 'fatwa' ordering Muslims to kill him. And the 2005 Danish cartoons of the Prophet Mohammed caused riots in many countries and several deaths).

It is ironic (maybe heart-breaking is a better word) to hear of the burning to death of school children in north east Nigeria by 'Boku Haram' - all in the name of God although nothing in the Prophet's revelations in any way condones such actions!

The Western reaction

Those of us who seek to explain how so many young Muslims 'come to hate us so' are not well regarded in government circles. There's an 'Iraq denial' syndrome among politicians. ('We voted only 'reluctantly' - Mr Cameron's excuse - for President G. W. Bush's and Mr. Blair's Iraq War). They don't like to admit that they voted for war without proper examination of the pros and cons - an obvious one being the likely effect upon Muslims already resentful of Western intervention in the Middle East. But the fact remains that little effective can be done to end the 'radicalisation' of these young Muslims unless one understands how they are persuaded to hold such extreme views and act on that belief even with suicide vests.

Germany, which opposed the Anglo/American invasion, is considering teaching non-salafist (and thus non-Wahabist) Islam for there are several other more tolerant interpretations of Islam, of the Koran, of the Hadith, and of Sharia Law. The idea is to show that there are ways of remedying injustice without resort to violence. Indeed, had there been a consensus of 'moderate' Muslims promoting a more tolerant Islam as opposed to Wahabism and its off-shoot Al Qaeda, that could have led to non-violent expression of the very real resentment of Western intervention in Muslim countries and the way Muslims are often mistreated. And that could have brought results that terrorism cannot. (One is reminded of Northern Ireland where swift action to meet legitimate Irish grievances might well have avoided IRA terrorism).

The problem here is that Islam is as split as Christianity, and in as many complex ways. Politically, Sunnis resent much of Western involvement in 'Muslim' countries since World War I. Iranians, majority Shia - whether religious or not - particularly deeply resent US and other Western backing for Saddam Hussein's horrific war against Iran with its World War I scale losses. Theologically it is hard to agree on what 'moderate' Islam is - although some version of 'tolerance and moderation' is the dominant persuasion among followers of this vast religion.

All this means that making the case for non-violence requires far greater knowledge of Islam if extremism is to be countered - and of how 'moderate Muslims' can be encouraged to help. As Saudi Arabia has so influenced the formation of clerics in many all countries, it is often no use to look to them for any real assistance. Among deeply religious Muslims, both Shia and Sunni it's common to hear some version of 'it's the clerics who are the problem' (both mullahs and imams). So it's in communities of Muslims that 'moderates', as concerned as non-Muslims at today's violence, are to be found who are ready, indeed eager, to give advice on how to promote toleration and cooperation in combatting the extremism which is giving Islam such a bad reputation.

Unfortunately, the US/UK and Russia - and Al Qaeda and its ever more extreme progeny - chose violence and many of the world's dictators chose repression over reform. The result is that much of the world - the Middle East, Africa, and even South East Asia - is embroiled in a conflict with extremist Islam. Indeed it is 'home grown' Muslims in Europe (including Russia) and even in the US, that may well present the greatest danger.

The sorry road from something near peace to today's pervasive violence

So to sum up, my answer is: we arrived at the present world of conflict largely because of the precipitate ending of European colonialism as a result of the two World Wars and the Cold War - and latterly because of our unwise military interventions. In my opinion it was necessary to intervene in Korea to show Stalin's expansionist Soviet Union that the 'West' was prepared to use force to stop Soviet post-war expansion at the partition lines, particularly in Germany, as established at the end of World War II.

But I believe that the disastrous war in Vietnam could have been avoided if blind anti-communist ideology had not prevented the Americans from looking at the situation pragmatically. That would have involved not only finding out the position of the Ho's Viet Minh, but benefitting from French knowledge of the country, its culture and its leading personalities.

One revealing incident about that. When I was briefly en poste in Saigon in 1954 just after the French had left (I had been desk officer for Vietnam in Sir Malcolm Macdonald's office in Singapore when he was UK High Commissioner for South East Asia) I was invited to a reception given by the American Ambassador for the newly arrived Military Attaché. In the course of the evening I spoke with the Attaché and found him very open minded about his mission. So I offered to introduce him to the most senior French security officer still in Vietnam - not just a contact but a personal friend of mine who was married to a Vietnamese. The Attaché's mood changed instantly. He replied - and his words remain graven in my memory: "I don't need to meet any French. They lost. We are here to win".

OK, so much for the past. And what about today's Al Qaeda, ISIS, and the 'war against terror'? Isn't that the main cause of the instability and violence in 2014 as compared with 1928?

What Bin Laden counted on but did not get from '9/11'

Al Qaeda's 9/11 was not an 'act of war' like the Japanese attack on Pearl Harbour in 1942 intended gravely to weaken the US at the outset of a war. This was a provocation. The aim was to use the opponent's own weight to achieve his fall (as in Ju Jitsu). The ultimate aim of Osama Bin Laden's then Afghanistan based Al Qaeda was not to bring down the U.S. government, but to bring about conditions which would forward Al Qaeda's ultimate aim: the take-over of Saudi of Arabia, so achieving worldwide leadership of Islam and restoring the Caliphate). Bin Laden was counting on so excessive a response by the United States to his '9/11' that Muslims worldwide would take that as an attack on Islam leading to massive disorders in the Muslim world in support of Al Qaeda.

But at first that did not happen. President G. W. Bush examined his options with care and elected to invade Afghanistan and root out Al Qaeda there. There has been much criticism about how this was done, but - given the fury of the American public - any American President would almost certainly have been obliged to do the same if he had been able to.

In the event Al Qaeda's leaders escaped to Pakistan and, after the victory over Afghanistan's Taliban government, the US was left in control of the country with the backing of almost the entire world, notably including the Muslim countries. Perhaps more importantly, the US enjoyed the support of 'moderate' Muslim governments (here meaning those who accept that Islam, like other religions, does not require some form of its religious law to be imposed on others). None wanted to see a confrontation with Al Qaeda degenerate into an anti-Islam 'crusade' (a word G. W. Bush had unfortunately used immediately after 9/11, but as immediately disowned).

Several countries had pledged considerable sums towards the rebuilding of Afghanistan. Even Iran's Islamic Republic was cooperative (despite the rupture of diplomatic relations after its gross violation diplomatic privilege by occupying the American Embassy in 1979). The Ayatollah Khamenei, Iran's second Supreme Leader, was glad to see the end of Iran's unfriendly neighbour, the Taliban's Afghanistan.

Al Qaeda had got only a rational and limited response from their attack, not the wildly excessive reaction it had counted on. The outlook, not just for Afghanistan but also for American foreign policy in the Middle East and the other Islamic countries looked good.

Bin Laden's delayed success

But the neo-conservatives, led by Vice President Dick Cheney and Defense Secretary Donald Rumsfeld, had long been looking for a pretext to invade Saddam Hussein's Iraq. The Ayatollah's Islamic Republic had paid a terrible price for taking over the American Embassy (indeed a barbarous uncivilised deed - ironic when you consider that at the time of the Romans the Persian Empire was the only civilised power on their borders) for, as I said, the US had supported Iraq's President Saddam in the murderous Iraq/Iran war.

But when Saddam occupied Kuwait the US and allies ejected his forces in the First Gulf war 1990-1991. President George H. W. Bush permitted him to survive. French forces advancing on Baghdad to depose Saddam were ordered to stop on the grounds that there was no UN mandate for regime change. Ironically Saddam Hussein's rule ended with the Second Gulf War which began with the Anglo/American invasion which George W. Bush, George H. W. Bush's son, ordered without any UN authorisation.

It was immediately after '9/11' that preparations for an invasion of Iraq were begun. The ostensible reason was Saddam's supposed possession of 'weapons of mass destruction' (which was very much in doubt after prolonged UN inspections), but the real reason was to reshape the Middle East in America's image: Iraq would be transformed into an American style democracy which would become a 'template' for the democratisation of other countries in the area. Al Qaeda would be upstaged in its Middle East heartland. Of course, control over Iraq's vast oil resources was an important subsidiary motive: indeed when Cheney was asked how the war would be paid for he replied: "with Iraq's oil".

As planning for an invasion became known security experts and diplomats became alarmed. In August 2002 Brent Scowcroft - the Republican Party's internationally renowned security expert and National Security Adviser to Presidents Ford and George H. W. Bush - warned that an invasion would "set the region on fire". His article in the Wall Street Journal (15 August 2002) set out his reasons, but the G. W. Bush administration paid no attention either to Scowcroft or to the Senate's veteran Senator, Robert Byrd's, forceful speech of 19 March 2003, pointing out that the Senate was rushing into war without any proper discussion. Despite this prescient warning the Senate went on to authorise the invasion without serious consideration.

Likewise the UK's Prime Minister, Tony Blair, ignored a similar speech by his former Foreign Minister, Robin Cook. Blair also ignored the extra-ordinary 'million man march' through London against an invasion: the only popular demonstration of its kind in British history. Not only were the warnings of the experts ignored but the facts were 'manipulated' both by the G. W. Bush White House administration and Tony Blair's 10 Downing Street. The invasion went ahead.

The disastrous results of the US/UK invasion on the Middle East's Christians

Both President G.W. Bush and Prime Minister Tony Blair make much of their Christian beliefs but, before launching their invasion of Iraq they do not appear ever to have taken into account the likely result of their action on the substantial Christian minority in Iraq or indeed in the rest of the Middle East, and Syria in particular. At the beginning of the last century under the 'Sublime Porte' (Islamic Turkey) it is estimated that Christians accounted for some 20% of the population of the Middle East. This number dwindled as Britain and France took over from Turkey after its empire collapsed following the First World War, largely because the Christians were resented as being of the same religion as their new European overlords.

In Iraq the Shia/Sunni civil war that the US/UK invasion sparked, found the Christians in the middle with devastating consequences. Many were killed and there was a large exodus such that (though the figures are disputed) since 2003 invasion, of Iraq's million or so Christians only about half that number are still there and many more are leaving as I write.

In Syria, when President Assad refused to make the reasonable reforms that the opposition demanded, civil war broke out and the Shia/Sunni conflict in Iraq caused by the inept US/UK 'raj' boiled over into Syria, with the Assad government taking the Shia side (backed by Shia Iran). The armed opposition led by the Sunnis (supported by Saudi Arabia and associates of Al Qaeda) rapidly became more and more extreme. The Christians found themselves between two fires. As they had benefitted from toleration under the Alawite (a version of Shia) government they came to believe that survival depended on an Assad victory. That, of course, made them even more of a target for Sunni forces - and for Al Qaeda-type jihadists: notably ISIS.

This has once again prompted a massive exodus. Just as the civil war in Iraq overflowed into Syria, so the Syrian civil war has spilled over into Lebanon which had a Christian majority in the 20th Century. So the self-styled Christians, Messrs Bush and Blair, have through sheer incompetence after overthrowing Saddam Hussein's regime, been ultimately responsible for the deaths, torture, and exile of a majority of the Middle East's Christians. And still further reduced their often very beneficial presence, in the very part of the world which had been the cradle of Christianity.

Some reasons for not invading Iraq

After an e-mail exchange with Leon Fuerth, (Vice President Al Gore's one time National Security Adviser), I attempted unsuccessfully to publish my 4 September 2002 article setting out eight reasons for not invading Iraq. I was only able to get a letter of 10 September 2002 into *The Independent* warning that an invasion of Iraq could bring Al Qaeda the victory from '9/11' which until then had eluded them. Here are those reasons culled from several sources:-

1. Giving priority to Iraq would jeopardise the success of the occupation of Afghanistan and lose the worldwide goodwill and pledges of financial support for Afghan reconstruction that America had won after '9/11'.
2. Saddam kept Al Qaeda out of Iraq but an invasion could well let it in, and so into the rest of the Middle East.
3. An invasion without United Nations approval would split America's allies, split Nato, and split the West in the UN.
4. It would open up the divide between Shia and Sunni Muslims in Iraq's fissiparous society, with grave consequences for Iraq's stability.

5. It would set back negotiations for a settlement in Palestine - the priority for ending Al Qaeda's successful exploitation of that number one Muslim grievance.
6. It would put American forces to the west as well as to the east of Iran creating a potential threat which would end the nascent cooperation with Teheran over the Taliban and Al Qaeda. Moreover no Iranian government could remain indifferent to the governance of Iraq.
7. Saddam's non-existent nuclear capacity would distract attention from the need to deal with North Korea's already existing nuclear weapon.
8. Perhaps most serious of all, it would distract world leaders from facing up to the existential threats to mankind: climate destabilisation and over-population.

The historical importance of the invasion of Iraq

The Iraq war has already proved to have been a turning point for the fortunes of the 'West'. The war which began in early 2003 was finally lost when American forces were withdrawn in 2011. Shia Iran and Sunni Al Qaeda became the main beneficiaries. The traditional Shia/Sunni hostility, resurrected in large part by the invasion, has boiled over into Syria and is also playing out in Bahrain and in Yemen, and so is surrounding Saudi Arabia itself. The moment Iraq was invaded, Afghan leaders lost confidence in US determination to rebuild Afghanistan and, as I write, the return of the Taliban to Afghanistan is a distinct possibility: that would mean the third war that the US has lost in the last half century.

The Taliban is deeply unpopular in most of Afghanistan but whether Afghan security forces will have the morale and the weaponry (particularly helicopters) be able to prevail once the bulk of the US forces have departed, or whether they will collapse as South Vietnam did when the US withdrew, is now in the balance.

Al Qaeda's 'franchising' has spread virtually worldwide – but with weakening direct control by Al Qaeda. The disastrous fallout from President G. W. Bush's 'War Against Terror' has now gone on for over a decade. The costs of the two wars in Iraq and Afghanistan had already risen to at least some two trillion dollars by 2007. This expenditure was a major, though largely forgotten, element in the financial crisis at the end of that year. (Indeed, estimates now suggest that, taking into account treating the wounded and those with post traumatic stress, the total cost of the two wars could reach $6 trillion).

In sum, the invasion of Iraq without UN approval has proved precisely the extreme over-reaction to 9/11 that Al Qaeda counted on. More than that, it has marked the end of the 'American century.' The US, with the UK's help, thus greatly accelerated the 'West's' relative decline in today's emerging multi-polar world. I believe 2003 will go down in history as the year when the United States followed the Europeans in 1914 and 1939 in hastening *'The Decline of the West'* - Oswald Spengler's famous title for his 1918 and 1922 world view (incidentally, the German 'untergang' is more accurately translated as 'downfall' rather than 'decline').

You've hardly mentioned Syria?

Syria gives me a chance to start talking about Russia which, as I'll explain, is very important to my assessment of the international scene. As I see it, the original peaceful protests were primarily against excessive repression by the Assad regime but beneath that lay the deep resentment of the majority Sunni Muslims against harsh minority rule by the Alawites who follow the 'Twelver' school of Shia Islam. In 1982, following the end of the Syria/Egypt union of the two countries under Egypt's President Nasser, the pro-union Muslim Brotherhood rose against President Hafez al-Assad in Hama. This rebellion was ruthlessly suppressed with at least 10,000 deaths. That degree of repression remains in the memory for decades.

In 2011 (during the so-called 'Arab Spring' notably in Tunisia and Egypt) initially peaceful protesters in Daraa demanded release of prisoners of the regime and reforms, but instead of addressing their legitimate grievances shared by many thoughout Syria,

Hafez's son Bashar Al Assad and his Alawite cronies, chose to act with his father's ruthlessness in putting down his opponents.

The outside world did nothing although the situation gradually developed into a full scale civil war. The Islamic Republic of Iran (extreme Shi'ite) provided support and weapons to the Assad government and Saudi Arabia (Wahabist Sunni) did the same for the rebels.

Russia and the US on opposite sides

The matter was complicated because of the United States' extreme reluctance to get involved in any further conflict (in December 2011 it was just completing its humiliating withdrawal from Iraq and President Obama had been elected in large measure to end both the Afghan and Iraq wars and not start any more). US sympathies were with the rebels against a vicious dictator - particularly in the context of the 'Arab Spring' where the US was engaged in the delicate task of preparing to end its support for Arab dictators if the popular revolts were to lead to the emergence of democratic governments. Also weighing heavily in the balance was its relationship with Saudi Arabia, the supplier of a vital percentage of the 'West's' oil.

Russia, on the other hand, was in the last year of President Medvedev's term and under the effective control of strong man Vladimir Putin. Russia had two principal reasons to prevent the overthrow of the Assad government: Syria permitted the use of the port of Tartus as a 'warm water' base for its navy in the Mediterranean. And Assad's Shia-associated Alawite Government, with the close support of Iran, was a bastion against (Sunni) Islamic terrorism in the Caucasus.

As a result, the Russians and the Americans were on different sides of the developing civil war in Syria yet both had a major interest in preventing it. So a number of observers, like myself, strongly urged immediate US Russian discussions about Syria with the aim of bringing pressure to bear both on Assad and on the rebels to negotiate before the conflict escalated uncontrollably.

Moreover Russia was well placed to bring Iran into the picture just as the US was well placed to influence Saudi Arabia. For a stable Syria was also in the interest of both Iran and Saudi Arabia.

The Russian option was not taken. The European Union, which could and should have brought Russia and the US to together, was paralysed by its lack of coordinated diplomacy. As it so often is, Europe was absent from the stage except as a Greek chorus lamenting destruction. In the absence of great power intervention, the civil war became, as one diplomat put it, 'a towering inferno' on the world scene attracting Al Qaeda-type terrorist groups largely manned by 'jihadists' from outside Syria - some of them came from Europe and the UK in particular, creating that security threat in Europe as they return.

Russia did at last join with the US over Syria's chemical weapons. Behind the scenes there was discussion on how the conflict could be 'wound down'. This followed the US's awakening to 'Al Qaeda and Clones' playing a major role in the Syrian conflict. The US' lessened dependence on Saudi oil makes possible a more nuanced role with Russia over Syria particularly now there is a degree of détente with Iran over its nuclear ambitions. But US/Russian relations are currently blighted by the Ukraine crisis.

As one Syrian put it to me in 2013: "so much blood has now been spilled that there can't be any good outcome". At least the Syrian tragedy is a further reason why there must be some procedures for avoiding such catastrophes in the future. As it was, the UN Security Council was paralysed by Russia's determination to keep the Assad regime in power. Given President Putin's strong man image and Russia's inferiority feelings as a result of the collapse of the Soviet Union, it was clearly for the 'West' to make the first move towards getting Russia 'on board' over Syria. But American and European diplomacy let Russia become the 'villain' blocking the 'righteous' Syrian opposition, while insisting on the replacement of Assad.

This only confirmed President Putin's 'irredentist' attitude towards the former constituents of the USSR, notably Georgia and the Ukraine. So the conflict escalated on religious sectarian lines bringing Islamic extremists to the fore - including those from Al Qaeda and its progeny. Indeed, as I have suggested, that 'progeny' is increasingly wagging the rotweiler that was once Al Qaeda.

It was this, rather than Syria's chemical weapons which provided the excuse for the United States at last to approach the Russians, though far too late. Unfortunately it's not only Putin's insistence on Russia's reputation as a newly recovered world power that is making concessions hard to achieve, but US politics (at the time of writing) is against bringing Iran, the Assad regime's key supporter, into negotiations on Syria.

Yet Iran and Saudi Arabia are the regional powers most involved with both Syria and Iraq. The two countries' divergent interests are behind the renewal of the Shia-Sunni sectarian conflict within Islam. The essentially Sunni-majority uprising in Syria is intimately related to the Sunni-minority opposition to the Shia government in Iraq with its close relationship to Iran. Hence first Al Qaeda in Iraq, and now ISIS.

As the Syrian civil war dragged on and these international implications have become clearer, the United States (now with much less reliance on Saudi oil) has awoken to the fact that, given its opposition to 'jihadism' and to related Wahabism, a hard line Islamic state in Syria is not in its national interest, but that improved relations with Iran certainly are.

So, even after the 'Crimea' annexation, some positive results may still be hoped for from US/Russian discussions over Syria. Though it is too late for any *'restitutio ad integrum'* in Syria, maybe it is possible for the war there to be 'wound down'. But it seems more likely one side will eventually 'win' with terrible consequences for the losers. Whatever the outcome, both Russia and America have, as a result of 'Syria' and now the Crimea/Ukraine, become more aware that in todays' world nothing much positive can be achieved without the other - a sentiment expressed both by President Obama and Foreign Minister Sergey Lavrov when the former was attempting to "reset" US relations with Russia after the damage done by President G. W. Bush's eight years in office.

MAINLY ABOUT RUSSIA AND EUROPE

You did say Syria would lead on to your views on Russia and why it's so important to your take on the international scene. We know you have a love of their language, their poetry - and much else. Yet Russia is in the dog house right now.

Europe as the key to shifting the world from confrontation to cooperation

I said at the beginning of this Part I that it was originally, and still is, my intention in this essay to bring out the importance of Europe, both the EU and Russia, cooperating and taking a major stance on the world stage, speaking with one voice on the great issues where the national interests of both the east and west of Europe coincide. I would go so far as to suggest that Russia is the key to world cooperation over those existential challenges. Given the hegemonic ambitions of both the US and China - the one waning, the other waxing - Europe as a whole is best placed to encourage the 'non-aligned' to cooperate in meeting those challenges.

Russia, as the eastern prolongation of our western part of Europe, has much history, much culture and many other interests in common with the EU. True, at present under President Putin, Russia is going through a xenophobic nationalist reaction to its humiliation after the collapse of the Soviet Union and is taking an anti-EU stand. (Curiously this coincides with the UK, at the other extreme of Europe, suffering a fit of 'Euroscepticism'). But the case for Russian cooperation with Europe is exceptionally strong. To make progress though, the EU too, has to play its part. It must act on its own behalf instead of leaving it to the US to act for it. There need be no contradiction in forwarding cooperation with Russia while continuing close relations with the US on other important matters. Indeed President Obama, like other US presidents before him, encourages America's allies to take a lead and not always wait for the US. And if the EU can bring about the 'reset' with Russia that he attempted, it is acting in the best interests of the US as well as of the EU.

There are many reasons why the voice of Europe, east and west, needs to be heard on the world scene - for one thing imperial Europe, east and west, is no more. Unlike America and China with their neo-imperial interests, Russia too, is an ex-Imperial power. It may be concerned about its former 'colonies' just as the ex-western imperialists are about theirs, but after its 'double suicide', the preference of Europe as a whole is for cooperation in place of confrontation whenever that's possible.

The present situation where China's power is waxing while that of the US is waning is fraught with potential conflict no matter that there are strong economic reasons for cooperation between them. But there is no such predisposition for conflict between the EU and Russia - it is bad diplomacy that has led to the present 'stand-off'. Both have a supreme national interest in enlisting the cooperation primarily of the US and China (but also of all other countries) in meeting the existential challenges the world faces.

This message of European cooperation needs to be put across both in the media and in private discussions, for it trumps the nationalism Mr. Putin is whipping up. And that gives credence to the current 'politically correct' position in 'The West' that Vladimir Putin, Russia's ex-KGB man is incorrigible and anti-West and that he runs a 'katascopic' state (*katascopos* is ancient Greek for 'spy': Edward Lucas' book *'Deception - Spies Lies and how Russia dupes the West'* goes a long way to validating this description).

But even the Czars - 'Supreme Autocrats of all the Russias' - were not omnipotent: they had to balance conflicting interests of their élite to maintain their supremacy and sometimes to bow to the need for reforms. Mr. Putin is their nearest equivalent and, as with the Czars, he too, must bend to the same pressures: in their case from the aristocracy, in his case from the oligarchs - and also from

Russia's now large and essential well-educated middle class concentrated in the major cities.

The fact is that Russian foreign policy has always had two strands - the one being isolationist, nationalist and confrontational, and the other pan-European. President Putin's is no exception. It is no mystery why, for the time at least, he has abandoned the second and adopted the first. I've mentioned his speech complaining of the misuse of American power - much followed from the 'West's' negative reaction to that.

Putin's Munich speech, 2007

President Putin made this speech in Munich on 13 February 2007 at the 43rd Munich Conference on Security Policy. He made it clear that Russia was no longer to be treated as a defeated nation and that it would defend its interests, explain its views, and invite the 'West' to cooperate in resolving international concerns through the United Nations. Speaking "frankly" - which he said was the best way - he made a forceful case against an American unipolar world. It was in this speech that he complained of American use of force, saying: "Today we are witnessing a hyper use of power, military power, in international relations which is plunging the world into an abyss of permanent conflicts" - (remember he was speaking in the fourth year of the murderous Iraq war which even France and Germany had opposed). He said Russia was concerned about tyranny, internal conflicts and the proliferation of nuclear weapons and that Russia would cooperate on all these issues in accordance with international law and the UN.

I immediately put the full speech on my website as expressing the views I and other observers had long been trying to promote. (It would have been even more of an outstanding speech if Putin had mentioned Russia's excessive use of force in Chechnya when deploring the 'hyper use of military power' by the US - but how many rulers ever criticise themselves!)

But Nato described the speech as 'unhelpful' and media pundits in the 'West' even suggested he was starting a new Cold War! This realistic, reasonable, and helpful speech bears the imprint of Foreign Minister Lavrov. Since this rejection - a rejection not just of Putin but of pro-Europe Lavrov and of Russia at its most reasonable - it is not surprising that US and EU relations with Russia have gone pretty well downhill ever since, greatly exacerbated by President G. W. Bush's push for the Ukraine and Georgia to join NATO, a clear challenge to Russia. Since then Putin has increasingly listened less and less to Lavrov and more and more to the hard line 'silovki', his secret service chums (the equivalent of the US neo-conservatives) that he brought in with him when President Yeltsin chose him as his successor.

It would be tragic if the reckless east Ukrainian authorities, egged on by those US neo-conservatives, used their military to try to wipe out dissent in west Ukraine so provoking not just Putin but the great majority of Russians who see a Russia-friendly Ukraine as a vital national interest - into a military response. That could easily end in a Russian takeover of all or part of the Ukraine. And that would end 'the great opportunity' that Lavrov sees to create General de Gaulle's 'Europe from the Atlantic to the Urals' that was so long 'on hold' during the days of the USSR: a Europe where the Ukraine is a hyphen between the EU and Russia and not a bone of contention.

The war in Georgia

It is hard to believe but in 2008, barely a year after Putin's speech, ignoring Russia's interests altogether, President G. W. Bush called for Georgia and the Ukraine to join NATO. This was in flagrant disregard for the solemn US promise in 1989 that NATO would not extend to the east of a reunited Germany. The north European countries, the three Baltics, that had suffered Soviet occupation did join NATO in 1999 but with Russia's tacit acceptance. Extending NATO to former constituents of the Soviet Union to the east was an entirely different matter for the US promise most certainly did apply to them.

So it was no surprise, indeed many of us had expected it, that

Russia reacted with force when Georgia imprudently attacked South Ossetia that same year - 2008. President Mikhael Saakashvili apparently believed he had firm American backing. A US military mission and, of course the CIA, were in Georgia at the time but the US made no attempt to stop him. In a matter of days Georgia had lost the war and its remaining presence in both Abkhasia and South Ossetia.

Even after that humiliation for 'pro-Western' Georgia, quite incredibly for those of us who had foreseen this fiasco, the US and the EU did not learn the lesson that Russia too, has very important interests notably in the former states of the USSR - most of all the Ukraine. There Russia had fundamental interests - not only for its security but culturally and historically, the 'Kievan Rus' being Russia's 'birthplace' in the 9th century.

A bit about Russia as a European Country

Russia is a European country geographically as far as the Urals. (And far more so than Turkey which retains only a sliver of Europe from the Ottoman Empire, yet is considered European enough to apply to join the European Union). The Slav peoples spread north in the first millennia BC and Russia's population descend in large part from Scandinavian (Viking) as well as other Slav expansions north and eastward - most Russians are racially essentially European.

Russia is also, historically at least, a Christian country. It was at Kiev the present capital of the Ukraine, that Czar Vladimir the Great (officially in 988) was baptised and decreed that Russia would follow the Orthodox rite. Last year, 2013, was the 1025th Anniversary. President Putin stated then that "the adoption of Christianity… helped Russia to turn into one of the largest world powers". Putin identifies himself as an Orthodox Christian and has backed the revival of Christianity in Russia after the atheist persecutions under Lenin and Stalin.

Putin sees the Russian Orthodox Church as what it has been in previous centuries: a close supporter of the government of the day and a pillar of Russian nationalism. (Stalin had to bring it back during the Second World War to recover support because the communist regime was anti-Christian and had all but destroyed the Church). Sergei Lavrov, half Armenian and half Georgian so from two 'Christian countries', has done more in practice. He is a member of the Imperial Orthodox Palestine Society and was awarded the Patriarch's prestigious Order of the Holy Prince Daniel of Moscow for 'services for the revival of spiritual life in Russia'.

Although, as in the rest of Europe, a majority of Russians identify as Christians (a poll in 2013 suggested 64%) only a small proportion attend the Orthodox Liturgy (acknowledged by the Catholic church as a valid form of the Mass though the two Churches are not formally in communion). Nevertheless it was with funds from the people that the Orthodox Church was able to rebuild a near exact replica of the Cathedral of Christ the Saviour blown up by Stalin in the name of communist atheism. This was done with surprising speed and was largely completed by 2000. In the eyes not only of the faithful but quite likely of most Russians it is the 'St. Peter's' of Russian Christianity.

Russia's deep Christian roots showed when many were shocked by the Pussy Riot anti-Putin protest (and prayer: "Mother of God chase Putin away") in that cathedral. (He took advantage of this to put the girls in prison but it was partly because they had chosen the cathedral for their impiety that they gained world attention such that criticism of the President resounded both in Russia and worldwide. And who knows how many Russians privately echo that Pussy Riot prayer!

Russia's status as a European country goes far beyond race and religion: even before Peter the Great in the 17th century Russia was a part of the then very varied European brand of society, though separated by distance from regular contact. Peter the Great visited the western countries of Europe as a young man. As Czar he ended this quasi-isolation by building St. Petersburg - a port and thus in full contact with the rest of Europe. Russia became a European power politically, economically and culturally. It was a land power on the extreme east of Europe just as Britain was a sea power on the extreme west of Europe.

This meant a bond with Britain because neither country could countenance any one power dominating the area between them. This became evident when Napoleon sought to dominate Europe at the end of the 18th century - warring with Britain on the world's seas and invading Russia. Britain won on the high seas and the French were defeated in Russia. If it had not been for the terrible losses of Napoleon's Grande Armée in the Russian campaign, the Battle of Waterloo would almost certainly have been lost. As it was, Wellington remarked: "It has been a damned nice thing - the nearest run thing you ever saw in your life" (Captain Batty, who was there, in a letter).

In the first World War the threat came from the German and Austrian empires. So this time Russia was on the French side along with France's new ally, Britain. The 1917 Bolshevik revolution, possible because of Russian defeats in the field, overthrew the Czar and the Russian Empire became the Soviet Union. Nevertheless the campaign on Germany's Eastern front had helped the Allies significantly. But the emergence of a communist Soviet Union put it at odds with the rest of capitalist Europe. So much so, that neither Premier Chamberlain's Britain nor Stalin's USSR perceived in time that 'my enemy's enemy is my friend' as the old saying goes. For the national interest of both Britain and the USSR demanded a common front to contain Hitler's Germany.

Britain and the USSR

The British did approach Stalin, but half-heartedly and at too low a level. By that time Stalin was close to writing off Britain after Chamberlain's 'Munich' capitulation to Hitler over Czechoslovakia in 1938. So, after Nazi Foreign Minister Ribbentrop's visit, Stalin chose to deal with Hitler's Germany: the presumed victor to be. By agreement with Hitler, Stalin took over half of Poland when Hitler invaded. But, contrary to expectations Britain did not collapse like France in 1940 and by the end of 1941 was the only country still standing and fighting Nazi Germany.

Stalin's utterly disastrous error was to disregard British and several other warnings that Hitler was about to invade the USSR. So the USSR was unprepared for Operation Barbarossa - the German invasion of Russia on 22 June 1941. Hitler nearly defeated the USSR partly because of this and partly because Stalin had purged the army, executing it's brilliant commander Marshal Tukashevsky in 1937 and purging many other senior officers. Without most of its best top professional soldiers and without orders to prepare for an attack it took many months and massive losses of territory, men and material, before the siege of Stalingrad was raised and Russia went on to enter Berlin in 1945. Russian military and civilian casualties from all causes (including Stalin's purges and gulags) were of the order of 20,000,000. Over 90% of German military casualties occurred in the Soviet Union.

With the German invasion, both Britain and Russia at last saw that they had no choice but to be allies yet again. At great cost Britain sent 78 large convoys of vital supplies to Russia via the Arctic ports - notably Murmansk and Arkangelsk. Without them the USSR might well have succumbed. And the Anglo-American D Day landings in France in 1944 only succeeded with difficulty. If Hitler had not had to fight a war of attrition on the Russian front, they could almost certainly not have been attempted at that time: indeed the war could well have been lost by then.

Russia's contribution to European (and to world) culture.

But Russia has far more in common with Europe than race, Christianity, and military history. For in literature, music, theatre, ballet, and the fine arts the Russian contribution to European (and through European to world) culture the Russian contribution, particularly in the 19th century was immense. You cannot talk of European culture without the Russians. Think only of Pushkin, Dostoyevsky, Leo Tolstoy, Chekov, and Pasternak in literature (and so many more it's hard stop there!); and just Mussorgsky, Rimsky Korsakov, Rachmaninov, Stravinsky, Prokoviev, and Shostakovich (I must stop here!) in classical music. Ballet was virtually invented by the Russian court in the 1740s: great names out of a long list are Diaghilev, Balachine (who founded the New York City Ballet Company) and more recently Ulanova, Makarova, Nureyev and Pavlova. Russian artists are less well known - but Kandinsky and Chagall come immediately to mind, also the avant garde woman painter Natalia Goncharova.

Russian opinion

Today many of Russia's élite (including its 80 or so billionaires most of whom benefited by buying the communist state's assets at knock down prices) have bought some of the finest property in Britain and enjoy European culture as the Europeans they are. And as I pointed out, the middle classes, many in key positions, are also well aware of Russia's proper place in Europe even if, right now, they are keeping their mouths shut about that! Russians have a long history of 'reading between the lines' and of knowing what they shouldn't know, let alone trying to do anything about it. I found out about that during a visit in Soviet times.

They see that the United States will remain for some time to come the most powerful country in the world despite its decline as a result of serious mistakes and crippling internal divisions. They see that remaining the dominant power brings it in conflict not only with Russia but with the EU. And that, with the rise of China and the emergence of a multi-polar world, it is most important for Russia and the EU to work together wherever possible. For not only do many of Russia's interests coincide with Europe's but it shares western Europe's aversion to war since World War II (despite the Chechen 'civil war'). Like leaders in most European countries, members of this school of thought particularly want to avoid the use of force in resolving international disputes.

The European strand in Russian foreign policy

One of the most influential of these is, once again, Foreign Minister Lavrov. One of his heroes is Aleksander Gorchakov, Czar Alexander II's foreign minister, a supremely cultured man and close friend Pushkin, Russia's greatest poet. Gorchakov restored, without a shot fired simply by years of patient diplomacy, Russia's position as a respected leading power after the defeat of the Crimean War. Lavrov, who has remarked "nothing good comes of revolution", believes that patient skilled diplomacy, not armed force, is the way to resolve problems in our modern world. He points to the failures of the American interventions in Vietnam, Iraq, and Afghanistan, and the Russian intervention in Afghanistan.

Evolution, not revolution should indeed be the watchword of the statesman. To avoid tumultuous upsets, rulers must not jam on the brakes refusing evolution. How many rulers today won't listen to that advice? And of course Lavrov's boss, Putin, could be one of those.

Understandably, despite his acceptance that Russia is a European power and his desire for much closer cooperation with Europe, Lavrov does not have much regard for the EU's ill-coordinated and often indeterminate and sometimes non-existent policies. He will probably continue to be reviled in the 'West' for his role over the Ukraine and the annexation of the Crimea. But Lavrov will doubtless have advised Putin that Russia held the best cards, military, political and cultural, and needed only to divide the weak E.U. from the American neo-conservatives and their wrecking ball, by offering a solution satisfactory to both the EU and Russia before resorting to annexation or military force. But as we know, Putin's all but obsessive over-riding fear of the US and its dominance of the EU led him too swiftly to choose force over diplomacy, so misplaying his winning hand.

Return of the neo-conservatives

Indeed the neo-conservatives are back again after laying low following the disastrous invasion of Iraq that they persuaded President G. W. Bush to order. Just one example: Robert Kagan is the husband of Assistant Secretary of State Victoria Nuland. And it was her notorious "epithet NOT deleted" open telephone call on 28 January to the US Ambassador in Kiev that was intercepted, publically exposing American involvement in the

Kiev uprising and US disparagement of the EU. Kagan is a co-founder of the neo-conservatives 'Project For A New American Century' (PNAC). Dick Cheney was the key leader of this movement both before and after he became President G. W. Bush's Vice President ostensibly to provide 'safe hands' for a Commander in Chief with little knowledge of foreign affairs. The PNAC is the group which tried unsuccessfully to persuade President Clinton to invade Iraq but got their wish when Cheney and Secretary Rumsfeld were providing those supposedly safe hands.

Robert Kagan was a member of the State Department's Foreign Policy Board. And Kagan is the one who so succinctly summed up neo-conservatism with the remark: "Americans are from Mars, Europeans from Venus". But it could well be that Obama was not aware of just how far the neo-conservatives in the CIA and the State Department were involved in Ukrainian affairs. Neo-conservatism, which brought low the US under G.W. Bush, is now riding high and is once again an important element in American foreign policy. It prevents that move from confrontation to cooperation. Which makes it all the more important that the EU somehow finds its voice.

The Nuland phone call was an astonishing blunder - even in my day no one in an embassy spoke on an open line about policy. How could she today when the Russians are listening? As for the SVR (the KGB's successor), they are virtually on home ground in the Ukraine: did the US neo-cons really think it wise to try to outsmart the Russians there? The extent of American involvement in the Ukraine was advertised when Nuland in December 2013 remarked that to help the Ukraine 'achieve its European aspirations we have invested more than $5bn'. Surely that should have been contributed not by the US but by the EU in concert with Russia?

Despite the present confrontation, I think I have made my point: Russia is part of Europe whether they, or we, like or not. Russians regard themselves as European and it is to Europe that they come for tourism, second homes, business and finance and much else.

The fact is - they don't feel very much at home anywhere else.

Wasn't Putin always 'the fly in the ointment' at least since his war on the Chechens?

Western media commonly present President Putin as an ogre and, as I have suggested, there is more than a bit of truth about that. He is of course an ex-KGB officer who runs that 'katascopic' state which spies most expertly in both the political and economic domains while at the same time 'hoovering up' vast quantities of electronic information. But then who doesn't spy and hoover if they can get away with it? America, of course, doesn't get away with it - it leaks badly: think Snowden and Bradley. So the US gets nearly all the blame along with Britain (e.g. a photo showed a 'captor' on its Embassy's roof in Berlin listening to German Chancellor Mme Merkel's private conversations. But we don't hear about what's on the Russian Embassy roof!). Much more serious for Russians is his anti-democratic authoritarian rule, reminiscent of the czars. He runs a nasty 'Archipelago' prison system inherited from Stalin. (Nothing new - Dostoevsky languished in Siberia under the czars).

Quite apart from the Ukraine, this greater Russia outlook brings Putin into conflict, not cooperation, with the European Union. The SVR, like the CIA and other secret services today, do not merely spy, they conduct 'special political action' which may include assassinations. The finger of suspicion points to Putin's Russia in two notorious cases - that of Alexander Litvinenko in the UK in 2006 (he knew too much about Russian clandestine activities) where the poison was polonium 210. And that of Ukraine's President Victor Yushchenko (who opposed Russia's hold over the Ukraine) and was poisoned with dioxin (which, as TCDD, was contained in the Americans' deadly Agent Orange used in Vietnam).

Secret services: the CIA, the SVR and others

It is worrying that this awakening to Russia's vital interest in the Ukraine has come so late and that in the absence of the EU, the

Ukraine has become a battleground for US and Russian 'special services' marked by US loss of control over its neo-conservatives, its military, and the CIA, while Putin's Russia has pretty well full control over its respective services. For Russia (with its SVR) and the US (with its CIA) have secret services which stop at nothing to intervene in disputed places like the Ukraine and Georgia (and in many other countries) whether in the longer term interests of their respective countries, or not.

The attempted assassination of Yushchenko did bring Viktor Yanukovych to the presidency, but very indirectly. The former's long illness and resultant disfigurement appear to have cost him his former political ability: his popularity tumbled to single digits. Ironically Russia's choice, Yanukovych, a corrupt oligarch, so misgoverned the Ukraine that he needlessly brought about the present on-going crisis against Russia's long term interests. Just as Yanukovych's west Ukraine opponents failed to keep east Ukraine's interests to the fore, so did he fail to respect west Ukraine's legitimate concerns.

A bit about the Chechens

Maybe even worse from the international point of view, is the way Putin continued his predecessor Yeltsin's long history of Russian ruthless suppression of the Sunni Muslim Chechens, a quite remarkable warrior people: it is their enduring hatred of Russia that puts Russia alongside the US and the 'West' in 'the war on terrorism'. But, as I have said, Sunni terrorism from the Caucasus is the major reason for Russia's support for the Syrian government of Bashar al Assad. His Alawite (neo-Shia) government is seen as a line of defence against Sunni extremist Al Qaeda and clones. Indeed Russia was the first to fight against extremist interpretations of Islam: in 1785 Sheikh Mansour, a Chechen Imam preached a neo-Wahab Islam against Russian imperialism resulting in what was the real first Russian/Chechen war. Russian General Yermolov suppressed the Chechens with appalling brutality. Indeed Chechen guerrilla warfare was only suppressed in 1862 after a long 'Holy War' declared by another Imam in 1834.

The Chechens remained so bitter after being incorporated into the then new Soviet Union in 1921 that Stalin had his notorious secret policeman, Beria, deport around half a million Chechens to Central Asia in 1941 to prevent them collaborating with the Germans in World War II. After the collapse of the Soviet Union the Chechens declared their independence in 1991. It was Russia's President Yeltsin who waged the first (modern) Chechen War in 1994 which ended with a Russian withdrawal in 1997 when matters calmed down. When Putin came to power in 1999 he took the fatal step of starting a second Chechen War, virtually destroying the capital, Grozny in 2000 and installing a puppet government. In the West there was much sympathy for the Chechens and Putin lost much support internationally.

Ever since then Chechen insurgents have been mounting a series of terrorist attacks in Russia itself. (Indeed the Boston Bombing in the US was carried out by Chechen brothers Tsamaev). Which is why Putin ordered the use of the same 'hyper use of military force' that he decries when committed by America.

HOW CONFRONTATION RETURNED

All the same, in international, as well as Russia's domestic affairs, President Putin has, as I have suggested, had much to complain about from the 'West'. That explains much about his hard line over the Ukraine. But first, again a bit of history.

The Ukraine, lies between two great power blocks, Russia on the one hand and a European power on the other - before World War I that was the Austrian Empire, more recently it is the European Union. As in the case of Syria, where American policies did not take proper account of Russia early on, so the European Union - and its disparate members - failed to appreciate Russia's position in regard
to the Ukraine and a thoroughly unhelpful 'tug of war' has resulted.

I have explained how important the lands around Kiev are to Russia historically, culturally, and strategically. Only 65% of Ukrainians speak Ukrainian as their first language. In central Ukraine 25% speak Russian first, and even in the eastern part of the centre it's 59%. In the south, in the Crimea, and in the east 80-95 % are Russian speakers. Ukrainian is the first language of about 30m people, Russian is the first language of 150m and the second language of 110m. As the language of the former Soviet Union enjoying Russia's immense cultural heritage, it is the second language, where not the first, of many, if not most, Ukrainians - the two languages are very similar. As all the world's major works are available in Russian, it provides the easiest way for a Ukrainian to enjoy not only the world's culture but also to access its science and technology.

As the media have at last learned, the economy of east Ukraine largely depends on the Russian economy, the centre and west largely depend upon the EU's economy. In a word the Ukraine is a partially divided country looking both east and west. Even in religion it is divided - there's the Ukrainian Orthodox and part of that looking to Russian orthodoxy. And then there's the Ukrainian eastern rite church, a version of Orthodoxy in communion with Rome.

The 'carpet-baggers'

Obviously it behoved the West after the collapse of the Soviet Union, to take Russia's vital interests very much into account when deciding policy - after all Russia remained a great power, it was not a defeated nation any more than the UK after the loss of empire. But American and European business descended on Russia. That was reminiscent of the Yankee 'carpet baggers' who descended on the southern states after their defeat by the North. Unregulated capitalism was virtually imposed on President Yeltsin's Russia instead of the 'West''s brand and so helping a carefully controlled transition from Soviet style communism to the kind of strictly regulated capitalism then practiced in Europe and even, to a considerable extent, in the US. The result was that sale of state property at knock down prices creating that host of Russian billionaires and a society even more unequal than the United States - which can much more readily afford it. So a deplorable Western triumphalist thrust is in part responsible for the unsatisfactory state of Russia today.

The Russian people, although many hailed the end of communism, were at one with many of their politicians in feeling an overall sense of humiliation. All at once, with the coup against Gorbachev, they had lost the huge empire of the czars - including the Ukraine, the cradle of Russia itself. Putin was not alone in calling the collapse of the Soviet Union a disaster, a view not confined to Russians provided one meant the rapidly reforming USSR under President Gorbachev. For, looked at objectively, huge Kazakhstan and much of Central Asia have since fragmented into independent dictatorships - their allegiances up for grabs. Not democracy, but instability reigns in almost all Central Asia where the USSR had been a political unit with a single foreign policy.

At that time - 1989/90 - Russia was the only countervailing power to the US. It had been rapidly evolving under those reforms of Gorbachev from the Marxist-Leninist-Stalinist monster it had become after the Bolshevik revolution. That laissez-faire capitalist takeover followed his deposition. Indeed, not a few international observers saw the US, after the Soviet Union's collapse, as needing a countervailing power to limit its excesses. America no longer had to have regard to the interests of another superpower in the same way as the Soviet Union had been restrained by the US and vice versa.

German re-unification and NATO - the 'West's' promise to Russia

The unification of Germany was the first big East/West challenge when Gorbachev decided that the USSR would not intervene to prevent the USSR's European subject peoples' achieving their independence. East Germany was the first with the collapse of the German Democratic Republic. This was difficult not only for the USSR to accept, but also for the other members of the European

Union which shared Russia's memories of German occupation under Hitler. Now all these countries were to agree to a reunited Germany becoming the major power in the European Union.

Gorbachev agreed to what had been East Germany joining the NATO military alliance on the very border of the then Warsaw Pact members in Eastern Europe. He agreed on certain conditions - one of which was, as I mentioned, that NATO would not move any further to the east. There is still a lot of controversy about this agreement which was not made a formal treaty - there was no need for that then as the Warsaw Pact still existed. But in the Kremlin on 9 February 1989 James Baker, then US Secretary of State, declared that there would be "no extension of NATO's jurisdiction for forces of NATO one inch to the east" (of a reunited Germany).

Before the accession in 1999 of Poland, Hungary and Czechoslovakia and the Baltics in 1999 - all countries which had suffered Soviet occupation and understandably still feared Russia - Russian concern had been largely met by the formation of the NATO-Russia Permanent Joint Council in 1998.

But breaching the 1989 understanding by inviting former members of the Soviet Union to join was a quite different matter and a serious reaction from a by then much stronger Russia had to be expected.

Germany and France 'let down' by the US in Afghanistan

It is worth mentioning here that Russia is not alone in being discomfited by American belligerence. The NATO members loyally declared '9/11' to be an attack on America, and that it constituted, under the terms of the NATO treaty, 'an attack on one country being an attack on all', thus triggering a military response. So France and Germany among others sent armed forces to Afghanistan believing America would be with them all the way throughout the occupation. But when the US and the UK invaded Iraq, Afghanistan did, as I have said, predictably lose its priority. So the NATO members, who had acted in NATO solidarity with

America, found themselves over-extended in Afghanistan without full American support and, after years of losses, being forced to make a humiliating retreat.

This rankles today with France, Germany and some other participants in the occupation of Afghanistan - which turned into over well over decade of war largely because the US invaded Iraq against their strong advice. (The US and UK acted without regard to the UN because France, backed by Germany, as a member of the UN Security Council threatened to veto an invasion. Some members of Congress were so annoyed that they famously declared French fries to be 'Freedom fries'!)

The Ukraine - as an object lesson in how NOT to do diplomacy

I have spent so long on Russia and the Ukraine not only because of my belief that Europe as a whole has a key role to play in working for cooperation not confrontation in world affairs, but because the 2014 Ukraine crisis provides a quite exceptional object lesson in how not to do diplomacy. A lesson that surely must be learned if future confrontations are to be avoided.

The failure of both the European Union and the US to see the Ukraine through Russian eyes has led to worsening, not ameliorating the internal divisions within the Ukraine, and to exacerbating that historical 'tug-of-war' between Russia and the Ukraine's western neighbours. Yet that very first rule in diplomacy is to look at any problem through your opponent's eyes. It is Russia, not just its present president, that has a vital strategic interest in the Ukraine. Quite apart from history and culture, for Russia the Ukraine needs to be a buffer state between it and what is now Western Europe. And no matter what agreements were signed in 1991 (the Budapest Memorandum) and in 1994 (the Kharkhov Treaty) about Russia's agreement to the Crimea being part of Ukraine, any development in Ukraine that threatened Russia's black sea fleet in the Crimea took precedence over any agreements made when Russia was weak after the collapse of the USSR.

In February 2012, following the Russia/Georgia war in 2008, I wrote that even then it was not too late in the day to defuse a crisis over the Ukraine, remarking that there was an urgent need for the EU, the US, and Russia to have top level discussions making it clear that the 'West's' interest in the Ukraine is essentially the same as Russia's - namely its stability and prosperity. And that those can only be achieved by the Ukraine being militarily neutral while maintaining close economic and cultural relations with both Russia and the EU - Russia's Black Sea Fleet retaining its bases in Sebastopol and elsewhere in the Crimea.

As it is, the ramifications of the Ukraine crisis look (in May 2014) as if they will persist for a long time to the detriment of moves towards that so badly needed era of pan-European cooperation. It is a prime example of how dangerous it is to ignore diplomacy in favour of media 'sound bites', ignorant politicians' incendiary appeals, and failure to control one's secret services. That's so especially if one's ability and will to use force - or even sanctions - is minimal compared with an opponent who believes he has a vital national interest at stake and reasonably deduces that you pose a threat to this and have no interest in constructive negotiations.

The Ukraine story would have been very different if 'the West':

a) had not behaved like victors when the Cold War ended with the USSR's implosion and encouraged the 'carpet baggers' descent on Russia,

b) had appreciated much earlier that Russia would not allow such humiliation to continue and so had treated Russia with respect,

c) had taken Putin's 2007 speech with the attention it deserved instead of snubbing him - and those around him who were working for close relations with the EU,

d) had not pushed provocatively for NATO expansion to the Ukraine and Georgia,

e) had made a point of taking no action without first discussing with Russia not only matters in Russia's immediate environment but other major world problems. If it had, the 'West' could reasonably have expected real cooperation from Russia in the United Nations and elsewhere,

f) had Obama's US let the Europeans take the leading role as he had had the US do over Libya: the Ukraine is a Russia/EU matter and the EU should have taken a lead instead of once again dithering and letting the US act on its own in the Ukraine (as it had done in Bosnia with what have proved very unsatisfactory consequences),

g) if the Obama administration had curbed its neo-conservatives (and the CIA) in their brash attempt to haul the Ukraine into 'the West' thereby taking on the Russian 'special services' for an 'at home' match,

h) if the US and the EU had not confined their talks to discussions with the Kiev interim government but had also talked at a high level with Moscow. For, after the ouster of Yanukovych, the Kiev government did not represent the whole country. Indeed its 'law' removing Russian as one of the country's official languages was a red cape to the Putin bull and a major reason for many in the east to seek union with Russia,

i) had both the EU and the US warned the Kiev authorities not to take lethal measures against protesters in east Ukraine which would start a disastrous civil war dividing instead of uniting the country.

Yes of course professional diplomats need to carry their heads of government with them in gaining authority to put forward their recommendations for resolving differences. But Heads of government often have their political positions, popularity and prestige at stake. They may also have unhelpful personal preconceptions which need to be tactfully whittled away. So, if you want a positive diplomatic solution it is most important to make no statements, no matter how attractive, which will cause personal offence or harden those preconceptions. One must at the same time handle the media with care to discourage inflammatory coverage while simultaneously negotiating in secret.

THE UK & EUROPE SEEN FROM A BACK SEAT

You've mentioned the European Union several times rather disparagingly? But you had quite a lot to do with it during your career?

Yes, I was in the Economic Relations Department of the Foreign Office after my return from the Far East in 1958 when all the talk was about 'sixes and sevens' (meaning 'our' European Free Trade Area with six members and the then seven members of the European Economic Community as the EU then was. Then I served in our Paris Embassy from 1961 to 1965 when Edward Heath was attempting to get the UK into the Community and our application was vetoed by General de Gaulle in 1963.

When I joined the Foreign Service (now the Diplomatic Service) in September 1951 I found myself on my first day in the Office the most junior member of the American Department. The Head of the Department, Donald Maclean, had defected to the Soviet Union on 25 May. The Deputy Head of Department became the Head and everyone moved up one leaving an empty desk at the bottom which I came to fill! In the space of just a month I was to serve under both Clement Attlee's foreign secretary Herbert Morrison and Churchill's Anthony Eden.

The US, UK and Europe

One subject under discussion was how our close relations with the US fitted in with our relations with post war Europe now that the European Coal and Steel Community (ECSC) had been formed without us by the Treaty of Paris that April. Truman was the US President and Dean Acheson, his Secretary of State. Both were favourable to greater integration in Europe (and that included the UK). Ernest Bevin had been Britain's outstanding post-war

Foreign Secretary. He believed that Britain, the one European country that had come out of World War II as a 'victor', had an essential role to play in post-war Europe. He had seen military integration as the answer to the problem of ensuring that there could be no further suicidal European wars and his great achievement, with France and Benelux, was the 1948 Brussels Treaty foreshadowing a European Defence Force. (NATO was formed the following year so the Treaty became redundant).

France though, soon saw the cure not in military terms but in economic integration starting with coal and steel. But Bevin was terminally ill (he resigned on his 70th birthday, 9 March, the month before the Treaty of Paris was signed) and there was no one of his stature to overcome the reluctance of a government struggling financially - Britain was re-paying its huge wartime debt to the US (Lend Lease) while continental Europe was being bolstered by the 1948 Marshall Plan. This drain was one reason why there were grossly insufficient funds for tackling the daunting problems posed by an unraveling empire.

All this largely explains the political reluctance to take on major responsibilities in Europe. So, not having played a part in creating the ECSC, meant that Britain had lost the chance to lead, or even to get in on the ground floor in determining the direction post-war Europe would take.

The ECSC was Jean Monnet's and Robert Schuman's brainchild as the first move towards European integration. Both were French and their initiative was greatly welcomed by Chancellor Adenauer's defeated Germany. Unlike the Brussels Treaty, West Germany was an essential partner - it was the beginning of reconciliation between France and Germany.

The beginning of 'Euroscepticism'?

But Prime Minister Clement Attlee appointed Herbert Morrison to succeed Bevin. Morrison was against 'Europe'. So that may be the best date from which to date the beginning of British 'Euroscepticism'. (Later Morrison made his famous remark "If

Britain joins the Common Market that will be the end of Britain as an independent state").

Attlee's post-war Labour government fell with the General Election on 25 October and Churchill began his second administration. He appointed Eden as his foreign secretary, another Eurosceptic. The American department continued to try to persuade our seniors that Britain should play a major part in the direction western Europe should take, given that the Soviet Union, the only other European 'victor' in 1945, was in control of all of eastern Europe. It pointed out that Truman's and Acheson's US was much in favour of the UK, its principal ally, taking a lead in Europe. (Acheson, was later [1962] to make his famous remark in the context of British failure to take a part in Europe, "Britain has lost an empire and has not yet found a role" that so upset Macmillan and many other British politicians of his generation: they knew the truth and did not like its face!)

Pro-Europe Churchill defers to Anthony Eden

But the Foreign Office was brought to heel by Churchill's appointment of Anthony Eden, his Foreign Secretary during the war: the renowned foreign policy expert to whose judgment in foreign affairs even Churchill, then ageing perceptibly, had to submit.

In Opposition during the Labour government, Churchill had pushed for close relations with Europe and had opposed the Labour Government's failure to negotiate with France, Germany and the Benelux countries as they set up the ECSC. In 1946 with his famous 'Iron Curtain' speech in Fulton Misssouri, it was Churchill, half-American, who had first awoken the US to the impending Cold War and its need not just for the UK but for the free continental countries as allies. For him there was no 'either go with the US or go with Europe' - it had to be 'go with both'.

But Anthony Eden, the supposedly infallible UK foreign affairs guru, was unwilling to recognise how Britain no longer ranked with US and the USSR as one of the great powers. His 'no' to

Europe meant that was that - no matter the deep concerns of many of his diplomats. When Britain was invited to prepare for a second step in the making of Europe, a plan to create a Common Market, the Eden government declined and refused the invitation to go to the Messina Conference in 1955 which, despite much doubt, did indeed set up the Common Market. This was a blow to many of the participants who wanted Europe to develop with British participation - even leadership - rather than that be left to France which had the say over a still humbled Germany and an Italy, also defeated in 1945, which had a fresh government every year.

The three great British errors since 1945?

To my mind even more than Suez, and possibly even more than Iraq, the refusal to take part in the Messina Conference was the greatest mistake made by any UK government from 1945 to the present day. Without the UK, Europe was made as France wanted with the top down bureaucratic structure and minimal democratic participation that we - and many other European countries - so dislike today. The UK had fought many wars to prevent any single power dominating Europe - now Europe was re-making itself without the UK!

No to Europe, yes to 'Suez"

So this great chance was missed and the very next year, 1956, Eden made his second disastrous mistake. He opted (with France and Israel) to go to war with Egypt. The ensuing retreat from Suez forced by the American refusal to support the pound, brought home to us all - and to the world - the full extent of Britain's decline and how we could not depend on the US to bail us out after an adventure that displeased it. At the time I was on leave in Kashmir appalled by what had happened. Mine was not the only stay in Kashmir that was blighted: I saw Attlee, who had also been there, abruptly leaving after calling Eden's 'Suez' "an act of criminal folly". (I haven't been able to check this quote).

Suez changed the whole picture: Britain had either to go it alone or go it with Europe - the sun had finally set on the 'Empire on which the sun never set'. After 'Suez', Macmillan succeeded Eden as Prime Minister in 1957. He was our second half-American Prime Minister. He understood his mistake as Foreign Minister in deferring to Eden, and in 1961 the UK applied to join the Common Market. But, with a weakened Britain, de Gaulle's resurgent France was now able to veto British accession.

Heath and De Gaulle's veto

Nearly a decade later, I was in our Embassy in Paris when in 1964-1967 Edward Heath, then Minister of State in Alec Douglas-Home's government, made a desperate attempt to overcome de Gaulle's objections to British entry. I was detailed to accompany Heath to the airport in the Ambassador's Rolls Royce on his last visit to Paris. I was sitting on the occasional seat opposite him as he threw the newspapers at me as he read with astounding speed. Suddenly he put down the paper in his hand and asked me point blank whether de Gaulle would veto our application. In the embassy we had excellent contacts with several top French contacts who saw British entry as greatly in France's interest. From them we believed that a veto was all but certain. I replied that it was hardly for me to answer. At which Heath had me open the glass between us and the French chauffeur and tell him to stop at the next phone box. Heath and phoned the Ambassador who must have given a very guarded reply as the French were of course intercepting incoming calls.

Those were fraught times - we all knew what was at stake. De Gaulle did of course veto. By that time Europe was no longer a fief of France because Germany had rebounded from its post war ruins. De Gaulle explained his veto: Britain was so close to America that it would not be a loyal European but a stalking horse for the US. We would not be a loyal partner in building his 'Europe from the Atlantic to the Urals'. That sounds prescient - but it was de Gaulle who more than anyone else made this come almost true. (Indeed, nearly forty years later Prime Minister Blair claimed that keeping close to the Americans required British participation in the invasion of Iraq despite the French and German opposition).

As an observer in Paris at the time, I personally believe that de Gaulle vetoed British entry in 1967 because he was more afraid that Britain's membership would boost *German* influence (which was still diminished at that time by the existence of the separate German Democratic Republic under Soviet control). What I think he feared most was the UK and Germany prevailing over France's dominance of the Brussels bureaucratic system that it had created. Only with de Gaulle gone, was Edward Heath able at last to get Britain into the European Community in 1973.

How wrong renowned experts can be when in power

I tell this story because it reveals how disastrously mistaken even a world renowned authority can be if he does not check his preconceptions with those whose duty it is to advise him. Eden's inability to understand that (as times had changed and post-war Britain could do longer go it alone) a great tariff free trading bloc was about to emerge that Britain could not afford to be outside and which 1955 Britain, then the leading European power, could ensure that its structures took the form it wished. As I say, having fought war after war to prevent any European power from dominating the continent, Britain abdicated when at last it had the chance to lead in designing a new Europe of prosperity and peace enjoying a powerful voice in the world.

Today the Eden story brings former Vice-President Cheney to mind - that renowned expert in 'security' and foreign affairs whose 'safe hands' were intended to preserve President G. W. Bush from foreign policy errors. But, where Eden had a mind-set of empire, Cheney's was of a unipolar world where America could do as it pleased. His was the 'realpolitik' interventionist ideology of the neo-conservatives: he had signed the letter to President Clinton urging an invasion of Iraq in the '90s. Like Eden with Suez, he got America into Iraq. And like Britain, the US suffered a similarly grave defeat.

The wrong way to approach Europe

Not having made the European Union as Britain would have liked, there was dissatisfaction when it did enter. Here successive UK governments failed, and still fail, to see that several other EU members were, and are, also much in favour of reform. After Mrs. Thatcher arrived in 1979, instead of gathering friends and promoting much needed reforms, she made enemies in Europe with her loud complaints demanding special treatment for Britain, and when she got concessions, went on complaining. Indeed many politicians mostly Conservatives have still gone on complaining even to the extent of demanding that Britain withdraw altogether. Spoon fed by the popularist anti-Europe media and kept too much in the dark by others in the media who see Europe as a 'turn off' for the audience they need, much of the UK public have little awareness of the imperative for Britain of its EU membership. The fringe United Kingdom Independence Party (UKIP) has flourished. Britain could be sleep-walking to isolationist irrelevance if the promised referendum on continued membership of Europe is held as promised should there be a return of the Cameron government in the next general elections in 2015.

The role of Rupert Murdoch

Blair was pro-EU but, as I have explained, seriously harmed British opportunities in the EU by invading Iraq with President G. W. Bush regardless of the opposition of Germany and France - so dividing the EU on a vital issue of foreign policy. The once respected British lion was egged on in this policy of behaving as 'Bush's poodle' by the immensely powerful international, but primarily American, News Corporation controlled by ex-Australian Rupert Murdoch.

Murdoch was the owner then of *The Weekly Standard* - the neo-conservatives' newspaper used by Cheney to co-ordinate the neo-conservative line. In Britain he owned *The Times,* the former paper of record at the top end, and the Sun at the tabloid end. Murdoch was against Europe and successfully fanned latent Euroscepticism in the British public. Euroscepticism has now become so powerful even in some Labour circles that Prime Minister Cameron, though himself well aware of the disaster of a 'no' vote, felt obliged to agree to the referendum if re-elected.

The Euro - should Britain have joined?

Another lost chance, because it has led to a fundamental and enfeebling division within the EU, was the opportunity to join the European currency: the controversial Euro which was established in 1999. Again, Prime Minister Blair was in favour but his Chancellor of the Exchequer, Gordon Brown, was against. The idea of a European currency had long been discussed and the UK was present at EU finance ministers meetings. A lot of politicking had surrounded the negotiations for the birth of the Euro. For example, it is said on good authority that the French got the Germans to accept the Euro on their terms in place of the leading European currency, the Deutschmark, by making that a condition for French support for the reunification of Germany. Also Italy's credentials for joining were seriously flawed: their accounting was 'window dressed' - but politics won the day and Italy was accepted as a member. So the stability of the Euro was not achieved by the Stability and Growth Pact, 1997.

In the opinion of many experts, the primary reason for this was the absence of a single European bond - each country was allowed to sell its own bonds. Many, including myself, were dismayed after Greece joined the Euro to find that the Greek sovereign bond was earning higher and higher rates of interest. That meant there was increasing risk in purchasing a sovereign debt bond. But the big banks, counting on sovereign debt always being met in one way or another, seized on this opportunity to make easy money. When Greece was about to default one might have expected the Banks to lose - the whole capitalist ethos is that risk-taking brings profits but also brings losses if mistaken. But to our amazement the banks were bailed out by governments - to the detriment of the public! The banks were said to be 'too big to fail' - but that didn't mean that if they were rescued they didn't have pay a heavy price.

I believe that had the Bank of England been involved in the creation of the Euro along with the Deutsche Bundesbank, the UK could have bolstered Germany's position at a time of uncertainty and transition, and so demanded far stricter stability measures independent of politics: for example a single European bond and the prevention of Italy joining as a 'founding' member. And Greece would never have been permitted to join in 2001. Free of politics, a stability mechanism negotiated between British and German central banks would, I believe, have resulted in a highly successful world currency uniting the pound, still a major world currency, with the prestigious Deutschmark.

There would then have been no sovereign debt crisis for any of the Euro countries. There would have been no London vying with New York - each offering the world's financiers deregulation as a plum. Europe would have been saved much of the effects of the American financial meltdown in 2007/8. And Italy and Greece in particular would have been obliged to put their houses in order before joining.

Once again, anti-Europe prejudice, lack of imagination, and lack of leadership has, I believe, caused Britain to miss yet another appointment with destiny. And, for once, we can't blame Tony Blair for that! What a tragedy when, as I keep pleading, the world needs Europe to take a lead in meeting the challenge of that existential double helix. With the US all but ungovernable and China a very dubious alternative champion, this is another reason for grave concern that financially and politically Europe lacks the leadership to act for mankind.

Let's assume the 'Europeans' among us win any referendum on the EU and Britain remains a member - or even if it doesn't - how do you see the EU progressing?

The language problem

It's a tower of Babel - that's Europe's biggest challenge. 24 official languages, also in important measure 28 different histories and 28 rather different cultures, though we all have much of history and much of culture in common. When I was in Paris the Ambassador asked me to try to arrange for British teachers to come to France to teach English in exchange for accepting French teachers to teach French in the UK. I was surprised to find the French government very keen on this project - it wanted to preserve French as the international language that it had been before 1914, or at least to confirm it as the chief alternative to English.

The idea also appealed to our government at the time - we were supposedly about to join Europe, and were hoping English would emerge as the main language of the Community - as is indeed has happened. But the UK Ministry of Education advised that this was impossible because British teachers, unlike French, are employed by local governments, so could not be given the assurances that their pay, promotion, and retirement prospects would be the same as if they had stayed in the UK. Despite appeals at a higher level, this remained the case. So despite Edward Heath's then ongoing efforts to join the Community, the UK Government was not in 'Europe mode'!

My own view is that reasonable fluency in a second major EU language (English, French, Spanish, German and perhaps Italian) should be a requirement for the equivalent of the French baccalaureate for all students of the EU countries unless they are fluent in a non-EU language (Thai or Urdu for example, or the particularly useful Russian or Chinese). Quite apart from communication, a second language has been shown dramatically to increase the ability to acquire an international outlook, the understanding and appreciation of the thinking and culture of other peoples - it can be valuable for doing business too! It is also said to be 'good for the brain'. Certainly it helps to be able to express, even discover, one's meaning if one can put a thought in more than one way.

Since language is largely a question of practice, reception of satellite television (motorized to receive from four or more satellites) needs to be encouraged. TV can do much to introduce the different countries to each other, and also to prevent government or 'self' censorship'. Twitter and Facebook are also doing just that while providing a lot of language practice. The last Labour Government's obsurantist de-emphasis on language teaching did much damage. There's been a major breakthrough: if you know enough Romanised Mandarin for what you want to say, you can now write the equivalent in characters thanks to a highly sophisticated algorithm which produces as first choice the character you probably seek depending on what you have previously been writing, then other choices in order of the likelihood you'll need them.

Poetry

Music and the visual arts cross language barriers, so do good translations of fiction as well as non-fiction. Poetry though, is largely confined to the linguistic group which produced it: little gets translated, and when it is, all too much is inevitably lost. Yet poetry is hard to beat both for getting an understanding of another culture and for bringing out how all peoples share much the same human concerns. One problem is that poets make use of rare words and difficult constructions. But if one knows even a little of a language one can often get very near to appreciating the original if one has an accompanying literal English translation.

For English speakers Penguin published from the 1950s to the 1970s a whole series of very well chosen anthologies of the best foreign poetry with word for word translations just beneath - these can still be found. I owe a great deal to these volumes and some others not only for the pleasure they have given me but also for helping me to be much more aware of the richness of other cultures mainly in the European languages but also in Chinese. There are a surprising number of books with the characters on one side and literal English on the other and even knowing a few characters helps greatly in working out the Chinese.

Reforming the EU

As regards reforming the EU - I'm among the many who believe that far greater 'subsidiarity' is needed. So far as possible each of the 28 countries should be able to make all the regulations and laws required provided they achieve the same fundamental norms set by the community. That would do much to lessen popular objections to 'being ruled by Brussels bureaucrats'. It would get rid of such absurdities as the famous (infamous?) regulations on 'curved cucumbers and bent bananas', since repealed, which gave Eurosceptics an ideal opportunity to ridicule Brussels and get popular opinion behind the call for a referendum on the UK leaving the EU. This is far from the only case of counter-productive daftness that politically deaf bureaucrats in Brussels have imposed leading to popular resentment in the EU.

If the British government went to Europe in a spirit of cooperation rather than with 'Thatcherite' confrontation and unilateral demands, I believe major reforms could be achieved. De Gaulle is long gone and the demand for reform of the Brussels organization is shared by many other countries, including France itself. Britain could take a lead in getting reforms instead of churlishly demanding this or that 'or we leave'.

Just as important as internal reform to make Europe more popular with both governments and peoples, is the need to restructure European foreign policy for, as I keep arguing, it is essential that Europe have a proper voice in world affairs. I have already pointed out that wherever possible EU foreign policy should be coordinated with that other essentially European country, Russia, if 'greater Europe's' policies are to be given the weight they deserve on the international scene.

As I write during the Ukraine crisis this looks utopian, but where long term national interests are concerned, they tend to prevail if not in the shorter, then in the longer run. And leaders change. The obvious answer is for the fledgling European diplomatic service to coordinate European policy and for the various EU countries' embassies to be abolished in favour of just one EU embassy in each country. Maybe this will be the shape of European diplomacy in the long term. But much improvement is possible using the individual embassies as 'inputs' for arriving at a coordinated EU foreign policy - as is supposed to be the case today. Lady Ashton, as High Representative of the Union for Foreign Affairs, is quietly making some progress in creating a European Union Action Service and has already done something to give substance to EU foreign policy in world affairs - but there is long way to go, as this crisis showed.

For any European High Representative is up against a daunting problem - what is the European foreign policy that the High Representative is attempting to carry out? Henry Kissinger's 1970s alleged remark 'whom do I call when I want to call Europe?' remains just as true today - not just for the Americans but for the Russians and others too. For EU foreign and defence policy is determined by the Common Foreign and Security Policy (CFSP) council chaired by the High Representative. It meets once a month. All 28 members of the EU belong, each has a veto where a decision has 'military or defence implications' which most matters of importance do. This unwieldy body is supposed to act to 'prevent a crisis arising', or 'to manage a crisis if one occurs'.

Not altogether surprisingly, as I've explained, it failed lamentably even to foresee the risk of a crisis over the Ukraine, let alone 'prevent such a crisis arising' - and that, despite many warnings that one was clearly brewing after President G. W. Bush urged NATO to admit the Ukraine and Georgia as members in 2008. When the predicted crisis did arise the CFSP council came up with absolutely no proposals to manage it. It was, as I've said, into this vacuum that America intervened in the Ukraine in a most unhelpful manner.

Yet the Maidan protests in Kiev lasted for months giving the Council ample opportunity to decide policy and make proposals to Russia in regard to this primarily East Europe/West Europe matter. Instead, many of its 28 members bleated its own sheepish bleat. I've explained how the EU even failed to impress on the west Ukrainian protesters that they must carry the east with them if they wanted a unified Ukraine, and how the EU stood by as the final match was lit by the interim Kiev government's astonishingly provocative 'law' depriving Russian of its status as Ukraine's alternative language.

Both President Obama and President Putin had each other's phone numbers but tragically neither yet has the EU's!

Writing in May 2014, in the absence of the EU as an effective player, it is hard indeed to see how the Ukraine crisis can turn out constructively. Particularly as the EU, the US, and NATO all claim that the blame rests solely on Russia. 'Putin bashing' is Politically Correct right now - those of us who tried to show how the 'West' bears much of the responsibility have mostly been timorously 'self-censored' by our media. This has brought about confrontation when there could so easily have been cooperation. And, as I bore you by repeating, cooperation between the east and the west of Europe is of immense importance for having Europe's voice heard on the fraught international scene if any progress is to be made on the many challenges the world faces.

Lord Curzon's 'Great Game' is over - indeed it was over in 1914. For both Russia and Britain have lost their empires. As I've explained their basic national interests now largely coincide and the hope is that before too long those genuine national interests will resurface as national interests tend to do. So, despite appearances, it may perhaps be not so very long before the EU finds its voice.

MY OWN MINI-PARTICIPATION IN EVENTS: BOSNIA, CAMBODIA, LAOS

You were in Bosnia during the siege of Sarajevo -people are saying the lessons of Bosnia need to be applied to resolving other conflicts. What's your take on that?

Mrs. Thatcher and the Falklands

I must put in a few words about Mrs. Thatcher and the 1982 Falklands War before answering. That's because it's the perfect demonstration of how an able leader can err seriously and yet benefit immensely politically. She came to power in 1979 in the wake of the OPEC oil crisis which fatally damaged her predecessor Edward Heath. She embarked on controversial reforms - some much needed (like limiting the power of the trade unions) some less so. By 1982 she and the Conservatives had lost much popularity and it was widely expected that she would not win the next election: by then, for the first time since World War II, there were 3,000,000 unemployed, much of British industry had been scrapped, and the economy was in the doldrums.

Her Foreign Secretary, Lord Carrington warned her of the danger that the notorious and highly unpopular Argentine military junta might use force to assert its claim to the Falkland Islands, 300 miles from Argentina but 8,000 miles from the UK, and so regain much 'patriotic' popularity. Mrs. Thatcher indignantly turned down the suggestion that the population of the islands - less than 2,000 - might be happily relocated in the Western Isles of Scotland as Britain no longer had a strategic interest in the Falklands as it had in the two World Wars. For her Britons had a right to live where they were born!

The one, but until then adequate, deterrent to an Argentine attack was HMS Endeavour on station in the area. But in 1981 the Thatcher government, ever looking for savings, announced the intention of taking Endeavour off station to save some £1 million a year. Given Mrs Thatcher's determination to hold the islands and not resettle the handful of islanders, this was disastrous: it gave a green light to the Galtieri junta to 'wave the flag' to their advantage by taking over the islands. Believing it would be a push-over the junta did invade. Mrs. Thatcher though, stood firm and ordered the immense strategic difficulties to be overcome and the invaders removed. Winning the Falklands war (at the cost of 255 British lives, 6 ships and £3bn - plus a large indeterminate bill for holding the islands into the future) - yielded no economic or other benefit except the prospect of finding some offshore oil.

But, though the junta was doomed by this failed attempt at 'flag waving', Mrs. Thatcher's 'flag waving' in response earned her a huge boost in popularity. A year later she won the 1983 election with an overwhelming majority. In collaboration with a BBC documentary maker, I submitted a piece about the origins of the war. The project was rejected on the ground that this would be politically impossible to air given the strength of patriotic feeling. This kind of 'self-censorship' is one reason why it is so hard for countries to learn from their mistakes.

There's a lot to be learned from the Falklands affair. External adventures tempt so many rulers when things are going badly: Admiral Galtieri tried one and it boomeranged. Mrs. Thatcher had one forced on her - and came out victorious. What about President Putin and the Crimea? In the longer run will the annexation be a feather in his cap - or the opposite? Sadly once again it is politically correct in the West as in Russia to suppress knowledge of 'our side's' errors, instead of learning from them about how crises can be resolved.

Bosnia: Mrs Thatcher ignored

But, getting back to Bosnia, Mrs. Thatcher most decidedly had it right in 1991 when Serbia invaded Croatia across its frontier in South Slavonia. But most unfortunately for Bosnia (and for Yugoslavia's survival), she had been removed as Prime Minister the year before - over the politically unwise matter of a misguided poll tax! She wanted tanks sent down by rail from Germany to Slavonia (the inland 'arm' of Croatia) to warn the Serbs that Europe would not permit another Balkan war. She wanted the EU members themselves to keep the peace in Europe: for her there was no need to have recourse either to the United Nations or to the United States. Her advice to the Conservative cabinet which she had led the year before, was ignored. Indeed her advice was ignored not only by the UK but by almost all the other European Governments - except the newly reunited Germany which, with its Nazi past, still could not act in the absence of allies.

Germany was much concerned at the EU's inaction - and particularly when the declared neutrality of both France and Britain as the war spread to Bosnia led to an arms embargo which greatly favoured the Serbs. The Serbs were in control of most of the Yugoslav armed forces, had a significant arms industry, and could readily import more arms illegally via the Danube and Serbia's southern frontier. Bosnia and Croatia at first had no armies and had to rely on defectors and seizures of Yugoslav army arsenal.

The UK and France were thus tacitly giving very significant support to Serb aggression. They did provide their own forces to serve with the United Nations' 'Unprofor' - the United Nations' small neutral force with the sole mission of protecting civilians. It was a largely toothless force which the Serbs humiliated whenever occasion arose. It was very useful to me and other pedestrians in Sarajevo: a large white armoured vehicle was available to hide behind whenever one wanted to cross a major road where a Serb sniper operated. But it did nothing to stop Serb atrocities. Indeed at Srebrenica, as all the world knows, the small Dutch UN force, without a single shot fired, simply handed over some 10,000 Bosnian men and boys to be slaughtered by the forces of General Mladić (who at the time of writing is defending himself at The Hague against a charge of genocide).

The British and French did not in any way favour the Serbs for religious reasons. (Though the self-styled Orthodox Christian Serbs did try to curry favour with the 'Christian West' by pretending that their war was somehow a 'just' one against the non-Serb Bosnians, who were then in majority very 'moderate' Muslims). Britain and France were stuck in a 1914/1939 mind-set - for Serbia had been an ally of the 'Allies' in World War I and their Yugoslavia had been an ally in World War II. The British Ambassador in Sarajevo, who had been most helpful to me, was moved elsewhere when he drew attention to these facts and others. Just as in the case of Eden over Suez, ambassadorial reporting and advice from senior Foreign Office officials went unheeded by a Foreign Secretary who had himself been a diplomat - in this case Douglas Hurd.

My own involvement in Bosnia

Because of all this, when I came back from Cambodia I felt that, just like little Cambodia, little Bosnia too, was the victim of mistaken Western policy. So, after helping the Bosnian Information Officer in London upgrade his office to an Embassy - with the enthusiastic support of both Protocol Department and the geographic department concerned (they hoped, by getting

Bosnia's voice heard in Whitehall, to acquire information that might persuade Mr. Hurd to alter his policy) - I went to Bosnia at the invitation of the government of President Ilya Izetbegović and Premier Haris Silajčić on a UN military flight in uniform lent me by a British officer. The only other way to get to besieged Sarajevo then was by the not so secret 'secret tunnel' under the airport which I later got permission to use. (Although more of a mouse hole than a tunnel, one could push, on a miniature railway, small wagons through it - vital for keeping Sarajevo supplied with absolute necessities. With 1m60 headroom I discovered that it wasn't good for the back of any one taller!) The tunnel gave access to the un-asphalted road over Mount Igman which itself could be interdicted by Serb shelling.

Although, as I say, the Serbs did present their aggression as a 'Crusade' justifying the murder of Muslims (and Christian Croats and anyone else who stood in their way) Christian/Muslim relations had been good when both were subjected to Yugoslavia's Communism (which ultimately became fairly benign under Tito). Indeed there were quite a few Muslim/Catholic and Muslim/Orthodox marriages (one such 'mixed' couple I came to know well escaped to Croatia as the siege began). The Croats in Istria received a large number of Bosnian Muslim refugees and did much to support them. When the Serbs in Krajina (along the old Croat frontier with the Ottoman Empire) revolted they were expelled, sometimes very roughly - though I found that often their Churches and houses were carefully preserved for their possible return).

As President Izetbegović explained to me, it was the British and French led arms embargo which had forced him most reluctantly to obtain arms elsewere - mostly from the Islamic Republic of Iran which flew them in by night. Its large, heavily barred Embassy on the Miljacka river brooded malignantly over the city as it organized these flights which came with specialist cadres who not only brought military training but their extremist form of Shia Islam. Izetbegović and Premier Silajčić presciently warned that Britain and France would come to regret their embargo which had brought extremist Islam to Europe - that was the best part of a decade before '9/11'.

Prime Minister Silajčić accepted my offer to interview him for the Financial Times. In Cambodia I had worked to its Foreign Editor so I felt sure of a positive response. But as luck would have it he was on leave. His deputy told me – "we know all about Silajčić, we don't need to hear any more from him!" Here was a besieged Prime Minister of a friendly European country offering, at no cost, to explain why French and British support for the undoubted aggressors was imperiling his country's survival!

I had met before this unwillingness to listen to anything which clashes with current preconceptions. So it was nothing new. I first encountered this kind of 'self-censorship' when reporting from Vietnam in that war, then again in Bosnia, and now I find it once more over the Ukraine crisis. In a democracy though, it is surely the function, even the duty, of the media to raise informed doubts as to the wisdom of one's own government's policies. Sometimes, of course, the media don't get such information because of the government's use of 'national security' to suppress what the public should know. For example when I offered evidence to a court (relevant to a friend's defence) about British backing for an invasion of Cambodia which the Khmer Rouge hoped might provide a way for their return, the Ministry of Defence told the judge, in the interests of national security, not to hear it.

It was, we all know, by a bridge over the Miljacka river in Sarajevo, that a young Serb had shot dead the heir to the Austrian throne thereby striking the match which set fire to Europe. The still smoking embers hamper Europe even today in playing its proper role in world affairs. An end to such self-censorship would certainly help the EU to come to terms with its mistakes, learn from them, and form radically improved policies.

My time in besieged Sarajevo

In the Ministry of Health the Minister was a Muslim and his Vice was a Croat. I had an office there: one job I had (because of my work in Cambodia) was to try to upgrade orthopedic care for land mine victims with the help of a young German orthopedist who had set up a clinic in Zenica. Bosnia's Ministers could not travel around the country but I was able to drive round and observe the human situation in the part of the country under Bosnian Government control. Often I found no front line - Serbs lived in part of a street, Bosnians in the other. Some Muslim friends living in such a situation told me of the break-up of Bosnian society: they couldn't safely cross the 'line' to see their Serb friends and vice-versa - but there at least neither had any wish to kill the other! In other places where there had been fighting there were fortified but barely marked front lines which one crossed at one's peril.

I did spend some time in self-styled Republika Srbska and found those in charge to be hardline zealots. They did not care that France and Britain were effectively helping their cause and that I had come to offer the same help over orthopedics that I was arranging for the Bosnian government. They simply refused it and would not allow me to visit their capital Banja Luka to show the documentation I had brought and discuss what could be done to help their war wounded. I found less senior Serbs privately very unhappy with having to work under such leaders. I was reminded of my visits to China during the Cultural Revolution. In no tyranny can humanity be entirely suppressed even when supposedly 'brain washed'.

Quite often I visited the American Embassy in Sarajevo. The US agreed with Mrs. Thatcher - it was not for the US once again to intervene in Europe for the fourth time in a century (after World Wars I and II and the 'Cold War'): the Europeans ought by then have been able police their own part of the world. Western Europe had had half a century to lick its wounds and come together in the EU. And militarily, a police action to stop the Serbs at the beginning of their aggression would have been a push-over for France or Britain alone: they had those tanks and much else in Germany which was no longer needed now it was reunified - a huge arsenal to be drawn upon at most only a couple of days' train journey away. And Milosović had counted on a push-over for him, not a war.

The mere threat of immediate intervention by the EU powers would most likely have been enough to dissuade the Serbs. It is scarcely conceivable that the actual arrival of tanks would not have caused even Milosović to desist. As the Americans had no desire to get involved yet again in a European war the US Defense Department jokingly remarked "we don't do mountains" - in fact there was no question of mountains, the Sava river valley is absolutely flat: ideal tank country which the Serbs fully exploited. Their tank-led advance was particularly ruthless: after the war I drove mile after mile along roads where every house had been shelled to destruction from a safe distance before infantry easily secured a by then totally abandoned village.

The US and Germany dragged in and the war ends

British and French effective support for the Serbs irritated the Americans. Once the Ambassador, at a meeting in the US Embassy, asked me with wry humour 'why are you here?'- meaning my country was making things worse instead of stopping what had by then had become an all out war in Europe. (A good, but controversial book about this is *Unfinest Hour. Britain and the Destruction of Bosnia'* by Brendan Simms. His anger, maybe sometimes a bit extreme, reflects my own feelings). The slaughter of Bosnians and Croats and their starvation in concentration camps went on while the Americans (with German help), exasperated by British, French and UN ineffectiveness, quietly 'created' a Croatian army, trained it and armed it - all over a period of about a year.

The war was then brought to an end after Croatian operation 'Oluja' ('Storm'). This quickly expelled the Serbs from the frontier area with Bosnia (Serbs had long settled there, refugees from Turkish Bosnia). Speed was essential to 'Oluja', hence its name, and although a Croat friend of mine who took part in the operation was given orders not to harm or even displace Serb civilians, the Serbs fled and there were what is now called 'breaches of human rights' (today's euphemism which, like 'collateral damage', can hide much horror). That led to the Croatian General in charge, Ante Gotovina, being judged and convicted at The Hague - to the dismay of a number of European and American senior officers. I myself protested remarking that our Generals and Air Marshals were not tried for war crimes after defeating the aggression Hitler had started.

After 'Oluja' the Croats quickly launched a twin operation: 'Operation Mistral' (Operacija Maestral), descending into Bosnia and joining up with the Bosnian forces. Within a week the Bosnian/Croatian 'blitzkrieg' was near the Sava River thus almost completing the division of 'Republika Srpska' and enabling Croatian forces across the river to reinforce and resupply the Mistral forces whose supply line was dangerously long. That would have enabled the taking of the 'Srpska' capital Banja Luka, and ending the war as projected. But when the Mistral forces were only a handful of kilometres away from the river, the order came to stop.

I still do not know what led to this order - was it a 'Srbska' counter-attack, when supply lines had become too long and insecure? Or did the order come from the Americans who had planned and made possible both 'Oluja' and 'Maestral'? For reasons of realpolitik transcending Bosnia and Croatia did the Americans not want a total defeat for Milosović's Serbia? Maybe Milosović was to be allowed to survive just as Saddam Hussein had been allowed to survive the First Gulf War in 1991?

Whatever the reason, that order to halt meant the fightingr ended with 'Srbska' and Milosović in a remarkably good position on the ground and so with a strong bargaining position. Thus the war ended with the Dayton Agreements negotiated by the Americans with little say from the impotent Europeans - even from Germany which had played such an important role. I visited 'Republika Srpska' a couple of years ago after driving through a part of Croatia like the one I have just described - utterly destroyed by the war. Srpska, just the other side of the Sava river, was doing fine - undamaged and the people without any contrition for their appalling war crimes of which I had seen the results at the time. The Bosnian Serbs had won nearly half of Bosnia, though not the whole of it as they had wanted. Today, in 2014, Bosnia is in reality a divided country like Korea and Vietnam after World War II and - because of 'Srpska' participation in the government of the rest of the country - it is all but ungovernable after the hatreds unleashed by the Serbs in the 1990s.

After the lessons of Bosnia and the Ukraine, my conclusion is that Europe must be able to police itself - not leave a vacuum for America to fill with its own rather different interests. Second - all international armed interventions should be of a police nature and organized in concert with the United Nations unless the disturbance to world peace is so grave as to demand immediate armed action despite a veto in the Security Council.

That would mean a complete overhaul of UN 'peacekeeping' which not only failed in ex-Yugoslavia but since in other conflicts like those in today's Central African Republic and the South Sudan. There's a need to have a permanent international police force, planning ahead for potential trouble, and powerful enough to be 'a deterrent in being'. And that force must be in close liaison with diplomacy which, with adequate force behind it, can often settle disputes by negotiation without a shot fired. That needs UN Security Council and General Assembly support - another reason why the EU and Russia should speak with one voice and three vetoes on the Security Council.

Before you went to Bosnia, of course you went to Cambodia?

Yes, Prime Minister Hun Sen - a former Khmer Rouge officer who is still in power and has since become a controversial dictatorial figure - invited to Phnom Penh a retired French Ambassador and myself. (Both of us had served in our respective Embassies in Phnom Penh between the withdrawal of the French in 1954 and the outbreak of the American Vietnam war). Clearly his aim was to persuade both of us that the time had come for the 'West' to accept that Cambodia's independence from Vietnam should be accepted and Cambodia officially recognised by the 'international community'. We were allowed to go without 'minders' wherever we wished. We were both soon convinced of Hun Sen's government's real independence from Vietnam which, to the continued displeasure of the US, had invaded Cambodia and defeated the 'auto-genocidal' Khmer Rouge.

As expected, we did find the country almost entirely isolated from the non-communist world due to lack of diplomatic recognition. One example - you could only make international phone calls, and that with difficulty and long delays, via either the Soviet Union, or Vietnam.

I was much disturbed by the appalling number of casualties - added to every day or so - caused by the tens of thousands of unexploded land mines. So on my return to Britain I and two others founded the Cambodia Trust (now renamed Exceed). Today it has branches in other countries providing prostheses for mine victims and others in need. In Cambodia anti-personnel mines still explode and the Trust continues to provide a European standard orthopedic service run almost entirely by Cambodians with European qualifications after training by the Trust.

Helping Cambodia return to the world

Both my French colleague and I were impressed by the young Hun Sen as a genuine patriot who, whatever his other aims might be, had no intention of returning to any form of communist rule. Although he owed his position to the Vietnamese, he was a determined upholder of Cambodian independence. And we found the Vietnamese accepted this. So on return we set about convincing our respective governments that Cambodia should be recognised and helped to recover from its terrible years.

We had no success although we pointed out that the American bombing of much of Cambodia with more bombs than it dropped on all countries in World War II, had made this little country the most heavily bombed in history. As already remarked, the blind, violent and impotent hatred that was aroused in the countryside had re-juvenated a moribund 'Maoist' Khmer Rouge and brought it to power, entering Phnom Penh in 1970. Those living in the towns which had been spared the bombing were the natural targets of this hatred - and so the auto-genocide began. In many cases just to wear glasses was a death sentence.

So Nixon's and Kissinger's US had created an extreme communist monster which ruled Cambodia until chased out by communist Vietnam in 1979. And that was against the wishes of the Americans who, with British help (as I mentioned) were then training Cambodian refugees on the Thai frontier to return and fight the 'Vietnamese occupation'. (Today, the parallel with the 'war on terror' is striking: as I've explained, US 'shock and awe' invading Iraq, indirectly brought in Al Qaeda and its progeny where Saddam Hussein's tyranny had kept them out).

I was able though, at least to provide Cambodia with direct dial telephone communications with the whole world - a crucial asset when seeking international recognition. When we had set up the Cambodia Trust and I had become its first Director, we asked a Jewish Charity for the funds to purchase the then new Inmarsat satellite telephone that had been developed in Finland but was made under licence in Britain. The Jews agreed with the simple remark "We don't like genocide!" I went to Basingstoke, placed our order, and was trained in the setting up the satellite system. But the CIA got the British authorities to ban the export. So we purchased the big telephone in Finland and had it sent via Air France to Ho Chi Minh City (Saigon). I joined the flight in Paris and we were met at the airport by a Cambodian army truck. To my amusement, when we reached the long queue for the ferry over the Bassac (before the bridge was built one could wait several hours) the Cambodian officer in charge of us shouted in French "Make way for the British Ambassador". With my magic promotion we caught the next ferry!

I set up the telephone on the roof of the Présidence du Conseil and invited Premier Hun Sen to use it. His first call was to thank the head of the Jewish Charity in London. His second call was to a United States Senator in Washington! Cambodia was direct-dial touch with the world - not just the Cambodian government but Cambodian business too. The government paid for the then quite high cost of satellite calls by charging those who used the telephone. Our Cambodia Trust had the communications essential to its operations and paid nothing for them!

Here I must put in another word about preconceptions which are something of an ideology in themselves. The Cambodia Trust's insistence that Cambodia's thousands of land mine victims should have the latest in European orthopedic prostheses involved a struggle not, for once, with the US and UK governments but with other charities. These provided leather and wood prostheses made in Cambodia. They argued that the Cambodians were too behind the times, too backward to be able to make European largely aluminum prostheses and fit them to European best practice. Fortunately Premier Hun Sen personally gave us the necessary backing. At first the Trust made below the knee prostheses with aluminium from drink cans, only requiring knee joints from Germany for above the knee prostheses.

What are your views about foreign aid after your experience as first Director of The Cambodia Trust?

Never give money - except for paying the salaries of those you employ. Money always goes astray, then it fuels corruption which, as I said, is one of the great scourges of our world today. And your organization too, must be squeaky clean keeping its accounts and setting salaries sufficient to get and keep qualified staff, but no more. At the beginning any charity will have to spend most of its income on its premises, paying its own small staff, and other essential items, but, as soon as it begins performing, its aim should be continually to reduce the proportion of operating costs as a proportion of income. A problem arises when deciding how much to spend on fund raising: you have to advertise the need you are seeking to meet. Many big charities spend what appears to be an inordinate proportion of income not only on fund raising but on lobbying governments. Finding a balance is hard.

Expect to make both enemies and nay-sayers and be ready to counter them and their arguments. And try, at the highest level, to obtain the approval and backing of both the national country and local governments. Make sure your successes are known.

I believe governments should be very careful in giving charitable status to NGOs - there's a lot to be gained in taxation and in other ways. Accounts should be rigorously scrutinised. Governments themselves are by far the most wasteful of aid money. They almost always give money, not 'things' and so fuel corruption to such an extent that it may negate what a government is trying to achieve. Governments give contracts, without due scrutiny, to their own contractors and do not bring in the country's own contactors.

By fuelling corruption aid may actually bring more harm than good - Afghanistan is the prime example. I saw this as long ago as 'Vietnam'. But with advanced countries where monetary payments can be properly supervised, aid can change if not 'everything' then at least 'a very great deal' as the Marshall Plan demonstrated.

You once said that it was your time in Laos that prompted the founding of the Cambodia Trust?

Yes. I had never seen victims of anti-personnel mines before and I was awoken to this scourge by the sight of Laotian army victims in the very basic conditions of Vientiane's hospital. They had been fighting 'the communists' in those two northern provinces, Phong Saly and Sam Neua. They relied on their families for their food which was often cooked on the floor of the hospital. French army doctors did remarkable work so most survived complications and infection and were discharged with wood and leather prostheses. After talking with the French, I tried to interest the outside world to get modern prosthetic aid with the help of my ambassador, Lord Talbot de Malahide - but no one sparked. When, years later, I saw far worse in Cambodia I found those two colleagues in Oxford and between us the Cambodia Trust was founded. It has gone on to work in some other countries.

But a word about Laos where I spent many of the happiest days of my life as a Third Secretary. I think that only in Laos and in those days, could such a lowly diplomat have been given a leaving party (and a gold plated Buddha) by the Minister of Foreign

Affairs in person! I had a particularly fine Laotian style wooden house 'sur pilotis' (it was later destroyed by the Ministry of Works in favour of air conditioned bungaloids) on the banks of the Mekong, across which I once or twice swam to Thailand on the opposite bank. I could go on and on for I was very fond of the Laotians and their simple way of life as well of their varied and beautiful country. But I will confine myself to one trip I made with a good friend of mine, the then head of the Laotian radio.

The Ambassador, Lord Talbot, asked me to visit the countryside far away from the towns and report on the day to day life of ordinary Laotians. He lent me his boat with a powerful outboard engine to beat the current and so get many kilometres upstream. Well away from the capital Vientiane we walked inland along tracks often impassable even to bicycles. From time to time we would hear far off the haunting notes of the khène, the bamboo national instrument. Then the khène player would come in sight on the winding path, followed by wife and children all dressed in plain sarongs (not the beautiful ones with gold and silver thread worn by the more opulent town dwellers). When we neared a village we first passed the phi house - a little wooden structure on a pole provided for the forest spirits so that they would not trouble the villagers.

At each village we were courteously received and always our arrival led to a village meeting. One question I always asked - what did they lack? These were people with little use for money. They lived as they had done for untold generations: very simply, poor but not crushingly poor as, say, peasants in much of India. Typically they took some time to discuss their answer. Always lack of health care came top of the list. Even for those living in Arcadia, sickness and injury is what blights their lives.

You got your degree in economics: what do you say about the 2007/8 'meltdown' and the response?

THE BANKERS - LEADING ON TO ISRAEL/PALESTINE

I agree with those who point out that the recent bail-outs for failing banks demonstrate how the vast sums paid out have let risk taking capitalists avoid taking the losses of the disastrous investments they made. The bankers walked away with their personal wealth paid out in bonuses over the years - in effect a prize for what later proved to be their mis-management and illegal, maybe criminal, practices.

I regret very much not having followed financial matters as closely as I have followed international affairs. I can though claim to have been among those who warned in 2003 that the huge unprovided costs of the two wars (Afghanistan and Iraq) would dangerously increase the US government's deficit. This was indeed a significant factor not only in bloating US government debt, but also politically. This has led to unreasonable Republican demands for across the board austerity to achieve balanced budgets. Ironic, when it was the Republicans and their President G. W. Bush who were the ones who went to war without provision for the costs, and so ran up a trillion or so of debt!

As I see it, for many years after World War II, essentially Keysian economics, which as I've mentioned John Maynard Keynes developed during the Great Depression, were dominant. It was accepted after that war that, for capitalism to be successful both economically and socially, there must be strict government controls, and at times government intervention, in both banking and the stock market.

Before World War II the world had already experienced a disastrous international banking 'meltdown'. In 1931 the largest of Austria's banks, the Kreditanstalt, failed. It had taken on far more debt than was safe sparking a dramatic loss of confidence in European financial circles. This debt concern spread quickly from Austria, via France, to the UK forcing the pound off the gold standard. That led to a rush on banks in the US - over 2000 banks with dollar deposits failed. That greatly exacerbated the, until then, still limited effects of the famous Wall Street crash in 1929. The worst of the Great Depression then followed in Europe and in the US. I have suggested that this, perhaps more than anything else, enabled Hitler's rise to power.

To prevent such a disaster in future, the US enacted the Glass-Steagall Act in 1933, the first year of Franklin D. Roosevelt's Presidency. This prevented banks from acting also as securities firms - the vital legal provision which prevented the reckless behaviour that led to the 2007/8 'meltdown'. But so great was enthusiasm, started under President Reagan, for deregulating capitalism, that three Republicans, Senator Gramm and Representatives Leach and Bliley, got Congress to approve their disastrous Gramm-Leach-Bliley Financial Services Modernisation Act which repealed those key provisions of Glass-Steagall.

There is controversy over why President Clinton signed the GLB Act in the last year of his presidency. He said recently that the Republican majority in the House together with their votes in the Senate meant he was presented with a veto-proof bill which he had to sign. It is true that he signed the partially deregulatory Riegle-Neal Act in 1994 before the Republicans took over both Houses in the mid-term elections that year, but he seems not to have been personally involved. Anyway, after those elections Clinton was obliged to make concessions to the Republicans to gain their cooperation. And after the Lewinsky affair (1995/6), which ended with the Republican attempt to impeach him, he was still further weakened politically although his public popularity barely suffered. So his responsibility for bringing on the 2007 meltdown is certainly far less than the Republicans driven by their ideology of strict de-regulation and a return to unbridled laissez-faire capitalism.

A propos Miss Monica Lewinsky: we know that the Israeli intelligence service, the Mossad - perhaps the best in the world - commonly uses Jews (either 'conscious' or 'not conscious' - meaning they either know or don't know they are being used by Mossad) to forward what Israel believes are its interests. Israel's governments usually find Republican policies preferable those of the Democrats. That was the case with Clinton. Despite his stated support for Israel there was much friction, in particular because of his 'negative' position on the key question of Israeli settlements in the occupied territories.

So it quite possible that Mossad, once it became aware of the matter, exploited the Jewish Lewinskys - mother and daughter - as 'not conscious' actors to weaken Clinton politically as he worked to achieve an Israel/Palestinian solution which had to have Republican acquiescence. But despite the proliferation of enquiries - including the exhaustive Starr Investigation - this line of enquiry was never followed up: indeed that would have been politically impossible given that near-unconditional support for Israel was, and to a considerable extent still is, all but unquestioned in American political circles.

And what about Israel?

Slaughter, whether on the battlefield or of civilians, and particularly by genocide, leaves great hatred, great fear and immense social disruption which typically lasts for many years, even generations. Kill my child and I will want to kill you. Only the intervention of the state prevents mayhem or at best some kind of *lex talionis* ('eye for an eye, tooth for a tooth') as under Sharia law. For anything as devastating as the Nazi genocide of the Jews reducing the number of Jews in the world from a mere 17m to as little as 11m, you have to go back to the Mongol invasions of China, where some put the killing at 26 millions, and of Persia under Genghis Khan in the 13th century: the slaughter of millions of Persians was such that it took at least a century for the country to recover and even then it was much changed. Or you have to go forward to the Cambodian 'auto-genocide' and the Ruanda massacres.

The Europeans (from the Netherlands in the West to Russia in the East) who had suffered much themselves under the Nazi occupation, cared little for the survivors of the Holocaust. Indeed all of Europe including Great Britain, had persecuted the Jews for hundreds of years before Hitler. A malignant 'Christian' ideological mind-set went a long way to making his 'final solution' possible. The Jews therefore had nowhere to turn except to Palestine under the British Mandate where Zionism was building that 'homeland for the Jews' promised by the Balfour Declaration, 1917. This was a letter from Arthur Balfour, Lloyd George's wartime Foreign Secretary, to Lord Rothschild the doyen of British Jewry ('HMG views with favour the establishment in Palestine of a national home for the Jewish people'). It is ironic that the Declaration came about through Herbert Samuel, a Jew who had 'renounced all religious belief', who in 1915 (the year he was Postmaster General) put forward the idea of a British Protectorate over Palestine which would favour Zionism. And it was Balfour, a Christian deeply ashamed by Christian persecution of the Jews, who took it up. In 1920, after World War I, Samuel was appointed High Commissioner for Palestine - the first Jew to govern what had been Israel in 2,000 years (over Arab and Christian protests).

So by 1945 the stage was set for a mass attempt by Jewish survivors of the Holocaust to join the Zionists already in Palestine under the 1922 British Mandate from the League of Nations. I have friends still alive who served as conscripts in Palestine and remember the appalling dilemma of the British authorities - let in the Holocaust survivors or preserve the traditional multi-faith nature of country in accordance with the both the Mandate and the Balfour Declaration. That stated: 'nothing should be done which might prejudice the civil and religious rights of existing non-Jewish communities in Palestine'.

Of course no one in 1922 could even imagine the Nazis would murder 6 million Jews and that the survivors would be desperate to come to Palestine. Because of their attempt to limit the illegal immigration, the British were faced with the Jewish terrorism of Irgun Svai Leumi and Haganah, both of which had existed even before World War II as resistance to the Mandate. So it was, in a cruel sense, a relief when Irgun blew up the British headquarters in Jerusalem's King David Hotel prompting Britain to leave, abandoning the Mandate. Israel is thus the child of the holocaust which inevitably still dominates Jewish thinking, and of Zionist terrorism, which in the context of Jewish history and particularly of the Nazi genocide can at least be understood.

The state of Israel was proclaimed in 1948 - the very next day it was attacked by the surrounding Arab armies and defeated them. As we all know, despite later wars with its Arab neighbours, Israel took over all the territories of the former Mandate and the country is now divided into Israel proper and the occupied territories.

The 'Nakba' and the 'running sore' on international affairs

For the expelled Arabs, 1948 is the year of *'an Nakba'* - 'the Catastrophe'. Since then Israel/Palestine has been a running sore in international affairs. It has over and again poisoned even the relations between the great powers. The 1978 Camp David accords led to Israel/Egypt mutual recognition which did much to remove the worst tensions. But all attempts to resolve the problem by creating a separate Palestinian state in the Occupied territories have failed to date despite a major effort made by President Clinton, also at Camp David, in 2000. His failure, despite his investment of much 'political capital', deterred President G. W. Bush from getting involved despite the crying need to settle the problem after '9/11'. For, of course, 'Israel/Palestine' was then, and remains, the ultimate grievance of Muslims throughout the world encouraging many of them to become 'radicalised'.

And of course, instead of tackling Israel/Palestine, President Bush invaded Iraq making matters far worse. At the time of writing President Obama, to his great credit, is making another major attempt to oblige both sides to compromise on the lines long since formulated. I very much hope I am wrong, but I see no possibility that the present Netanyahu government of Israel even desires a 'two state solution'. If that's so, there will likely be another Palestinian 'intifada' uprising and more bloodshed. In such circumstances all the Palestinians can do is to draw their plight to world attention exploiting the inevitable Israeli crackdown in both the UN and the media.

Any possibility of a change appears now to depend on the assessment of US national interest in continuing to subsidise Israel: a severe cut, or threat of one, could make all the difference in awakening Israelis to their true interest in resolving the problem with the Palestinians. Many Jews in America look askance on Israel's present policies. It is said that over 70% of them vote Democrat and want Israel to resolve the Palestine problem. More and more extremist, Israel is losing friends as they become aware that it is becoming more of a theocracy thanks to the power of its religious fundamentalists. If there were real 'give' on the Israeli side the extremists in Hamas could find themselves sidelined by a Palestinian majority with real hope of a 'two state' solution. As it is, the more violent the repression, the more Palestinians killed, the more settlements that are built - and the more the world's criticism of Israel reawakens dormant anti-Semitism in many countries to the dismay of Jews and their friends everywhere. All too many individuals, governments and other organisations fail to make the vital distinction between the present Israeli government and Jews.

The mantra, attempting to justify harsh Israeli reaction to Hamas and other attacks, that 'Israel has a right to defend itself'' (no matter how violently) only increases world support for the civilian victims and worsens Israel's longer term predicament. If meaningful negotiations are even to begin Israel will have to drop demanding that, before any negotiations, the 'terrorists' disarm and recognise Israel's existence. For weapons, terrorism, and non-recognition are its opponents' only strength and can only be abandoned when a successful agreement is reached.

But instead Israel is going even further in the opposite direction by demanding Palestinian recognition of it as a 'Jewish state' - a race/religion based country to the detriment of its considerable Arab and other citizens. This goes even further than appointing one religion as the state religion - as Church of England Christianity is the formal religion of the UK, but other religions are equally permitted provided they do not compromise 'the Queen's peace' or that nebulous thing 'national security'.

This move towards theocracy contrasts with Iran, Israel's great enemy, which has tried extremist theocracy, but due to ever-growing, ever-more open, dissatisfaction, its clerical rulers find themselves obliged to accept some secularist reforms. In the 21st century, with its nexus of communications, it does not seem that theocracy is 'on the side of history'.

But even the emergence of a Palestine state alongside Israel will no longer suffice to undercut the appeal of Al Qaeda and its even more extremist progeny for Muslim would-be 'jihadis'. The curiously named 'war on terror' is being lost in country after country. The one achievement is that these groups have so far been unable to mount another large scale attack on the United States - perhaps because they have now become too diffuse, even increasingly divided, and lacking the unified leadership Bin Laden supplied in 2001.

A hopeful initiative was the establishment of the so called 'Quartet' of the UN, the US, the EU and Russia. But President G. W. Bush scuppered any chances that this might have had by getting Tony Blair appointed the Quartet's envoy against Russian wishes - that was on 27 January 2007, the same day he resigned as British Prime Minister. Blair had already gone of record as firmly on Israel's side. This was another reason for President Putin to mistrust the 'West' in international affairs.

It was in 1947 that the United Nations General Assembly called for a partition of Palestine - 67 years later that is still as elusive as ever. The dire state of the Palestinians, particularly those in the Gaza strip which used to be administered by Egypt but is now under extremist Hamas, is a rebuke to the world. Unfortunately Israeli governments, after the Holocaust and persecution by both Muslims and Christians for upwards of a millennium, have reacted by treating the Palestinians in much the same way as Jews themselves were often treated. Aren't the Occupied Territories one big ghetto? This needs to be remembered when condemning the Israelis for being unreasonable. As I keep saying - kill enough people and the result is a deformation of history for decades if not centuries.

Many in Israel, Palestine and the world are working for a peaceful solution and friendship between Jews and Arabs - just one example is Daniel Barenboim's initiative in providing musical training for both Israelis and Palestinians. His West-Eastern Divan Orchestra is now world famous. Barenboim is a national of both Israel and Palestine, as well as of Argentina where he was born.

SOME WORDS ON DIPLOMACY

All the way through your tour d'horizon of the international situation you've suggested that diplomacy is superior to armed force. But what is this diplomacy you advocate?

A view of diplomacy

Sergey Lavrov says a diplomat must have "a deep knowledge of world history not only during recent years but over the centuries, even the millennia. He should also be an erudite person with fluency in several languages, as well as having a profound knowledge of his own, in order to work with precision". He adds that a 'feel' for the psychology of those he has to deal with is also essential: he must assess their openness, truthfulness and motivation. Above all he must serve his own country to the best of his abilities, giving the best advice he can irrespective of the opinions of his superiors - something that often requires great tact and calm perseverance.

Provided he - or she - has this knowledge and outlook I personally don't think a diplomat needs much formal training beyond knowing how his Foreign Ministry and its Embassies operate. Whatever training he or she may get, they must largely learn on the job as I was obliged to do. More important than the diplomats, I believe, is the ethos of the Foreign Ministry and the Diplomatic Service themselves. As I have suggested, it is not only in dictatorships but often in democracies that the Foreign Minister and the government fail to get the advice that might prevent them from making disastrous mistakes. Among the service's guiding practices there must be a readiness to permit officers at all levels to talk frankly to their superiors if they consider a mistake is likely to be made: you are serving your country, not its government of the day.

Iron discipline enforced by fear has led many a dictatorship to pursue disastrous policies. Messengers don't like being killed - they keep their doubts to themselves. And even in democratic countries like Britain, diplomats may fear for their promotion and prospects (for example bad postings instead of ones where their abilities could be most useful) if they draw the attention of their seniors to what worries them. And seniors right up the hierarchy, though they may believe their advice is the best, must be ready to consider that they might be mistaken. In the British service Ambassadors are the Queen's representatives not of the Secretary of State for Foreign Affairs to whom they work. That is, they are supposed to be giving the best advice they can in the interest of the UK not of a government or of a political party.

This was the ethos in the Foreign Service when I joined the American Department. Twice a day at morning and afternoon tea breaks, the Head of Department and his Deputy joined us desk officers in the 'Third Room'. Then nothing was off the agenda. Without having to commit anything to paper that one might regret, we had the opportunity to discuss any concerns or problems we had. This ethos was particularly valuable when one was appointed to work directly to a Minister (as I was to the Minister of State in the '60s when desk officer for South Africa). The problems we faced over Apartheid and Ian Smith and his Southern Rhodesia (now Zimbabwe) were delicate and complex. Being able to discuss such issues informally and without a record was immensely helpful to me in understanding his political concerns and also, I believe, to him in understanding the preoccupations of the Service.

Overseas Chinese

These informal consultations also greatly helped me when, in the Cold War 1950s, I was appointed Overseas Chinese officer for South East Asia under Malcolm Macdonald when he was based in Singapore as UK High Commissioner for that area. This too, was a particularly delicate subject because it involved many influential overseas Chinese whose loyalty Peking was trying to win. On one occasion I had to point out that the government's effort to prevent the communists getting control of text books for Overseas Chinese children in all South East Asia had led to a pro-Peking firm taking control of 'our' publisher' which was receiving a subsidy from HMG. We were spreading Mao Tse Tung's communism, not combatting it! But influential shareholders friendly to the 'West' naturally wanted the company to profit. I believe Malcolm Macdonald, who had excellent relations across a wide spectrum of Chinese, resolved this himself by arranging for Peking's secret interest in the Company to be quietly bought out.

After I left the Service I kept contact with some of my contemporaries who had achieved high positions. All of them had open minds ready to question policy, no matter how entrenched, if persuaded that would be in Britain's and the 'West's' best interests. To my surprise I found the same in Mao's China which I visited 12 times.

The value of 'back channels'

Of course, on my visa applications I always answered the query about previous employment stating that I had been a British diplomat. Once, on a visit to Peking as a businessman my 'minder' asked me "what are you doing this evening", I replied that I was going to a reception given by some business colleagues. "I don't think so," was the reply, "please be down in the hall at 6.30". A large black Russian Zil, net curtains over the windows, arrived. I was a bit concerned as there was no one in it to greet me. I was driven to the Summer Palace alone. The compound still bears the name although the palace itself was destroyed by the 'Eight Power Alliance' - the major Europeans plus Japan - in 1900 when their Embassies in Beijing were besieged. The Imperial cuisine survived that, the Japanese occupation, and the Cultural Revolution with a prestigious restaurant frequented by top cadres. My host, a distinguished-looking gentleman in a well-tailored cadre-suit, accepted my business card but did not give me his as was the invariable practice. One of his party of ten told me only that this was

Mr. Feng - which means nothing without both the surname's character plus the other two characters of the given name. I was treated to an outstanding Chinese meal, a top interpreter, and a long and detailed conversation about China's foreign policy without any of the usual Communist jargon. I realised that what he was telling me was intended to go back to the Foreign Office - which it did at Deputy Under Secretary level.

In foreign affairs there is much of this 'back channel' communication where information is given by various sources to senior politicians and diplomats to 'back up' both embassy and media reporting. Contrary to what many people believe much delicate political information, which secret services are asked to obtain, comes not from them but through diplomats cultivating relationships on behalf of their Ambassadors. At Ambassador/Foreign Minister level there are limits to what can be said. I have already mentioned that our Paris Embassy was aware that de Gaulle would most probably veto British entry into the Common Market because not a few well-placed French believed that that would prove disastrous for France's true interests, and so had taken upon themselves to warn us.

A back channel need not be between governments. I was invited to West Germany (as it was then) by German friends who were Social Democrats. They told me many Germans were much concerned that the British Embassy, among others, was reporting that the East German regime - the DDR - was likely to last for years to come, while the Germans knew how fragile it was. They feared this outlook could lead to business and other contacts strengthening the DDR and could even lead to its recognition. So they were using unofficial channels to correct perceptions of the DDR. They arranged for me to meet their contacts in the West German government. After that they would arrange for me to visit the DDR. After a lunch at the British Embassy in Bonn where I was briefed on their assessment, I drove to Berlin along the 'causeway' autobahn slap through the DDR and thence via the famous Check Point Charlie through 'the Wall' into East Berlin. On my return I gave my reasons, again at Deputy Under Secretary level, for believing that East Germany would not outlive its leader

Erich Honnecker. By chance I had it right for Honnecker died in 1989 the same year that the Berlin Wall fell and with it the DDR!

Diplomats, Secret Services and 'too many cooks'

A personal example: when I was only a Second Secretary at our embassy in Phnom Penh (staff of six) the 'West' badly wanted to know what the maverick, mercurial Prince Sihanouk's policy would be towards China. I had got to know personally two members of the Royal Council. One day we were concerned by small indications that something might be brewing. The Ambassador asked me to see my two contacts. I found both intensely worried: the evening before the Prince had told the Council that he was going to recognise Communist China. But Cambodia did not have the means to neutralise the work of a Chinese Embassy out to use Cambodia's several overseas Chinese Congregations (there was one for each dialect: Cantonese, Hakka, etc) to forward Peking's policies and apply pressure on those that did not.

Although the decision was secret, so concerned were my contacts (who presciently foresaw that importing Maoism, even through an embassy, would prove catastrophic for Cambodia), that they confided in me. The American Embassy at that time had over a dozen CIA officers and diplomats but this news came as shock when my Ambassador's telegram was repeated to our Embassy in Washington. The American Ambassador was kind enough to remark, "You're a good citizen, John". (A kindly but misplaced comment! Though I hope I have been a 'good citizen' not only of Britain but of Europe!)

I have often noted that the very large numbers of diplomats and intelligence agents in US Embassies often do not lead to efficiency. Individuals have less influence, good ideas get lost in the crowd. Over-staffing creates an elephant not a cheetah when a change of policy is needed. Of course I've seen the UK too, out-manoeuvred by smaller more agile opponents. Size matters: keep as small as possible!

To return to the requirements for a diplomat

Being ready for the unusual is one of them. Two personal examples come to mind. In Laos in 1955 Lord Talbot, my ambassador, told me he could not properly meet the famous or 'infamous' but exceptionally well-informed pro-communist Australian journalist Wilfred Burchett, but as his Third Secretary I could do so. For a man of his evident ability I found Burchett strangely starry eyed about communism. He was though, personally remarkably pleasant, forthcoming and strangely anxious to tell us much of real importance that we did not know. As I, wrote the despatch for the ambassador to sign I reflected that the most junior must come prepared to do the work of the most senior!

In Paris each year the British ambassador, then Sir Pierson Dixon, gave a dinner for the Duke of Windsor. In 1966, though now a First Secretary, I was the most junior present. The Duke struck me as a singularly sad figure and I could not imagine how he could possibly have renounced the throne for love of the Duchess. Meeting him confirmed for me the judgment that we had been lucky indeed to have had instead his eminently decent brother 'Bertie' as our George VI facing Germany's Führer during World War II. The contrast certainly helped strengthen our appeal, and encouraged a number of foreign waverers to decide to back us. After dinner the ambassador came up to me: "the Duchess loves thrillers - you've write them so I'd like you to talk to her". Clearly he wanted some time with the Duke. So we spoke about some thriller writers and in particular we discussed intelligence officer David Cornwell's ('John Le Carré') *'The Spy Who Came in from the Cold'* then still a runaway best seller. (It was Cornwell's book that had spurred me to write *'Diplomatic Cover'*, which had then just been published).

Whether to resign or not

All too often the diplomat, no matter how senior - he may himself even be the Minister for Foreign Affairs - will find that his head of government cannot be persuaded to alter some damaging policy. If he regards this as likely to prove utterly catastrophic for his country - or maybe even the world as a whole, clearly he must consider resignation. But most big issues are not quite so critical and maybe his advice is being accepted on many other matters. In such a case it is far better for his country that he stay in place - maybe to help clean up the mess he is sure will result. Laudably Carne Ross, a middle ranking British Diplomat then with the British delegation to the UN, did feel obliged to resign in protest at the British Government's Iraq policy and gave vital and damaging evidence at the Butler review of the lead up to the invasion of Iraq, contradicting Prime Minister Blair's version of events.

In the case of Anthony Eden's premiership, Harold Macmillan obeyed his instructions as Eden's foreign Minister. So after Eden's disappearance with the 'Suez' disaster, he was able to achieve much with his 'wind of change' in Africa, and even with his doomed attempt to get the UK into the Common Market no matter how late in the day. It follows that sometimes a diplomat, (even a Minister of Foreign Affairs, like Lavrov), has to practice the art of diplomacy less on his country's opponents than on his superiors (or head of government, like Vladimir Putin) in persuading them against some dangerous, even disastrous, move - and if unsuccessful, stay on in the country's interest, to help try to remedy a gross error as Gorchakov did so patiently following the Crimean war.

What does the leader know?

It is hard enough today for a diplomat to follow happenings in the world which may be relevant to his own work. He has to read the telegrams from overseas missions, intelligence reports, and Top Secret intercepts (about which we now know so much!) He also has to scan his own country's newspapers and the digest of what the foreign press is saying. Now in addition there are the more important items of 'alternative' reporting and comment on the internet. He can't read everything in the hour or so he has before he starts on the papers in his own in-tray. So, even at a humble level - and this applies to foreign affairs experts, gurus, pundits and of course journalists and TV commentators on foreign affairs - there has to be strict self-rationing of what one reads. It is extremely easy to miss something of major importance.

At the top end it is worse. Ministers of Foreign Affairs have political and other matters to attend to. They must be briefed before meetings with 'the leader', or attend their parliament to speak, to vote, or to hold a press conference. At this level their choice of reading is to a large extent decided for them by the foreign service they head: they are dependent on the excellence of their senior advisers who are equally as dependent on the excellence of their juniors. So it is critical that opposing views are put before them and that those proffering divergent views are encouraged to do so.

But what does the leader himself get to know surrounded by his own staff in the White House, 10 Downing Street, the Kremlin, or the many other seats of power? For him or her too, there are, of course, only 24 hours in a day. Access to him has to be strictly controlled - there is so much that he must be told about both politically and from the professionals in the various ministries and other government organisations. If he does not ask about matters that do not come before him, he may risk political disaster. At the top there are always risks of disloyalty - for which he may get the blame. For instance, as I write some observers suggest that President Obama was not warned of the re-emergence of the neo-conservatives, notably in the State Department and the CIA, who were thus able to go a long way towards destabilising the Ukraine although it was in part to counter their disastrous foreign policies and end their two wars, that he was elected.

Churchill often saw gaps in his knowledge and asked questions (one, about post-war French and Italian communism, came all the way down to the bottom for me to answer. My two page answer, which I thought was as brief as it could be, was 'précised' by superiors into two short paragraphs, but came back with a note in Churchill's hand 'What I want to know is - is it getting better, or worse'). Edward Heath did not rely on press cuttings. As I related, he scanned almost the entire press himself to be sure of missing nothing important: but that was before Rupert Murdoch bought into the UK media, and before today's media self-censorship.

Perhaps the prime example of catastrophe caused by the leader refusing to consider what he is told is Stalin's reported belief in 1941 that he could trust Hitler not to attack the USSR. The messengers did not want to perish for bringing bad news, so no one dared contradict him when he shrugged off the warnings of Britain and others.

But the inability to accept that one has been disastrously wrong often dogs attempts to put things right. For example, neither Mrs Clinton (who could well be the next US president!) nor Premier Cameron - nor indeed all those other Senators and MPs who voted for the Iraq invasion - seem able to accept their responsibility for its effects, particularly on that curiously named 'War on Terror'. Must a whole generation of politicians pass away before politicians accept that 'our side' made so a grievous a mistake? It is vital to perceive one's errors before working out how a situation can be improved. Refusing to question that 'our side was always right' is a dangerous way to conduct diplomacy.

'In foreign affairs we know best': the denial that diplomacy is a profession

As I have stressed, another essential of diplomacy is to be able to see through the eyes of your opponent or those who disagree with you. This is all too frequently not practiced today by governments, ministers of foreign affairs and much less excusably by diplomats. The consequences are always serious and too often disastrous. Action is quite often taken without objective analysis by professionals. Indeed politicians, let alone the 'the man in the street', far too frequently think they know best about foreign affairs (although in most countries Mr. Average Man has little idea of where most other countries are - sometimes even after his own country is having war with one!) Most of us are ready to listen to scientists and to our doctors. And we admire our best artists, present and deceased, yet we do not believe that diplomacy is both a profession and an art to be cultivated.

That makes it hard indeed for the views of professional diplomats to prevail. Just one example, 52 UK Ambassadors, High Commissioners, governors and senior international officials, in their 28 April 2004 open letter to Prime Minister Tony Blair (mainly about the UK's failure to try resolve the Israel/Palestine problem), wrote: 'All those with experience in the area predicted that the occupation of Iraq would meet serious and stubborn resistance, as has proved to be the case'. But, as I have said Blair, like President Bush in the White House, had effectively divorced himself from informed criticism. Professional opposition was simply ignored - and, as in the US Senate, so in the House of Commons the Bush/Blair rush to war was 'rubber stamped' by politicians before any attempt was made to find out what the top British officials had to say. They evidently believed, like so many outsiders, that in foreign affairs, 'we know as much as the professionals'.

The media: nationalism, 'political correctness', 'giving both points of view', the owner's or the advertisers interests

The media often deliberately whip up fervor (often nationalist or 'politically correct') simply to attract attention (readership and viewership determine income and, maybe more important, advertising revenue). So our desire to read or view problems objectively in the press, TV, or on line is often just what we are not given. The media's other common fault (claiming to be true to that excellent journalistic precept of being fair to both sides) is to give all arguments equal space, so giving inordinate attention to ideologies that are demonstrably false, making them appear eminently plausible.

But it is the opposite for subjects that the day's political correctness requires be suppressed or self-censored. And if you are wealthy, or your corporation is wealthy, then by spending some money on scientists, pundits, and others ready to advance your personal views you can get credence for them, never mind how untenable.

Being 'fair to both sides' often leads to a more tenable 'middle' being over-looked

Deciding what is untenable, even in science let alone in politics, is not always easy. In many cases, particularly where foreign affairs are concerned, the 'middle' position' is not covered. It does not attract the same attention from readers and viewers - and that's bad for selling ads! On the one hand the 'traditional' media present the 'respectable' point of view, often reflecting nationalism ('<u>we</u> made no mistakes!'), the owner's interests ('of course there's 'freedom of the press - if you own one'), or 'political correctness' ('it's <u>we</u> who set today's agenda'). So with the 'traditional media' the middle position frequently doesn't get a hearing. On the other hand the (now usually on-line) alternative media too often reflects the other extreme - here that 'middle position' gets castigated for not being extreme enough, for instance in not being gullible enough to swallow some current conspiracy theory. A pragmatic, non-ideological, 'middle position' is often not exciting enough, not 'anti' enough, to meet the expectations of the 'alternative' media's aficionados - and so gets no airing even on the internet.

The media's dilemma - what is absurd and what should be known about?

But, as I say, it is often hard to know which opinions are absurd. So the media needs to be careful not to follow exclusively the current fashion in thinking, whether about science, medicine, politics, art, existential challenges, let alone about morality and religion. What appears today to be a view held by an insignificant number of people, may well be tomorrow's big news. Consider how few held Galileo's view of the cosmos, or how many held the 'earth, air, fire, and water' explanation of phenomena. Until the late 18th century one prevailing treatment for many illnesses was leeches: often the last thing the patient needed. And as for religion and morality one person with a handful of followers can attract enough followers to have a major effect on policy. Foreign affairs are no exception: to be able to observe matters objectively demands the suspension of your own preconceptions (whether derived from the media, the fashion of the day, or even from your own studies) for long enough to do so!

INDO-CHINA - MY TWO WARTIME VISITS

You were in Vietnam during the American War but you haven't really said anything about that?

Yes - but this is about what I've come to believe about world affairs, not to list my travels! Come to think of it though, my visits do bring out some of my present beliefs: not just my antipathy to war of which you know well. I knew Vietnam quite well in the '50s from my time in Singapore as desk officer for the country and my short posting to Saigon (Ho Chi Minh city now). I had a number of Vietnamese friends during my four years in Indochina - several were members of the Phnom Penh Yacht Club and took part in regattas on the Mekong and the Tonle Sap (where they regularly out-manoeuvred me in races - they knew the tricky currents where both rivers form the kilometres-wide surface on which we sailed). In Vietnam itself most of those I knew were overseas Chinese from my time as officer for South East Asia's Overseas Chinese.

I had a particular love of Vietnam and its people - quite sui generis with their complex characters and fascination with religion, but that only made them more interesting to get to know. I found the frequent American use of the term 'gooks', once even in front of a Vietnamese officer, as not only grossly impolite and pejorative but showing a dangerous mind-set: dehumanising the people the Americans had, ostensibly at least, come to help. That mind-set facilitates slaughter - like the use of the word 'Bosch' in World War I. ('It's all right to kill them because they're not really human like us').

<u>A bit about my to visits to Vietnam during the American war</u>

When I had a year's sabbatical in 1969 I spent some time in Vietnam about which I was writing a book looking at the war from the Vietnamese viewpoint. On arrival I called first on a former contact, who had become perhaps the richest Chinese merchant in Saigon. He had once told me: "we Chinese owe our success here because we can trust each other while the Vietnamese can't trust themselves. So we are the middle men for all big deals". (I don't necessarily underwrite the truth of that!) In addition to my own contacts from the 1950s, I obtained the names from him of Chinese and Vietnamese who could tell me about the way the war was going. He himself believed that, though 'Viet Cong' casualties had been extremely high and US bombing, particularly along 'the Ho Chi Minh trail had been massive, this had not affected the effectiveness of the North Vietnam's war machine. So he saw the war as going badly, adding that If the Americans left they would not continue to fund South Vietnam sufficiently to hold back the North.

He told me that the Chinese Congregations had arranged for a Boeing 707 in Taiwan to be on standby to come and collect as many prominent Chinese as possible 'when the time arrived'. (I don't know whether this happened before Saigon fell in 1975, seven years later - perhaps by then most Chinese with businesses had already quietly left).

Of those Vietnamese he had recommended I called first on the Vietnamese Colonel who was the liaison officer between President Thieu and the American Embassy. He took me to the Van Canh restaurant/night club - the height of decadence beyond anything known in Vietnam in the French days. With a 'lady' on his knee and another on mine, he painted an extremely pessimistic picture ending with the remark "you'll find everyone hates the Americans from the President to whom I work down to the peasant in the paddy field". And so I did! This was the result, in Putin's phrase, of 'the hyper-use of military power' (in which, as I say, the Russians have also indulged as well as the Americans).

I was accredited as a journalist. The Major giving me my press card held it moment as if he might withhold it and pleadingly asked, "You're going to write some good things about us, aren't you?" There was something approaching despair in his voice.

As a journalist I had the rank of Major when travelling with US transport and I was obliged to wear the required camouflage uniform. That 'hyper use of power' was concentrated at Than Son Nhat airport, then a vast US airbase where every journey started. On my travels with American forces I found two types - the first, mainly among airmen, were those with the mantra 'if it moves kill it' which all too often came down from on high (after all the number of bodies in body bags was one criterion of American success in winning the war). One incident I remember - taking off in a helicopter there were some kids throwing stones at us. A pathetic gesture of impotent hate. The gunner beside me swung his machine gun to target the kids. But, glancing at me, pulled up the barrel.

Second were the deeply unhappy enlisted men - black and white (and disproportionately black). On the way to some incident our plane would put down at a small airbase from which helicopters would come to take soldiers to the 'front'. It was there drinking Kool (made up from powder, so no need for Coke tins up front), that I had a chance to talk to these conscripts. Plenty of talk of 'gooks', but tempered with grudging admiration. I don't remember one who believed in a US victory, and I don't remember one that didn't yearn to go home 'when my time is up'. Most seemed to accept that the war would go on and on for years.

Morale was very poor. Once, when I was in Saigon to queue up with other journalists and telegraph (at immense expense) some item of mine to the Sunday Telegraph, a colonel attached to the US Embassy invited me to his home. During our talk two captains came round separately to the open French windows to the garden. He spoke privately to both and told me they had called to ask him what to say to their men. I said I hoped he had something cheering to say as I had found so much gloom. He just looked at me and changed the subject. Certainly he had nothing positive to say to me! He spoke very frankly confirming what my Chinese friend had said: that the Têt uprising, which had just happened, appeared to have cost the Vietcong dearly - but, even if it was severely weakened, the reality was the success of the North Vietnam army in mustering its troops along the border of South Vietnam despite the massive bombings of the 'Ho Chi Minh' trail along its Laotian and Cambodian sides.

South Vietnam was a strange place - it reminds me of Bosnia years later in the way civilian life carried on despite Vietcong-held enclaves. Many buses still worked but one had to pay tolls to the Vietcong. Locals paid a few dongs, French and British commonly paid a dollar.

Hué in the year of the Têt offensive

When I arrived at the US base outside Hué I overheard some soldiers loudly protesting an officer's order to patrol around the base that evening. Changing into civvies, I walked into Hué, the old capital of Vietnam and stayed with a French family at the town's electricity generating works. My French host told me that he had been able to keep the generators going during the Vietcong occupation and the American occupation that followed. The Vietcong had made him open his safe which he showed me, but took nothing. The Americans in contrast, had left graffiti including the name of their unit, but not the money! The Vietcong though, had gone on to murder quite a number of Vietnamese civilians.

I had gone to meet a member of one of the older aristocratic families who had surrounded the Emperor's court in Imperial days. He told me he had had narrow escapes moving from house to house during the short lived Vietcong occupation. He then took me to his home - a beautifully constructed wooden house with those traditional Chinese style upcurving roofs. There was a fine matching family altar in the centre of the compound which also housed a go-down. He said he had something to show me and opened the door to the go-down. Inside were some tons of rice in bags marked 'Hong Kong'. He explained that the Americans had sprayed from the air all the paddy fields in the coastal area around Hué with Agent Orange making them unusable. The Americans had made up for this by importing rice which, of course, had passed through Hong Kong from China via a Hong Kong merchant who had exported them to Vietnam. My friend had bought them for a very good subsidized price. Typical of the weird ironies of war. Typical too, of both American devastation and American generosity. In ways of this kind, Mao's China, while aiding the Vietnamese communists, earned a fair sum from Uncle Sam!

My visit to the High Representative of North Vietnam

One last story about the Vietnam War. After my first visit to Vietnam I went on to visit Cambodia where I called on the High Representative of North Vietnam. I was kept waiting awhile and was invited to play table tennis with one of the diplomats. Of course I was well and truly thrashed - that was certainly not a polite diplomatic gesture on my part! But ping pong broke the ice and my opponent laughingly showed me into the High Representative's office. He was far from as open as my Chinese host at the Summer Palace, but he did say one interesting thing.

Remarking that as the war dragged on in the South the Vietcong got more and more and more volunteers, he added that there was quite a problem enrolling them into the forces. "You see", he said, "they only come to us when the Americans kill a member of their family and not because they want to build a communist Vietnam. It's going to be hard to make communists out of them". Another irony! For it wasn't long after the Americans left that the victorious communists made capitalists out of themselves.

Chiming with my Syrian friend's lament is this remark about bloodshed being the motive driving people to join extremist organisations with which they have little real sympathy. Indeed it is ever-valid, but far too often ignored by the world's leaders. They commonly create monsters of violent opposition inspired by hatred when a little give early on could have appeased populations seeking reform. Here's a recent short list: Israel and the Palestinians; Russia and the Chechens; the Americans and the Vietnamese; Iraq's Shia government and the Sunni minority; Syria's Alawite government and its Sunni majority; Egypt's, Tunisia's, and Libya's dictators and the people they ruled; the Khartoum government and the south Sudanese; both east and west leaning Kiev governments and their peoples of west and east respectively. From killing and bloodshed decades of hatred are born. Evolution is blocked and revolution results and the old cycle of hatred and violence perpetuates. And Mankind's advance towards cooperation is delayed - maybe for many years. Maybe until too late.

My recollection of Afghanistan

I went to Afghanistan for a couple of days in Kabul, before the Russian or American occupations. I found it both uniquely attractive and, to me, the most foreign of all the countries I have visited. Kabul was small then. The clarity of the light and pure mountain air lent a strange enchantment as one looked down from a hill on the little drab looking capital city. The Afghans lived austere lives but were in no way as poor as so many in India. You felt their pride as they welcomed you as a rare visitor to their country, but you also felt they were not people you would want to cross! I remembered the first and second Afghan wars when the British, ever trying to pacify the North West Frontier, twice got a bloody nose. The First Afghan War, 1839-1842, was an East India Company war and utterly disastrous.

The second Afghan War was fought because of the strange but then fashionable idea of the 'Great Game': that the Russian empire was expanding south to threaten British India and that for both sides Afghanistan would be the decisive prize. This second war was a Pyrrhic victory for Britain. The Afghans accepted that they would only have formal diplomatic relations with the UK, meaning effective British control of their foreign policy. But this only lasted until 1919 after World War I. The cost was 10,000 men, 8,000 it is reckoned, from disease. And all to block Russia which was just as keen to use Afghanistan as a buffer to block British expansion north. Neither country had the means to take over Afghanistan! Curzon's Great Game was a non-starter from the outset. (This was Dr. Watson's war which led Sherlock Holmes, just by watching him, to deduce that the doctor had been thinking of the Afghan war and the wound he had received).

Imposing communism on the fiercely nationalist Muslim Afghans was a project which from the outset, given their history and geography, was highly unlikely to succeed. The Russians could have learned a lot from the story of the 'Indian Mutiny' in 1857 about how far one can go in imposing one's own culture on 'the natives'. Queen Victoria's government did learn - and the 'Raj' went from strength to strength.

Something like communalism could possibly be the form of Afghan society in the longer term: but as the Soviet Ambassador to Cambodia remarked to me - "some countries are simply not ready for communism". At present that would appear to apply to all!

A last word about diplomacy and doing one's homework

I mention this because it illustrates well what I've said about Lavrov and about diplomacy and foreign policy: one must do one's history thoroughly (and, I would add, one's geography) and always look at the situation through the eyes of your opponent. And one must consider realistically what a course of action might cost in life and treasure, and compare that with how much one would be likely to gain politically and otherwise from success.

Indeed it was failure to obey these really rather obvious precepts that cost the Russians their Soviet Union and has blighted the fortunes of the West. You might well conclude that, while diplomacy is certainly not 'rocket science', it does require a large dose of common sense which is an uncommonly rare commodity! Despite so many lessons of history, there still are too many top politicians who cannot see common sense for their ideological baggage, their hubris, and their personal ambition.

As I write, the Chilcot enquiry into the Iraq war is expected at long last to conclude that the decision for war was taken secretly months earlier by Prime Minister Blair with President G. W. Bush - in other words before the essential studies had been made as to whether all alternatives to war had been exhausted.

Above all, politicians and diplomats should heed Churchill's warning: "Never, never, never believe any war will be smooth and easy, or that anyone who embarks on the strange voyage can measure the tides and hurricanes he will encounter. The statesman who yields to war fever must realize that once the signal is given, he is no longer the master of policy but the slave of unforeseeable and uncontrollable events."

You've had something to say about many of the countries you've been concerned with, but you've missed out Cuba?

I went there mainly for curiosity - Castro's Cuba had been a thorn in America's side ever since the Cuba missiles crisis in 1962. I had had émigré Cuban friends in Paris who held very diverse opinions on the revolution. They had all initially welcomed the Castro revolution because it had got rid of the Battista regime with its corruption and had asserted Cuba's independence from the US. But they'd soon developed second thoughts and had ended up in Europe and not with the more extreme anti-communist Cubans in Florida. One lady, an Afro-Cuban, had stayed on as Castro's version of communism had been forced on the easy-going Cubans. She had been delighted when the Castro government had gone a long way to end the racial discrimination which had been so stultifying an affilliction for her as she had climbed the ladder of her profession. She had wanted to stay, but had found it impossible to live with the economic absurdities and ideological nonsense weighing on all imaginative efforts to make Cuba successful. So, with great reluctance, she had gone to France where she made a very successful career.

The nonsense started for me when I was told I could not have a visa permitting me to contact government officials but that I could have a tourist visa which would enable me to have talks with Cuba's institute for foreign affairs - the equivalent of Chatham House, the UK's prestigious 'think tank' for international affairs. I would be very welcome. And indeed I was - as a 'tourist'. The head of the Cuban foreign affairs institute was an Afro-Cuban. I found him, like Mr. 'Feng' in China, ready to discuss world affairs without any trace of ideology. He encouraged me to travel round the island because Havana was only one face of Cuba. So I made the train journey to Santiago de Cuba in the extreme west 750km and over 10 hours away by train, a journey which enabled me to quiz quite a variety of people.

What struck me was that, like the Afghans, the Cambodians and so many Vietnamese, the Cubans too were 'not ripe' for USSR style communism. They liked the good parts - like the remarkable health service, the virtual ending of racial discrimination, and, more importantly, independence from the US. They dreamt of a good hunk of America's wealth but they saw the US was far too powerful a force for Cuba to control. Some pointed out that the emigrés in Florida were mostly 'gringos' who had been the top class under Battista and might revive the pre-revolutionary racially stratified society.

I liked Cuba and its people and would like to visit again now that quite a few reforms have been implemented under Fidel's brother, Raoul Castro. Cuba is currently opening up to the EU in an attempt to counter excessive American influence. It appears that, just as much as during my visit all those years ago, neither government nor people want to be swamped by the US as they were before the revolution.

Once again I return to the point - to avoid repression, even revolution - the ruler needs to know how far he can go with his policies and always be ready always to make reforms step by step to meet his people's reasonable demands. Evolution is almost always better than revolution for the rulers, their country and their people. That's one glaring lesson of the 20th century which rulers need to practice even more in this 21st century. As the Tao Tê Ching remarks: 'knowing when to stop makes the ruler immortal'.

RICH & POOR

You've told us a lot about how you view the international scene and the existential challenges now facing us all. Now we want to ask about some of your beliefs about other problems - for example the increasing gulf between the very

rich and the rest of us?

For what it's worth this is how I see it. I have explained that I think 'directed capitalism' is the only way to meet the existential challenges of today's world. And I do believe that there must always be people with financial and political power who are able to accomplish things that the rest of us cannot. It is inequality of wealth that has enabled the increasing wealth of others. Only the better off farmer can experiment with new farming methods. Those on mere subsistence cannot afford to risk a new idea's failure. It is often the demand of the rich for better products which has led to break-throughs in technology to the benefit of humbler classes. Just one example, it was the arrival of the reliable Rolls Royce for aristocrats and the captains of business in the early 1900s that helped bring the motor car to the masses. Recently it has been the same with computers. In culture too, it was the largesse of a rich church and of rich connaisseurs that supported many of the composers of works of genius that we can all now enjoy on CD. There are so very many other examples where the discerning rich have benefitted the rest of humanity.

Class – and what those at the top owe to society

There was much wrong with the still pretty rigid class system that I was brought up with in the 1930s and 1940s - not only in Britain but in the US too. But the disappearing British aristocracy had by and large contributed greatly to society - from their sons going into the navy, the army, or the Church of England, to pioneering animal breeding and advances in crop growing agriculture. Their daughters, by and large, performed the equally valuable task of instilling into the children the morals and duties that the fortunate owe to society. Of course there were all too many exceptions. Quite a few just took what they could and gave nothing back. But these were not the ones who were looked up to. Then there were the wastrels - the great Dr. Johnson summed them up with his poem about the young Sir John Lade, Bart. '*Long-expected one-and-twenty/ Ling'ring year, at length is flown/ Pride and pleasure, pomp and plenty/ Great Sir John, are now your own./ Loosen'd from the minor's tether,/ Free to mortgage or to sell./ Wild as wind, and light as feather/ Bid the sons of thrift farewell....*'

The ideal of the gentleman not as a man of exceptional wealth, but as a man of culture, education and of high moral standards using force only as a last resort, a man setting the tone for society and winning the respect of foreigners is remarkably similar to the Confucian ideal of the gentleman (jün zi - 君子) in China. At its best this inspired the Mandarinate just as, at its best, the idea of the gentleman inspired the servants of the British empire. Morality, not wealth, were the ideals for both China and Britain - however much both societies fell short of them.

Records suggest that it was the sons of the aristocracy and the gentry that suffered disproportionate casualties as junior officers in the trenches of World War I. Indeed the slaughter of the aristocratic and landed gentry led to the commissioning of less exalted classes to be slaughtered in their turn! Death duties, the 1911 Parliament Act, and World War I were three nails in the coffin of the British aristocracy.

Lack of the same sense of responsibility among today's nouveaux-riches

But the new upper class, based almost solely on wealth, which has succeeded the old upper class in the UK, the US and many other countries has to a large extent lost that underpinning belief that if you are rich you have an obligation to the society which had made possible your good fortune - and that, irrespective of whether it was your birth or inheritance that gave you position, or whether you became rich by your own efforts. So many of the very rich today consider their wealth their right and thus see no obligation to give anything back to the world or even their own country. This idea of wealth as something akin to a divine right undermines the cohesion of society. Yet there are a hundred, even a thousand, ways that every society helps the rich man or corporation to arrive where they got - and many ways that society can claw back some of what it has contributed and so reduce inequality.

Taxation is only one of them. Just as important are public opinion, the consensus of morality, and a general rejection of the 'trickle down theory' (the idea that the wealthier the 'one percent', the more of their wealth 'trickles down' making everyone richer). That is the ideology of the rich, including the bankers who have amassed great fortunes through deregulation. Mr. Picketty's book, which I mentioned, has helped spur already growing skepticism of that theory.

And in today's world with those existential challenges, there are those unpaid for costs to the environment which can be huge - in some cases even as much as the mega rich, like the Koch brothers, earned from some enterprise like coal mining, supermarkets, shipping, air freight, beef farming and many others.

Inequalities and opportunities

There are two points here - a) how far inequality damages a society, and b) whether there are due opportunities for those at the bottom to succeed. Of course even in the most fair societies it is inevitable that those who start with wealth can more easily succeed.

Taking b) first: in England in the 19th and early 20th centuries the grammar schools, the Labour Party, the Trade Unions, and Freemasonry often greatly helped those from the lower classes to climb some way up the class system - not just to wealth but to positions of power and influence. (The remarkable career of Ernest Bevin is just one of many). But today there is less, not more, opportunity to climb the social ladder even in the advanced countries. That's bad for society if only because it wastes a large part of its 'brains pool'. (Thomas Gray, in his 1750 'Elegy in a Country Churchyard' meditates on what some of the dead might have contributed to society had they had the opportunity).

Now to consider a) - the damage massive inequality causes. Today's ever widening inequality (notably in the US where it is tarnishing 'the American dream') is disrupting the social structure. Some billionaires by their labours contribute immensely to society creating real wealth. But many do not - many of the very rich acquire it in ways that do nothing for society but often to harm it, lending some truth to Honoré Balzac's saying: 'behind every great fortune lies a great crime'. All too often true, but many of the super-rich actually do work and reap their due reward - this is particularly so since the industrial and technological revolutions replaced land-owning as the fountain of wealth.

The financial sector

Today perhaps the worst examples are those in banking after the repeal of the Glass Steagall requirement that banks must not also be investment companies. Banking may not produce things, but it enables others to produce. But much of investment banking does not, it simply enables those who speculate to make vast profits and to walk away with them - often in the form of immense bonuses paid yearly for 'making money' on paper which turns out to be a mirage, even bringing down the bank concerned. (Which then gets propped up with taxpayer's money because the bank is 'too big to fail').

Many of us thought that the financial world would have learned the lesson from the collapse of one of the UK's most prestigious banks, Baring Brothers, in 2005 when just one dealer, Nick Leeson, in its Singapore office left a $1.4bn hole in its accounts. But instead reckless trading became more common, not less. The financial sector has come to provide nearly 10% of the UK's GDP not far off the 11.6% for manufacturing, with maybe only half of this coming from traditional banking. The trading in derivatives etc. and deals based on sophisticated dealing like interest rate fixing provided the other half. This is just one example of how GDP does not measure usefulness or real value to society. Such an inflated banking system working largely for the benefit of banks and to the severe detriment of other sectors, is far too big a proportion of GDP sucking in some of the most able in the country who could be contributing real value to the economy. Unfortunately governments see only the prestige and taxation advantages of preserving a bloated financial sector. They do all they can to prevent these golden geese going to lay their dubious eggs elsewhere.

The LIBOR scandal

Right now the American Federal Deposit Insurance Corporation, (AFDIC) which guarantees bank deposits, is taking action for fraud in what is claimed to be 'the biggest financial scandal ever' against 'the largest cartel in world history' of 16 of the world's biggest banks for colluding to fix the LIBOR (London Interbank Offering rate) to their advantage and to the grave disadvantage of many of the world's institutions such as pension funds and local governments - those insured by the AFDIC which in consequence lost the billions of dollars for which it is now suing. (These banks, unlike traditional banks, make immense profits from interest rate swaps and so benefit by colluding to lower the Libor rate for the world. It's said damages may be measured in trillions of dollars. Just possibly this scandal will effect some changes).

'Tobin' tax, shares tax: a way of financing actions needed to beat that 'double helix'

Many observers of the banking scene see near instantaneous dealing in shares and other instruments as enabling massive profits (legal or not) to be made and recommend some very short delay be built in to the system. Also a very small tax - say .01% - on share transfers could yield hundreds of billions dollars as well as usefully dampening down speculation by retarding 'millisecond trading'.

Currency trading is another area of extreme volatility and huge profits are made through the near $2trn a day which is changed. Here, many experts recommend a very small 'Tobin tax' to be applied to all currency deals, smoothing rates and also providing hundreds of billions of dollars annually.

As well as doing much to 'tame' speculative financial dealings, these taxes could be used to counter 'global warming, disease and poverty' as proponents of a Tobin tax have long recommended. The difficulty, of course, is to get the world's governments to agree, leaving no loopholes for traders to avoid the taxes. Still, given the will, here is a way to pay for essential steps that must be taken in order to respond to the challenges of that double helix.

Philanthropy on the increase can make a real difference

No matter how much society properly owes the 10th of the 1% (individuals and corporations), so enormous is their wealth that they take an inordinate share of that GDP and there is less to go round for the rest of society. Fortunately more and more billionaires are following the example of Bill and Melinda Gates, Warren Buffet, and some other billionaires like George Soros, and devoting a large part of their fortunes to philanthropy, often achieving what no other organizations can. There is much criticism of billionaires' choices of 'glamorous' charities. No matter, for whatever their choices they leave more public money to be devoted to less eye-catching but often more important subjects.

The way capitalism works

There is immense discrepancy in the returns the 1% achieve and those earned by the less exalted. This is due, at least in part, to the way capitalism works: you take a risk with your money and, if you succeed, you make a sum much in excess of the work you put in. But it is hard to get on the capitalist ladder - on $2 a day you never do unless you can get a mini-loan. And, as I said, the man with just a little money has to be sure his first gamble will pay off, for he has to succeed first time, or he has lost his little capital. But the further you go up the ladder the more you can afford to be wrong part of the time - and so make much larger profits by investing in more risky and hence more profitable ventures. Money breeds more and more money the higher you are on the ladder. Capitalism is an example of "to him who has, shall be given".

But it is inherently unfair because potentially crippling risks get taken by those least able to afford them. This is why progressive taxation, even sometimes as high as 90% at the top end, is required to remedy, even partially, this injustice. But alas, with globalization, the rich - whether in individuals or corporations - can transfer their taxable profits to safe havens or where tax is lowest. Or they can make inordinate profits where labour costs are lowest and pay tax there - where poorer countries will give them tax breaks to keep them.

Inequality between countries

This brings me to the inequality between the developed and undeveloped countries. The great corporations and even quite small investors pour capital into 'backward' economies to produce goods (and services) which used to be produced in the 'advanced' countries. Provided fair wages are paid (and too often they are not) this can do much to increase the standard of living in the former although creating unemployment for the less skilled in the latter: this actually reduces their spending power and so reduces demand for what is sold. In the 'third world' much of the profit gets 'skimmed off' by the bosses and far less ends up with their employees - a vicious circle creating massive inequality in the 'developing' countries where little existed before.

Two results follow - the 'fair trade' movement to try to ensure that workers in the 'developing world' get their due for what they produce and to make sure that working conditions are reasonable in relation not just to pay but also for health and safety. The second result is that, as technology advances in the poorer countries, so, in the 'advanced' countries unemployment increases even among the more skilled. True, higher wages in 'developing' countries make it less profitable to send work abroad. But work will not return unless education standards in the advanced countries at least keep up with the fast increasing educational standards in the less advanced world. And at the moment that is not the case. For example in Shanghai, Hong Kong, Singapore, South Korea, Taiwan - and Finland the standard of mathematics of school leavers is markedly higher than in the US or even the rest of the EU.

Less of that 'American dream', not just for Americans

All this makes the 'American dream', (and the equivalent in many other countries), that ability to beat class barriers, ever less attainable. Only massive investment in education in the widest sense offers a partial way out of this dilemma. Ironically, the only people sure of a job are those whose jobs cannot be exported - e.g. electricians, plumbers, construction workers, garbage collectors, janitors and some manual labourers.

I say 'partial way out of this dilemma' because, as we have seen, the problem of the Luddites has not gone away as it did in the 19th and 20th centuries. With more and more work being done by computers and the machines they control, there is simply less work to be done by humans. Technological education cannot solve that though it helps. Ploys like reducing the number of hours worked, and two people doing the work of one, also can help. And if we are producing less to save the planet for humans, that means producing dramatically less, aggravating unemployment - at least until world population falls to a sustainable figure. Not just in the 'developed countries', finding something to occupy people looks like becoming a major problem even if the world does move towards a sustainable population. Though of course there's

178

always valuable work to be done caring for the sick and elderly, alleviating poverty and many other socially valuable occupations. The problem there is funding it - that's not impossible, but it would require a major, even revolutionary, rethink about how resources are found not just for the profitable, but for the socially desirable.

Meanwhile - in China and India and in several other 'developing' nations - the growth of a well-educated 'upper middle class' enjoying a standard of living more or less equal to their opposite numbers in the 'developed' nations. That gives a false appearance of 'development' for it hides vast numbers of poor, all but unseen, neglected and left behind.

Before we move on to what you call the 'beyond', there are a lot of other subjects we'd like to know your thoughts - but we realise we'll have to ration ourselves! We do though, want to have your views on sex, 'gays', and that same sex marriage we hear so much about.

SEX, PROSTITUTION, HOMOSEXUALITY, 'GAY' MARRIAGE AND POLITICS

Yes, there isn't room for anything like all the subjects I have views on - I told you I'd have to keep this book short otherwise you won't read it! But I agree sex and those subjects surrounding it obviously must be looked at. After that I'll allow you just one more question before we move on to 'the beyond' in Part II.

Sex

Obviously, for every form of life - animal or vegetable, from the simplest to the most complex - reproduction is the categorical imperative par excellence. For animals it is simply an essential vital function, neither good nor bad. But in humans sex reflects all aspects of life from the most degrading and cruel to the most exalted, even sublime. There is a divide somewhere in the middle between sex solely as an animal need and sex accompanied with affection or love. It is a bit like a rainbow without colours going from black to white: from total evil to utter good - to use moral terms. For that reason I had thought of dealing with it in Part II - the 'beyond'. But it is so important for society that I consider it here. Heinrich Heine puts it:

> Doch vielleicht ist dir zuträglich
> Nicht die wilde Lendenkraft,
> Welche galoppieret täglich
> Aus dem Roß der Leidenschaft.

(Perhaps it's not good for you - that wild power of the loins that gallops daily on the steed of passion.)

Ludovico Ariosto though, writes of the ecstasy that 'the wild power of the loins' can bring:

> O letto, testimon de' piacer miei;
> letto, cagion ch'una dolcezza io gusti,
> che non invidio il lor nèttare ai dèi!
> O letto donator de' premi giusti,
> letto, che spesso in l'amoroso assalto
> mosso, distratto ed agitato fusti!

(O bed, witness to my pleasures; bed, cause of my tasting a sweetness such that I do not envy the gods their nectar. O bed, giver of just rewards, bed, which was often moved, ruffled, and shaken by the loving tussle.)

Boris Pasternak was even more discreetly erotic:

Зимняя ночь

> Свеча горела на столе,
> Свеча горела.
> На озаренный потолок
> Ложились тени,
> Скрещенья рук, скрещенья ног,
> Судьбы скрещенья.
>
> И падали два башмачка
> Со стуком на пол.
> И воск слезами с ночника
> На платье капал.

(**Winter night**: A candle burned on the table;/ A candle burned./ Distorted shadows fell/ Upon the lighted ceiling:/ Shadows of crossed arms, of crossed legs -/ Of crossed destiny./ Two little shoes fell to the floor with a thud./ A candle on a nightstand shed wax tears/ Upon a dress).

Michelangelo Buonarroti, impressed by the strength of the sexual drive, asks the question:

> S'ogni affetto al ciel dispiace,
> a che fin fatto avrebbe il mondo Iddio?

(If every one of our desires is unacceptable to heaven, to what end did God make the world?)

Studies suggest that a majority of the healthy of reproductive age - especially men but many women too - seek a sex outlet around twice a week, but very often don't have one. Worldwide we are talking billions. Masturbation reduces the problem which otherwise gets resolved by abstinence, nocturnal emissions, casual - even forced - sex, or prostitution. Abstinence, for most people, is extremely demanding. And prostitution is a demeaning, and often tragic solution - whatever the politically correct with their 'sex worker' euphemism and bogus appeal to 'women's rights', may pretend.

For the euphemism 'sex-workers' for 'prostitutes' suggests a respectable career like being a nanny or even a lawyer. But this hides the realities of prostitution: from many personal memoirs we learn that even the upper class 'call girl' knows very well what damage it does to a woman - and indeed to her clients - to degrade her intimacy. And downscale very many are not making a free choice - they have been 'sex trafficked'. There's exploitation by pimps (often charging wildly exorbitant rents ensuring their lion's share); there's grinding poverty obliging a girl to support her family; there's heartless male coercion - often involving perversion, even sadism - for a moment's selfish relief. And of course there's the spread of disease.

Indeed it is a 'profession' which, for health and social reasons needs some degree of state control. Here, as the example of Sweden suggests, it is often the clients who should be sanctioned, not the 'sex workers'. The financial exploitation of sex can indeed be a daunting problem not just for individuals, but for society and for the state. Not least: the identification of abusers of children, traffickers, and pimps.

For the state, sex ensures continuity, the population of the future. So society and the state are inevitably involved - notably in marriage, divorce, adoption, and abortion. Both secular and religious organisations find it necessary to determine what sexual behaviour needs to be sanctioned and/or repressed. Rape is an obvious example. Another is the need for setting ages of consent for adolescents. This need not be the same for both boys and girls given their differing ages of sexual development, though the 'politically correct' claim that 'equality' - as they define it - requires the same ages for both sexes.

The state's essential interest, surely, is in promoting marriage as between a man and a woman, and encouraging, as far as possible, life long relationships in the interests of children. That surely implies making the legal requirements for divorce more demanding where there are children. But where there are none, the interest of the state is surely to avoid couples being denied reasonable opportunities to have 'a second chance'.

As I see it, problems arise because, although quite a few people have no great sex drive, many more do. A glance at the media shows that otherwise serious highly regarded people, often at the top of society, will commit self-destructive follies 'under the influence' of that imperious need for sex. Sometimes state, society and religion, all fail to make sufficient allowances for a drive from which few are immune. All too often politicians and religious pundits take a high moral position which can be destructive of their own wider interests.

Parnell and Katherine O'Shea

The tragic case of Charles Stewart Parnell and Katherine O'Shea (the derogatory 'Kitty' for Parnell's enemies) comes to mind. Parnell was a Irishman - a protestant and so able to have a seat in the British Parliament - who, in the 19th Century, was the leading politician seeking Home Rule for Ireland. A scandal erupted when it became publicly known that he was in a 'long term relationship' with Katherine O'Shea and had had children by her (she had for a long time been separated from her husband, Captain O'Shea who had, until then, always accepted that his separated wife had gone to live with Parnell).

The scandal led to a very public divorce and that cost Parnell his parliamentary support and almost certainly his life - he died in 1891 at the age of 46 soon after marrying Katherine. This incident may well have cost Ireland Home Rule in the 19th Century, the subsequent division of the island into north and south and, almost certainly, the resultant violence and misery in the 20th and this 21st century.

President Clinton and Monica Lewinsky

I have already mentioned the 'Lewinsky scandal' which had even more disastrous consequences not just for one country but for the world. President Clinton did not even commit adultery - yet his political enemies tried to impeach him for what used to be called 'heavy petting'. The President denied that he had had 'sexual relations' with Miss Lewinsky and was accused of lying - although 'sexual relations' are normally understood to involve coition. Particularly unpleasant was the hypocrisy - some of those who accused him were later found to have indeed actually committed adultery! Americans commonly claim to be extremely patriotic, but a large number, notably Republican politicians, gave no thought to the worldwide humiliation of their Head of State by subjecting him to a merciless and prurient public enquiry by Kenneth Star while much of the rest of the world looked on in amazement.

President Clinton's popularity with the majority of Americans was sustained. His high approval ratings actually rose in 1998 - the year the scandal broke and remained over 50% for the rest of his term. Nevertheless his Vice President, Al Gore, thought it best to distance himself from Clinton during his election campaign, and despite Gore receiving a majority of votes, the Presidency went to G. W. Bush. Had there been no 'heavy petting' the world would have been saved his calamitous two term presidency, for the Electoral College vote majority depended on a mere handful of votes in just one state - Florida, which Gore may actually have won.

But the Republican majority Supreme Court handed the Presidency to Bush. Never in history has the world had to pay so immense a price for a peccadillo, something most of the world would have either have ignored or laughed off. Even more important than the catastrophe of 'Iraq' has been the paralysis of US policy on climate. For Gore was the leading political voice, not just in the US but in much of the world, warning of climate destabilisation and calling for something to be done about it. And something certainly would have been done if he had been president - whatever other errors he might have made. As it was, under G. W. Bush his alter ego Dick Cheney preferred to indulge in that "hyper use of military force", abdicating the US's role as the world leader on 'climate'.

It reminds me of the ditty once quoted by Benjamin Franklin:- '... for lack of a shoe the horse was lost'. For in this case a bit of heavy petting led to the attempt to impeach President Clinton, so Vice President Al Gore thought he had better distance himself from the scandal despite Clinton's enduring popularity. Although Gore got more than half a million more votes than G. W. Bush that cost him votes and in Florida an indeterminate count suggested a shortfall of a tiny handful of votes. And Florida's Electoral College votes were critical to the decision whether Bush or Gore had won the Presidency.

To break the deadlock, the Republican majority of one on the Supreme Court declared G. W. Bush the winner despite the lack of a recount in Florida. So, for that peccadillo, the US lost the one leader who would have given climate change high priority. And under his opponent, G. W. Bush, the US abdicated its leadership of that cause. There followed a decade of inaction such that it just could now be too late to prevent the extinction of mankind!

Well, I hope not - but the Lewinsky affair is yet another lesson, like Princip's assassination of the heir to the Austro-Hungarian empire in 1914, of how a single young person can unwittingly change history quite disastrously.

The continuing use of sex for blackmail

I think this shows what a force sex can be not only in people's private lives, but in politics. It's worth remarking that despite today's more relaxed attitude towards sexual behaviour, secret services (and businesses too) nevertheless still manage to blackmail people into assisting them by threatening to publicise their sexual behaviour. For example many men do 'cheat' on their wives but will do much that they otherwise would not to prevent their wives (or anyone else) from knowing. And even today there are homosexuals who do not want to be 'outed' and are open to blackmail by their fellow 'gays'.

Homosexuality

Which brings me to homosexuality and 'same sex' marriage. At a time when humanity is faced with existential challenges and the world faces a host of problems of the first importance and urgency, we find politicians and the media giving high priority, valuable legislative time, and prime media space to this subject. 'Same sex' marriage is only of such priority importance because politicians have made it so. It is something of a fashion for the 'politically correct' in the West to be absorbed with 'gay' issues.

Indeed priority for 'equal rights for gays including the right to marriage' has become a dogma for the 'politically correct'. As I've said, 'political correctness' is normally associated with attitudes and ideas 'the left' want to impose on the rest of us, but now, a major part of 'the right', both in America and Europe (notably Conservative British Prime Minister David Cameron), has proved just as determined as so-called 'progressives' to change the legal definition of marriage to include the marriage of two people of the same gender.

The point I asked some MPs to make is that same sex marriage is not a matter of equality in the sense of 'equal pay for equal work' because homosexuals do not contribute to the state and society as do heterosexuals in the matter of marriage: they do not produce the next generation (in the normal way - excluding adoption and surrogate motherhood, etc.)

The other argument I made was that overturning the definition of marriage to accommodate a very small number of homosexuals (who make up possibly 5% of the population and only maybe

1/10th of these will make use of the law, maybe as little as 30,000 people in a population of about 60m). This is far fewer than the number of Jews, Muslims and Christians who opposed the measure, and the many whose freedom of expression is curtailed. The most controversial issue is whether homosexuality in schools is to be taught, even encouraged, on the ground that it is, according to the 'politically correct' an 'equally valid way of life' - something with which a majority of the population appears to disagree. (Typical reasons given: "I'd be much disappointed if my children don't have kids"; "it spreads diseases like Aids, doesn't it"; "it's distasteful and children shouldn't be led to try it").

Same sex marriage

As with so many matters of the first importance - like the invasion of Iraq - legislators pushed through parliament the Marriage (Same Sex Couples) Act, without any careful consideration of the facts, simply on a knee-jerk ideological belief that denying 'gays' the right to marriage would be to deny them their 'equal rights'. Today few legislators risk opprobrium for questioning this and so of being labelled 'homophobic' - for that means being prejudiced and hopelessly out of date in today's digitally interconnected 'with it' new world.

Since the passing of the Act, government and local government servants can lose their jobs if they criticise 'gay marriage'. And foreigners can be denied entry to the UK if they hold 'homophobic' (sic) views: (homo = same, phobia = an irrational fear). An American couple were recently refused entry although they do not in any way promote breach of the peace or violence and do not promote an irrational fear, let alone 'hatred of homosexuals'. I don't share their views, but then I don't share the views of many groups I want to be free to express themselves. Sadly the spirit of 'Hyde Park' is fast disappearing: there are things government won't allow, and for other things there is media 'self-censorship' - see *'You Can't Read This Book'* by Nick Cohen. (In the fifties I spoke in Hyde Park in favour of the Labour Party - my friend and I brought our 'soap box' in his ancient Rolls Royce to the amusement of the crowd. Our next door neighbour on his 'soap box' was a communist putting forward the Soviet party line in the midst of the Cold War - he competed with us to make himself heard!)

Secular arguments ignored

Secular arguments against changing the definition of marriage were largely ignored and organised opposition came largely from the Christian churches and a majority (but far from all) of their worshippers - and also from Muslims and some other religions. Neither politicians nor the media did much to inform a general public (largely indifferent to religion) about the issues. Thus too much was left to moral and religious arguments and too little to facts. The interests of the state and of society as whole were scarcely discussed and the fact that marriage is and always has been of fundamental importance to the state was largely forgotten.

Parliament did not discuss the need for this change, nor the likely legal and social consequences (now becoming apparent), nor even whether it would be beneficial or harmful to the interests of the state. Yet, surely, legislators should only legislate where there is some real advantage to be gained for the state and society as a whole. The debate in parliament was just between the religious opposition and those with the 'politically correct' ideology of 'equality' as defined by them.

Lack of knowledge about homosexuality

From what the polls and other sources have revealed it is clear that many of our legislators and a large proportion of the public know very little about homosexuality. This is hardly surprising given the considerable gaps in our knowledge. There are wide differences in sociological and medical figures for the percentage of the population in the UK who acknowledge being, or are reasonably to be included as, homosexual by nature: those whose 'sexual orientation' cannot be changed. There is no agreement about the incidence of homosexuality 'by choice' nor even how this should be defined. There is little recognition of the fact that there are two distinct forms of homosexuality - male and female.

Nor that male homosexuals can be divided into those that practice anal penetration, and those that practice forms of mutual masturbation (as do female homosexuals unless they use artificial "aids").

Then there are those of both sexes who have been, or are, sexually attracted in some proportion both to those of the same sex, and to the opposite sex - the so-called bi-sexuals. Here there is a greater or lesser degree of choice as to whether to pursue some form of homosexual behaviour. We don't know how many people of either sex fall into this category. Homosexuality is clearly an important sociological and medical phenomenon which deserves the proper study which it should have had prior to the Act.

As a result of the present media and political interest in the 'gay' adoption issue, and the campaign to change the legal definition of marriage to include same sex marriage, in the US at least, the public tends to guess a very high figure for 'born' homosexuals. One enquiry found that as a result of the immense attention the subject attracts, the public supposes 'gays' must number even as much as 20% of the population although several governmental and medical estimates suggest around 1% - 1.5% for male and about the same for female homosexuals: perhaps 2% - 3% in total.

A number of homosexuals declared that they were entirely satisfied with Civil Partnerships and had no desire to change the definition of marriage. I supported Civil Partnerships because it is clearly in the interest of the state to provide legal recognition for homosexuals in a long term relationship. This seemed to me not only to be just, but could encourage stable relationships and perhaps limit the public health problems posed by male homosexuals frequently having a large number of partners.

I was brought up to be tolerant of people with different ideas and ways of life which included homosexuals and I was sad to find that, particularly among the less educated there was deep prejudice against male homosexuals, and even physical attacks on them. I had no idea that homosexual behaviour was illegal and could lead to imprisonment until I heard that Alan Turing, the brilliant mathematician who had done more than anyone else to decrypt the German Enigma Code - and to whom Britain (and the world) therefore owed an immense debt - was found guilty and chemically castrated in 1952. That led to his suicide two years later - and all because he had performed consensual actions in private of which the law didn't approve. Unfortunately his war work was still top secret and so was not brought for his defence. He was pardoned in 2013 - absurdly late in the day! Our treatment of Turing seems to me something of a war crime.

The age of consent and adult predators

To return to the age of consent and the harm done by much older homosexuals seducing adolescent boys: although I drew this to the attention of some MPs none made the important point that, except in the case of the very few children who will prove to be homosexual by nature, both boys and girls, some even before puberty, often have 'crushes' on those of the same sex - whether for others of the same age or for adults. Therefore it was important to recognise that sexual orientation is by no means determined for all at birth and that homosexual relationships in adolescence are usually a passing phase and no indication of the person's later sexual orientation.

Today though, we see young people being encouraged early on to regard themselves as homosexuals often with lasting damage to their lives. The 'politically correct' dogma that homosexuality is 'an equally valid way of life' can do a lot of harm. I regard it more as an affliction (the word used by the BBC's founder, Lord Reith, about being excessively tall. He was 6'6") - but one which is often accompanied by rare and remarkable talent.

Boys in particular are at risk from older men who seek to persuade them that they have been born homosexual in order to seduce them. There is a much evidence about the severe psychological trauma this can cause. From what I have learnt about this I would prefer to see the age of consent for homosexual relations with boys to be raised to 17 in the case of consent to homosexual acts with men older than 21. Over the past decade or so we've learned that a far larger proportion of middle aged men will seduce children of both sexes, particularly boys in their early teens, than anyone had supposed.

Homosexual adoption

The Adoption and Children Act 2002 is another case where no proper enquiries were made before legislation. There is very little sociological and medical information about the effects of adoption by homosexual couples. There are, so far as I know, no studies based on children's experiences, only on adult perceptions. So we are reliant on what some individuals have said about their upbringing by homosexuals before homosexual adoption was permitted. One cannot draw conclusions from such a small sample but it would seem that most would have preferred to have been bought up by heterosexuals. And both boys and girls appear to have settled into female homosexual homes better than in male homosexual homes. While proper research needs to be done it does appear, prima facie, that once again the dogma of 'equality' rode roughshod over the well-being of children without any discussion, or recommendation that further research was needed before legislation.

Toleration

In my experience the aristocratic class was markedly more tolerant of homosexuality than the working, or even the middle class, where some with bi-sexual tendencies shouted the loudest to conceal this. The unfortunate Oscar Wilde would probably avoided prosecution had he not challenged the Marquess of Queensberry for libel for labelling him a paederast. It is good to see that this tolerance is now much more widespread. Indeed, though homosexuals do still face persecution even in the 'West', we are now witnessing the reverse: some intolerant homosexuals are taking advantage of the new law to sue harmless folk who offend them. The fate of Pete and Hazelmary Bull comes to mind.

THE MEDIA (TRADITIONAL & ELECTRONIC), ADVERTISING, SNOOPING

We've chosen our last subject - one that we really must have a few of your thoughts about, though it's a vast one! That's our generation's electronic world: the media and advertising, newspapers, TV, social media -plus state snooping and our privacy.

Yes, that's a really big one, and, of course, one you were brought up with but I wasn't! When I was young if you did something bad - as young people so often do - in a couple of years people would mostly have forgotten about it or put it down to 'sowing wild oats' or something like that. Today's young can't afford to do anything wrong - the world now has a near infinite memory. As a middle age job seeker the sins of your youth can be brought up remorselessly. Then there's so called social media like 'Facebook' - a single mistake, one sentence you may regret, and it can cause serious trouble, even worldwide. The indiscretion on Facebook of the wife of the man chosen to head MI6 comes to mind.

In the past you had to be careful what you wrote, even in private correspondence (for instance, your letters might be published after your death). But today there's little that's truly secret. If Google hasn't hoovered up your e-mails, the government has - I should say 'governments', for it isn't only 'Western' governments (who've got caught) but other governments, e.g. Russia and China. I've mentioned that the UK got caught snooping on Mrs Merkel, the German Chancellor but that both Russia and China were likely to have been doing the same. And you don't only have to be far more careful than we were about what you say and what you write - you have to be careful of where you go, and with whom! When TV arrived, there were cases when people were by chance shown doing what they did not want to be known. Now almost every street corner, every shop and office (and many homes) have Closed Circuit TV monitors - something that has become essential in our present less secure society with its criminals and terrorists.

As for the internet, it's an astonishing boon. I can look up anything, often on Wikipedia or a similar site in a matter of seconds: it takes up much less time than hunting through my library and is often indispensable when one wants the latest. But at the same time the search engines are picking up what they can about me on behalf of advertisers who want to sell me something - and that information gets sold on to governments who hoover up my political views! I don't myself care, but many people understandably do. Then there's 'social media', Twitter and Facebook - I've been unable to get much benefit from them: almost nobody follows my 'tweets'! But, subject to 'eternal vigilance' (never a click out of place) they are very useful for many (even the Pope!)

I've found having a website or two amounts to something of a revolution for one's work, though keeping them up to date is quite a drain on one's time.

The media and Rupert Murdoch

My views on the traditional media start with that old saw I've mentioned: 'freedom of the press is guaranteed only to those who own one'. Before World War II there were enough proprietors competing with each other to provide news, both home and foreign, to be able to say Britain had a free press. Even the communists had their say ('The Daily Worker', now 'The Morning Star'). 'The News of the World' (founded in 1843, provided much of the 'scandal' that we associate with tabloid journalism today - but less sensationally; it was a Sunday paper worth reading). This broad provision of the news, both home and foreign, went on until 1964 when that Australian, Rupert Murdoch, (I mentioned him as orchestrating euroscepticism in the UK) bought the 'Sun' - the former Labour supporting Daily Herald - for his international News Corporation.

Mr Murdoch's is quoted as remarking 'a paper's quality is best determined by its sales'. This was not just a cynical remark about profitablility: it hid his real aim. For sales determine political power. Huge sales promote, often even subliminarily, your particular line on political and foreign affairs. This gives you immense influence in politics and business. In 1969 Murdoch bought The News of the World, giving him commanding control of the 'popular' press which, to keep up circulation, now had to follow his 'populist' lead.

Instead of home and foreign news from a variety of sources, the public were force fed (French: *'gavé* - of geese for *foie gras*) with a diet of sensational crime, astrology, endless gossip about celebrities, and junk news. To this was cunningly inserted news, slanted to reflect Murdoch's views, for behind all this huge joint readership of the Murdoch media, was his scheme to get politicians and the influential come to him to ask him to back them. But Murdoch did not just set the tone for the tabloid lower end of the press, for in 1981 he bought The Times, the august and internationally respected 'paper of record' dating from 1785. That secured for him the commanding heights in the top newspaper market. His behaviour with The Times is recorded in *'Good Times, Bad Times'* by its former editor, Harold Evans.

But the deterioration of The Times as 'the paper of record' led to the launch of The Independent in 1986 edited by William Rees-Mogg who had resigned when Murdoch took it over after 14 years as editor. I was privileged to see a couple the dummy editions produced in the lead up to publication: they were most impressive. The paper's excellence for genuinely independent top end journalism soon gained it a circulation of 400,000 by 1989 overtaking The Times with some 300,000.

That was too much for Murdoch - he began a merciless price war in which his deep pockets could take losses that the fledgling Independent could not. The paper got into financial difficulties and was forced to abandon its position as heir to The Times as paper of record. It was obliged to follow The Times down market though remaining far more independent than The Times was once it had become a further member of Murdoch's stable. Murdoch's interests in the UK are not confined to the press. Among other things he also owns 39% of BSKYB television, and Harper Collins - one of the world's largest publishers. The list of his properties worldwide number more than 100.

Murdoch is now best remembered for his newspapers' involvement in hacking into the phone calls of royalty, celebrities and people in distress. This has reportedly cost News Corp approaching $1/4bn in legal fees and damages - but this is peanuts for this colossus.

Less attention has been paid to Murdoch 'the kingmaker's' success in UK politics. To him Tony Blair (New Labour) and David Cameron (Conservative) can credibly owe their positions as successive Prime Ministers, the former in 1998 and the latter in 2010. Both went out of their way to foster close relations with Murdoch and his aides. Perhaps even more significantly, Murdoch has managed greatly to increase' Euroscepticism' in the UK with his anti-Europe stance - he the 'Aussie turned Yank' with no stake in the UK's or Europe's future - would like the UK out of 'Europe'.

Murdoch's News Corporation has massive holdings around the world totalling some $15bn with an income of over $1bn a year. Much more important even than the political clout in the UK of this naturalised American, is his immense political, economic and business influence in the US. There he owns the prestigious Wall Street Journal (and its UK, Europe and Asia editions) and Dow Jones (the shares index and its subsidiary holdings). Probably even more importantly he owns 21st Century Fox which he recently hived off from News Corporation for strategic reasons.

That Hollywood film company owns Fox Television with what is said to be the most watched TV programme in the US, and Fox broadcasting with local stations widespread across the US. The political message is pro the extreme right 'Tea Party' and the now far right Republican party. It is also subliminarily racist at a time when the US President is a 'black'. As I've said, at the time of the Afghanistan and Iraq invasions Murdoch also owned The Weekly Standard - the paper of the neo-conservatives (and hence pro those invasions and other foreign adventures).

Fox television is openly partisan and has more than anything else brought about the 'Tea Party's' ability to bring the Republicans so far to the right as to make the United States partially ungovernable. No single individual not actually a top member of the G. W. Bush administration was as successful in forwarding the aims of both the neo-conservatives (e.g. in getting the US and the UK to invade Iraq) and of the 1% of the 10% - the billionaire individuals and corporations that are so dominant both in American, and in world affairs: that non-governing oligarchy.

Just as in the case of the UK, other media in the US feel obliged to tailor their products to vie with Murdoch's output. So perhaps I should amend that saying about a free press to read: 'of course freedom of the media is guaranteed, provided you own most of it'!

Self-censorship

Partly because Murdoch's heavy hand has made much of the rest of the media timid; partly because the media mustn't offend advertisers who now keep it afloat; partly also because of the power of 'fashion' in politics, there's massive self-censorship. Now it is far more difficult than it was a couple of decades ago to put forward views that are not 'politically correct'. That's so not only in the regular media but even on-line. I've mentioned that I was among the many observers unable to place, in 2002, pieces making the case for not invading Iraq the next year. Indeed over and again my warnings have gone unheard. Correctly foreseeing the future but so often being unable to get my voice heard, it is not surprising a colleague dubbed me 'Cassandra'. I am far from alone. Today there are many thousands of Cassandras! But it's no fun watching the disasters you've predicted come to pass.

Even in March 2014 it wasn't 'politically correct' to voice an opinion of how the Crimea crisis might be resolved by EU negotiation with Russia. ('Putin and the Russkies are baddies and that's that'). Connected to that is the reluctance to publish much about the errors made by the US, the UK, the EU, and the rest of 'the West' in foreign policy since the collapse of the Soviet Union in 1991. But then it has always been the case that governments, like most people, cannot bring themselves to contemplate their most serious errors - and, as I say, that makes it difficult to learn from them.

Truth is often not a welcome commodity. All too often people pay with their lives for telling it! Even in the 'free world' it comes at a price. Nevertheless it can help - like the 'truth and reconciliation' process in South Africa. And, because of its apology for the Nazis, the German government and people have in very large measure recovered the respect not only of governments but of the peoples who suffered. Germany now plays a valuable role in Europe and the world on the side of negotiation where at all possible, and using force only as a last resort. I have mentioned how Germany joined with France in opposing the invasion of Iraq, and before that played an important role in seeking the rest of Europe's support for ending the Serb conflict with both Croatia and Bosnia. Only when no one would listen did Germany back the US in using force to end the conflict.

Sadly the Japanese Government's refusal for six decades to apologise formally to China, Korea, South East Asia and the world for its appalling record of aggression, slaughter and gross inhumanity in the 1930's and '40s still heightens the mistrust of Japan not only by China's government and people, but by many others who are still bitter. Japan of course is not alone - has the US government apologised for slavery? (It's no real excuse that it took place in a Confederation that no longer exists). Britain, and other countries involved in the slave trade - including the African states whose forbears sold their own people - have not apologised formally, though some have 'regretted'. And, of course, in parts of the Muslim world slavery effectively still continues. And cases of human trafficking and effective slavery blight Britain and other European countries today.

There are number of subjects that are self-censored in our UK media, some are totally taboo. I've mentioned Freemasonry which is deemed 'too delicate' to touch even by the Catholic media. (This has led to the curious situation where Catholics are still officially told that they must not join the Brotherhood but cannot be told why). I've mentioned the near awkward silence about 'the

Craft'. Yet this secret society, nominally headed by a Royal Duke, remains one of the most important institutions in England (whence it has spread over much of the world - it is said to number some 5m members). The UK government (both Conservative and Labour) did attempt to oblige Masons in the police and judiciary to register their membership - but those two powerful bodies fought back. Finally, the United Grand Lodge of England threatened the government with legal action citing an Italian 'equality' precedent of the European Court. The government then abandoned this effort to 'out' some of the Masons in public employ. Even this retraction was barely noticed in the media.

And as I've also mentioned, understandably given the international violence against Salman Rushdie as a result of his *'The Satanic Verses'* and of the Danish cartoonists in 2005, the media are quite literally afraid of Islam. This leads to a serious lack of balance in covering religion because nothing is off limits when discussing Christianity or even Judaism. Both can be severely criticised provided one is not openly 'anti-semitic' (a curious word when Arabs are also Semites!) This failure of the world's media to discuss Islam makes it far more difficult for those 'moderate' Muslims who oppose violence in 'promoting' their religion, to win any understanding of, or respect for, their pacific, yet deeply held beliefs.

Then there's that need to avoid offending advertisers: where journalists previously were once the élite in the media, advertising staff now often enjoy greater prestige and influence: they are the ones who bring in the lion's share of income and warn the journalists not to offend the advertisers. That explains much self-censorship and even connivance in forwarding advertisers' interests in journalists' copy.

I have mentioned too, how vested interests play on the journalists' credo of giving equal coverage to both sides of an argument, by giving prominence to the stance taken by the 'extreme right' and so moving the middle ground further towards the 'far right', however absurd its view may be. Then it's easy to claim that it's the moderate 'left' rather than the 'lunatic left' that is extreme.

Hence the joke that equal time must be given to 'flat-earthers'! This is difficult - for who is to say that some new or minority subject should or should not be 'given an airing'. There is a real danger today of failing to examine important new thinking particularly about politics and foreign affairs. We are forgetting that quite often 'every new idea faces disbelief, then acceptance, then enthusiastic promotion'.

GETTING OLD

A word about old age before we move on?

As one ages so the question 'who are we' becomes more insistent. Who is one? The grumply old lady or tetchy old man that one has become - or some earlier incarnation, the young girl dreaming of a family, or the young man seeking adventure? Or one of many variations as adulthood advances? Some suggest that we are no more than our memories. Is the essence of me just my ever dimming and sometimes false memories, or something else? Years ago an eminent professor at Bristol university, recounting on TV the immense advances in our knowledge of the brain, ended by remarking "but what makes you you and me me - of that we know nothing whatever". We do know that our very character can change dramatically - even for example with certain medications. Interestingly the Toxocara infection from cats has recently been shown to make those who are normally very careful take risks - a change of behaviour of great importance in certain professions like airline pilots. This has now come to the notice of insurance companies. So we can well ask 'who am I?'

Despite this uncertainty, all prehistoric civilisations we know of made ritual arrangements for interring the dead, frequently burying with them items (or substitutes) that they were presumed to need in an after life. This culminates with the Egyptian pyramids and the terracotta army buried with Qin (Chin) Shih Huang, the first Emperor whose name gives us China. Until modern times, the belief that some essence of a person survives death was all but universal. Ancestor worship in China and Vietnam I found not altogether dissimilar to our beliefs about an after-life for our loved ones. Is this all but universal and still seemingly prevailing belief in some sort of an afterlife mere wish-fulfilment, or has it some foundation? (The earliest scientific study of burial practices and associated beliefs is Sir Thomas Browne's *Hydriotaphia or Urn Burial,* 1658 - something of a first for a scientific book being written in elegant English rather than in Latin).

And as you age you will ask ever more wistfully - in Alphonse de Lamartine's words:

> 'Ne pourrons nous jamais sur l'océan des ages
> Jeter l'ancre un seul jour?

("On the ocean of time can't we ever drop anchor even for a single day?')

Here are some thoughts I find useful:-

"Do not resent old age, few are granted the privilege". (David Niven)

"Don't let your clumsiness and forgetfulness make you angry, laugh it off. Get used to it".

"Old dogs can still learn new tricks, but they have to work a lot harder to do it!"

"Don't fret about failure - only one athlete wins gold in his event. But he couldn't have run without the 'also rans'. And that's who nearly all of us are".

Whether you believe in some form of an afterlife or not, I suggest it could be wise to adopt the maxim 'live each day as though it were your last, and as though you are going to live forever'. Both could possibly be true!

As General de Gaulle said, "old age is a shipwreck". Go down with your ship as gracefully as you can.

And there is much to savour as the sun goes down. Here I'd like to end with my own 1997 translation of Russian diplomat Fedor Tyutchev's poem 'Last Love'. (He was serving in Venice when he wrote it):-

<u>Last Love</u>

How we, in our declining days
More fondly love, more magically...
Glow on, glow on sun's ebbing rays,
Last glint of last love, pray dally.

The sky's a deepening cast of grey
But from the west yet roves a gleam.
Wane slowly, slowly dying day,
Live on, live on enchanting dream.

The sky's a deepening cast of grey
But from the west yet roves a gleam.
Wane slowly, slowly dying day,
Live on, live on enchanting dream.

The blood runs thinner in the veins
But the heart is still as tender.
Last love, last love - commingling pains:
You're brightest bliss and dark despair.

Here's the original, for those with Russian who can see
how far my translation fails to do it justice –

ПОСЛЕДНЯЯ ЛЮБОВЬ

О, как на склоне наших лет
Нежней мы любим и суеверней...
Сияй, сияй, прощальный свет
Любви последней, зари вечерней!

Полнеба обхватила тень,
Лишь там, на западе, бродит сияье,
Помедли, помедли, вечерний день,
Продлись, продлись, очарованье.

Пускай скудеет в жилах кровь,
Но в сердце не скудеет нежность...
О ты, последняя любовь!
Ты и блаженство и безнадежность.

ca 1864

And with that, let's move on to Part II

Appendix to Part I

Out of the hundreds of papers I've generated as a diplomatic consultant I have chosen, as an appendix, just this one - my letter to The Independent published six months before the Anglo-American invasion of Iraq. That is the event I have mentioned as the turning point in the fortunes of the West. It is one of my credentials as a Cassandra! None of the MPs with whom I was in touch shared these thoughts. That is not surprising for, with praiseworthy exceptions, the entire political class ignored the 'million man march' through London on 15 February 2003 against the invasion.

The Independent (London, September 10, 2002)
Letter from John Pedler

Sir:
Isn't a US attack on Iraq just what Osama bin Laden's flagging plan requires? After 11 September it was widely suspected that al-Qa'ida's plan was to provoke a massive ill-directed, unilateral, anti-Muslim retaliation from the United States. This would release extremist Islamic forces, destabilising the already precarious Middle East and compromising the West's oil supply. That in turn would create economic and political havoc in the developed world. When the dust eventually settled a new extremist Islam would face a debilitated West.

With political skill and military luck the Bush administration avoided such a scenario with a measured, internationally accepted response in Afghanistan. Now though, the President is squandering the world's good will in a series of unilateral actions. He declines to ensure stability in Afghanistan, and refuses his vital support in settling the Israel/Palestine problem on the lines now acceptable to all interested nations.

In these circumstances a war in Iraq, followed by some questionable nation-building, makes 11 September look like a gamble al-Qa'ida might yet win.

JOHN PEDLER, Volosko, Croatia

Part II - The 'Beyond' Guide to contents:

p 211 MY COURSE IN COMPARATIVE RELIGION
p 217 STARTING TO PUT TOGETHER WHAT I HAD LEARNED
p 223 FROM 'AHOR' TO GOOD AND EVIL
p 228 FIVE THINGS THAT STRIKE ME ABOUT RELIGION
1. A plethora of superstitions leading to human sacrifice - leading to religion
2. Few conversions, much doubt but little searching, the appeal of atheism and barbarism
3. The prevalence of empathy and compassion among the religious
4. Religions and the state suppress freedom of religion
5. Beyond dogma, much similarity in the apprehension of the 'beyond'

p 244 A BRIEF OVERVIEW OF SOME RELIGIONS
Hinduism, Buddhism, Sikhism, Bahai, Mormonism
Judaism, Christianity, Islam
The Prophet Mohammed and Jesus of Nazareth, their scriptures
The Koran and 'higher criticism'
Jewish and Christian scriptures and the Koran
Islam – a religion with political implications
The Jews as a people
Evil and Religion

p 263 COMING TO A CONCLUSION
Peace

p 267 MY SEARCH ENDS
Suffering and prayer
The Holy
Envoi

The postscript is at page 273

PART II
'The Beyond'

Naturally many of the questions my children asked me over the years were about 'my philosophy' and my views on religion. When I told them I was writing this essay about my weltanschauung they said that, for them, this might be the most interesting part. Of course they already knew quite a lot about my conclusions about religion but they were still eager to hear how I had arrived at these. For this was such a controversial subject which so divided people and led to such violence. There were so many different religions, and so many variations of each one - and then were the atheists and agnostics. What a tower of Babel!

As my mother had been going through an altogether agnostic phase, I was brought up with no religious instruction. Of course at boarding school we all (unless we were 'something else', like Jews or Catholics) had to attend Mattins - a Church of England service where one sang hymns and listened to a sermon. This was a bore for us kids as it spoilt 'free' Sunday mornings. And of course in 'English' we absorbed hunks of both Shakespeare and the King James Version of the bible. Both of these greatly impressed me for their literary merits - as they do everyone else who studies the English language as something more than just a means of communication for some particular purpose - like acquiring a military vocabulary.

When still at boarding school I chanced on that famous remark of James Joyce, which for me as a teenager had landed like a punch between the eyes: "history is a nightmare from which I am struggling to awake." History was my best subject which later helped get me to London University. It struck me then that, when looked at dispassionately, history is indeed a nightmare - one from which there is no awakening. I concluded that the Romans had been right about life. Stoicism was the answer - one just had to accept the bad bits and 'grin and bear it'. The Romans were soldiers par excellence, and wasn't this the soldier's creed:

"pack up your troubles in your old kit bag and smile, smile, smile" - that message from the 'Great War"?

Teachers of course said that there is much more to Stoicism (Epictetus, Marcus Aurelius and all that) but the dictionary assures me that 'the essence of the English adjective stoical is not utterly misleading with regard to its philosophical origins.' After that I forgot about the whole subject of religion: I'd heard the cynical remark attributed to Seneca: 'religion is regarded by the common people as true, by the wise as false, and by rulers as useful. And hadn't Spinoza summed up religion as just 'a desperate attempt to ward off God's wrath' - in other words not worth thinking about.

And why should I? After all, I was still young enough to wake up each day full of the thrill and wonder of life - the first part of Alexander Pope's "where every prospect pleases, and only Man is vile". Of course I was already aware of the truth of the second part, but somehow that just didn't concern me with my animal energy and joy in living.

By the time I was sixteen though, and leaving school, I began asking myself what I thought I knew of the world, not just the material world but what lay behind it - surely there had to be something beyond it? Or wasn't there? Our physics master had said there were basically two theories about the universe - steady state and sudden creation. But neither theory answered what was behind creation and why there wasn't nothing? Each time I thought seriously about the idea of 'nothing' I was plunged into a strange and fearful mental state, asking myself such questions as would numbers too, cease to exist if there were nothing, yet how could they not 'be'? And where are numbers anyway - you can't see them or touch them but you can use them - and our civilisation is built with them. I couldn't get away from the thought that numbers existed eternally in a world beyond our material world and what else existed there? That started me on a mental trek to find out.

I won't try to retrace my thinking any further, but rather to put together what conclusions I have come to so far, for the quest never ends except with death - or perhaps Alzheimer's syndrome! At the same time I'll try to show, with a few quotations from different cultures, how universal are thoughts and feelings about life and the search for something beyond our everyday experience.

MY COURSE IN COMPARATIVE RELIGION

When, just 17, I arrived at the London School of Economics with these thoughts recurring every now and again with their unanswered questions. I discovered there was a course in Comparative Religion. And it occurred to me that maybe I shouldn't just ignore such a vast, and so controversial a subject: maybe it could help my perplexity. In addition to the courses on economics proper we had to include others like economic history or statistics, but we were free to sign up to courses in other subjects. So I signed up for this one.

And during the course I found myself beginning to ask myself which - if any - of all these religions, or none, might I adopt? Which might best help me find some clue to that most basic and eternal question: 'why are we here' - and, as important, its corollary: 'what ought I do'. And that of course implies some answer to those other questions: is there a 'moral' element in the 'beyond' - is there 'right' and 'wrong', do 'good and evil' exist? And if they do 'exist' then what does that imply about the 'ultimate Beyond'? And what is that for Hindus and Buddhists, and for monotheists like Muslims, Jews and Christians?

Comparative Religion as a starting point

Dr Hilde Himmelweit, the social psychologist who gave the course (she was one of the distinguished Jews who had come to Britain before the war to escape Hitler) began her first lecture by asking us to suspend so far as possible our belief in any religion we might have if we wanted to benefit fully from the course. After all, most of us held the same religion as our family did. But whatever religion we held, the great majority of the rest of the world held quite different views. So we ought to be open to the possibility that some other religion might answer the question 'why are we here?' more satisfactorily than the one we had happened to be born into. This advice applied to atheists too - for atheism was also a belief that needed to be considered by sociologists. For the duration of the course we should all be agnostics. This approach to the course pleased and intrigued me.

The origins of religion

To begin, we had an introduction to superstitions through Frazer's 'Golden Bough' and his proposition that religions evolve from myth and superstition, and lead eventually to a scientific approach to both and thus on to the objective study of religion as a branch of anthropology. That made sense to me.

For we all, or almost all, have at some time been superstitious: as a child I had picked up superstitions like, when going to school, not walking on the joints between paving stones or having to touch some particular lamp post. Doing that seemed somehow necessary to avoid something going wrong that day. Then at the end of the month I'd find that I'd acquired so many of these compulsions that I risked arriving late at school! That had made me give up all of them and start the new month without any - only to find I'd begun collecting another lot of quite different ones!

So I'd already been introduced to the fact that superstitions are surprisingly powerful even for people who claim not to be superstitious. I had noticed that many adults feel obliged actually to touch something wooden when jokingly saying 'touch wood', and that they actually cross their fingers when saying 'fingers crossed'.

Superstition, as a means of controlling, or at least mitigating, the cruelties of 'fate', seemed to me a plausible origin for religion. You could see how, as each superstition failed to diminish the impact of some disaster, an even more powerful action seemed to be required. And logically that ultimately led to human sacrifice.

In remote antiquity Man found himself a 'waif and a stray' in thrall to the unforeseeable forces of nature. So a primary part of the life and culture of his tribe was to try to find some actions that would contact with them and influence them, rather than be forced to accept total impotence.

Then beside superstition there is myth. Frazer's initial emphasis on the myth of the Golden Bough - making that the title of his book - seemed to be pointing to some psychological necessity hidden deep in all of us. Frazer adduces the mystical Sun King, who was married to Earth and had to be killed each autumn by his successor and come to life again with the latter's resurrection in the spring. As it is the same king who is resurrected in the autumn he kills his previous self and, in effect, commits suicide. The parallel with Christianity is striking. This idea also fits in with Carl Jung's proposition that there is in Man a collective unconscious which contains the 'archetypes' - primordial patterns of thought innate in all of us.

This insight offered a peep at a deep mystery - the eternally slaughtered and resurrected god - opening the way to an understanding of creation. Do we see here something intelligible to be found about the workings of the universe, a reason for things beyond its cruel indifference to Man and his fate?

Differentiating between superstition and religion

In the lectures that followed sketching the major religions I was struck by the element of superstition which creeps into the practice of all religions and how hard it is to draw the line between superstition and ritual. Indeed, how, even in the recent past, we lacked sufficient knowledge of science to reject certain superstitious practices. A good example today is the widespread belief in horoscopes based on the effects on humans of the planets, the nearest of which is at least 38 million km away. Even when all the planets are aligned as in 1982 their combined gravitational effect is as near nil as to make no difference.

So the idea that some tiny planet or even a huge one like Jupiter could have any influence on the people born under the 'sign' of that planet's month, but not on anyone else, is all but absurd. Yet even quite serious newspapers print a horoscope section where, depending on your 'sign', you are told what that day is likely to bring for you. And the practitioners of this 'art' often have quite different outcomes for their particular followers! This leads believers to choose their own newspaper's 'seer' or some private practitioner - rather in the way people choose (or more likely are born into) a branch of their particular religion (e.g Orthodoxy or Calvinism; Sunni or Shia). Astrology - and the advertising in support - is a profitable profession and a surprising number of well-educated people have belief in it: the figures for the UK and North America suggest that at least around a quarter have some belief in it - and one needs to add the many who don't want to admit it. If correct, that makes it the largest belief system in the UK!

It is not easy to differentiate between superstition and ritual (the acts religious people perform in both individual and collective worship). For example the Muslim practice of symbolic washing before praying is clearly ritual expressing the need to approach Allah with reverence. A parallel is the Catholic priest's symbolic washing of his hands during mass. It is harder though, to differentiate between the many apparently religious practices and superstitious acts - examples are footballers crossing themselves before a match, Catholics hanging St. Christopher medallions in their cars, Mahayana Buddhists who pass prayer wheels and spin them. All these actions may well involve sincere religious belief, but they may just be superstitious gestures. Quite apart from religion - is avoiding walking under a ladder a superstition or is it common sense in order to avoid the man above accidentally dropping something on you? The answer of course depends on why you didn't walk under. How much more difficult it is to differentiate where religion is concerned!

As I related in Part I, coming to a village In Laos - the Laos are Hinayana (little vehicle) Buddhists - you first pass the 'phi house', a miniature house on a pole perhaps with a little sticky rice by the entrance: this is to provide a home for spirits from the jungle so that they don't come into the village and bother the inhabitants. This is entirely sensible if there are such spirits, but a pointless superstition if there are none. Who is to say - a great many highly educated people throughout the world believe in spiritual beings: angels and suchlike?

A great many Hindus are superstitious - indeed there are long lists of their superstitions - but, like superstitious behaviour all over the world, belief in it diminishes markedly with education. The most rigid opponents of superstition are some Islamic theologians who condemn all superstition as denying the unity of God - for them it is 'shirk' and unforgivable. But no one who has visited Islamic countries can fail to be impressed by the many superstitious beliefs that persist. What is superstition after all but an irrational belief that some action will ward off evil - and the desire to liberate ourselves from 'evil' lies at the root of all the major religions.

More importantly, in the case of some leading religions, much superstition, superfluity, even distortion has developed surrounding their original basic beliefs. Two examples: typically both in Hinayana and Mahayana Buddhism many superstitions have grown up obscuring what we know as Gautama's teaching. And in Taoist (Daoist) temples and among believers it is hard to recognise precepts from that ever-untranslatable numinous classic, the Tao Te Ching (Dao De Jing). But, observing Taoist rituals I realised that the need for some form of ritual is seemingly built into Man.

Dualism as an answer to the great problem of monotheism

Crucially - is there an on-going combat between the force of evil and the force of good? Zoroastrianism, an example of such dualism, seems to have developed from aspects of Hinduism in India. It is recorded by the Greek 'father of history', Herodotus, in the fifth century BC as the religion of the Medes (and Persians). It is an example of such dualism - of a struggle between the forces of good and those of evil. Zoroastra appears to have lived around the 6th century BC and there is no even near-contemporary documentation. So it is all but impossible to find out his teaching. Zoroastrianism is on the one hand called the world's first monotheistic religion and the first clear case of religious dualism. I was fascinated by the explanation, for some, that this contradiction is resolved through Ahura Mazda, the creator, the supreme spirit and neither good nor evil, creating two lesser spirits Spenta Mainu, the good spirit of wisdom - and Angra Mainu (better known as Ahriman), the evil spirit of destruction and that, so long as time endures, these two spirits are in constant combat. It is said this derives from Hinduism's 'supreme essence of existence' Brahman, which is beyond the gods who number the beneficent Vishnu and the destructive Kali (Shiva is too nuanced a god to be described as evil).

I say crucial, because religious dualism resolves the great problem of monotheism: how can a good omnipotent God tolerate evil? In dualism there is no god with responsibility for what Edward Fitzgerald in his famous translation of Omar Khayyam's Rubaiyat calls "this sorry scheme of things". In dualism, God (god?) is a combatant like us, and so 'our ally' in his cosmological battle to defeat Evil.

Dualist beliefs appear in many places - for example in Gnosticism, among the Bogomils who emerged in Bulgaria in the 10th century, and the Cathar (Albigensian) 'heretics' in the south central France whom the Catholic Church found so hard to suppress. But perhaps the purest form of dualism emerged in ancient Egypt: the opposition of Set (disorder, death) and Osiris (order, life).

STARTING TO PUT TOGETHER WHAT I HAD LEARNT

At the beginning, a universal note of anguish and despair

But all this was just an introduction to the study of beliefs - merely a *vorspeise*, an appetiser in comparative religion. I had to start putting together what I was learning from the course.

And as good a place as any to start is Edward Fitzgerald's remark about his translation of the *Rubaiyat* of Omar Khayyam: "It is a desperate sort of thing, unfortunately at the bottom of all thinking men's minds, but made music of."

In his preface to Fitzgerald's work Arthur Dewson explains: "The soul asks what the meaning of it all is. It finds itself in a world full of beauty and delight, filled with every kind of desirable sensation; after the first child-like ecstasy is over, it begins to perceive woven into the texture, the dark lines of sin and suffering, of shame and grief, which transform what might be tranquil and beautiful into something harsh and unbearable; and then too, there opens a still darker and mistier prospect upon the view. Whichever way it looks, death closes the prospect like a wall, till the spirit, disillusioned and terrified, asks itself why it was placed in so congenial a sphere and with so immortal an outlook, only to be confronted with the blank mystery of extinction. The only answer to such questionings is the answer of faith, and that, to the distracted and melancholy mind, is nothing more than a faint hope, a light of sunrise seen across dark valleys and cold mountain ranges."

The blank wall of personal death torments the bereaved - witness Fedor Tyutchev's poignant cry on the anniversary of the death of his beloved:

> Завтра день молитвы и печали,
> Завтра память рокового дня…
> Ангел мой, где б души ни витали,
> Ангел мой, ты видишь ли меня?

(Tomorrow is a day of prayer and sorrow, tomorrow is the anniversary of the fatal day... My angel, wherever souls may dwell - my angel, do you see me?)

The Japanese Lady Heguri has the same thought:

> A thousand years, you said,
> As our hearts melted.

> I look at the hand you held,
> And the ache is hard to bear.

Sir Thomas More, in his poem on the vanity of this life observes:

> Damnati ac morituri in terrae claudimur omnes
> Carcere: in hoc mundum carcere nemo fugit...
> Jam quoque dum carcer non tamquam carcer amatur,
> Hinc aliis alii mortibus extrahimur.

(Condemned and doomed to die, we are all shut up in the prison of this world. In this prison no one escapes death... While the prison is loved just as though it were not a prison, we are released from it some by one death, others by another.)

And those valleys Dewson talks of are dark, dark with the Weltangst, the Weltpein - the anguish and atrocious sufferings of mankind throughout the ages. We have only to turn on the television to have this truth invade our living room, prompting us to ask what are we ourselves doing but waiting, if not for our death sentence to be carried out, then for some interim disaster that will devastate our lives? Assessing our situation we find with bitterness that even our greatest pleasures seem pale as compared with our potential for pain and suffering. Even the intense joy of copulation is seen as but a momentary ecstasy in compensation for blind nature's imperative to reproduce.

So what faith is it that enables us, as Dewson puts it, "to find that even the darkness of the pit is illumined by rays of sweetness and tenderness... which can form the first steps by which the soul can climb a little way out of the abyss?"

Next comes melancholy

Keats puts rather the reverse of Dewson's first thought pithily:
> Ay, in the very temple of Delight
> Veiled melancholy has her sovran shrine...

Lucretius too:

A strange melancholy emerges from the heart of every pleasure
and disturbs us already in the midst of our delight.

The Lady Hou (China, early 7th c.) observes,

> To dream of happiness is in itself a grief.

Count Aleksey Tolstoy asks:

> Какая сладость в жизни сей
> Земной печали непричастна?

(What joy in this life has no part in earthly sorrow?)

In the *Nineteen Old Poems* - perhaps the most ancient in Chinese literature - we read,

> Life's years do not fill a hundred,
> But always they embrace a thousand years' sorrows.

John Crowe Ransom observes,

> We are one part love
> and nine parts bitter thought

The anonymous song sums up a whole poetic literature on mutability,

> Fortune, honor, bewtie, youth ar but blossoms dyinge
> Wanton pleasure, dotinge love ar but shadowes flyinge.

Miguel de Barrios, a 17th century Amsteram Jew from Spain, mirrors this,

> "Ay!" dice, "gozo incierto! gloria vana!
> mentido gusto! estada nunca fijo!
> ¿Quien fia en tu verdor, vida incostante?

('Alas' says he, 'how uncertain joy! How vain glory! How deceptive pleasure! How precarious our situation! Who trusts your green promise, o capricious life?')

Fr. Cantalamessa, preacher to two popes observes:

> Suffering adheres to pleasure as to its shadow.

Imogen Stubbs pins down the parent's dilemma:

Our children ask us – "If life is only about getting from now until death as lucratively and as divertingly as possible, what is the point?"

And Leopardi -
> ...e in sul principio stesso
> la madre e il genitore
> il prende a consolar dell'esser nato.

(And right from the start mother and father console their child for being born)

Another of the Chinese *Nineteen Old Poems* has similarly,

> If I had known what would come,
> I would have preferred not to have been born.

Heine repeats the Satyr's even more doleful words:

> Gut ist der Schlaf, der Tod ist besser - freilich
> Das beste wäre nie geboren sein.

(Sleep is good, death is better - of course, best of all is never to have been born)

Much quoted is T.S. Eliot's – 'Humankind cannot bear very much reality.'

Then there is that ultimate overwhelming experience purely of the mind - true pathological depression. "To those who have experienced it, the horror of depression is so overwhelming as to be quite beyond expression" says the American novelist William Styron, a sufferer, in his *Darkness Visible*.

"I wasn't ill, I just saw too clearly," a patient told her psychiatrist, he replied: "That, in humans is an illness".

This brings us to those deep, and disturbing words of Renan: 'Il se pourrait que la Vérité soit triste.' (It could be that Truth itself is sad.)

Fitzgerald's *Rubaiyat* ends,

> Ah love! could thou and I with
> Fate conspire
> To grasp this sorry Scheme of
> Things entire,
> Would not we shatter it to
> bits - and then
> Remould it nearer to the
> Heart's desire!

And this 'sorry scheme' is so unbearable for many that they bury themselves in work, or in the pursuit of pleasure, just in order to avoid so long as possible facing up to the human predicament. Some indeed take up the most dangerous of professions for this very reason. And when this does not work and what is to us reality intrudes, very many take to drugs making their predicament even worse. So strong though, is nature's drive for self-preservation that the suicide rate is well below what might be expected - except in such extreme conditions as China's Cultural Revolution where the suicide rate jumped considerably though any statistics remain secret. And of course in prisons where there is suicide watch, the comparatively low figures conceal the real figure of those who would have killed themselves had it been possible for them to do so.

Yet somehow for us life has overwhelming value

But yet in Measure for Measure (III, i) Shakespeare puts it,

> The weariest and most loathed worldly life
> That age, ache, penury and imprisonment
> Can lay on nature is a paradise
> To what we fear of death.

Heine in Der Schneidende:

> Der kleinste lebendige Philister
> Zu Stukkert am Neckar, viel glücklicher ist er
> Als ich, der Pelide, der tote Held,
> Der Schattenfürst in der Unterwelt.

(The lowest little Philistine in Stuttgart on Neckar is happier than I, son of Peleus, the dead hero, now the shadow prince in the underworld. [Achilles was the son of Peleus])

William Cory (Johnson) in 'Mimnermus in Church' puts it engagingly:

> You promise heavens free from strife,
> Pure truth, and perfect change of will;
> But sweet, sweet is this human life,
> So sweet, I fain would breathe it still;
> Your chilly stars I can forgo,
> This warm kind world is all I know.

So yet it seems there are those 'rays of sweetness and tenderness' that Dewson perceived even in the darkness of the pit. For example, when we contemplate calmly but intently the fine arts painting, sculpture, architecture, music and poetry, including the performing arts - theater, ballet and dance, including too some exquisite artefacts like Chinese porcelain - all creations of man - we sometimes experience a quiet ecstasy quite different from our day to day world view. We appear to have been led, by men of genius and 'inspiration' up to the sublime - the very frontier of experience where we have a tantalising glimpse of a 'somewhere' beyond.

We note that, independent of any religion, Man - though left that waif and a stray on an insignificant and none too friendly planet - has found his own way to the brink of a mystery to which we give the name 'spiritual'. Found his own way? But then what is inspiration? What though are the Muses of Greek myth, instigators of the arts? Did Man alone reach these heights? Many of the greatest artists had the impression that they had 'outside' help - that 'somewhere' there is an external arbiter of excellence which in some way acts as a magnet to those of talent.

> Thou, silent form, doth tease us out of thought
> as doth eternity.

Keats on The Grecian Urn.

FROM 'AHOR' TO GOOD AND EVIL

<u>The extremes of suffering inseparable from Man's grandeur</u>

Cruel and murderous Man may be - reflecting his environment where nature is so 'red in tooth and claw'- but we cannot deny that he has a grandeur. He can overcome his animal nature shaped by the survival of the fittest. And like many others we too, come to appreciate that, if the conditions of existence were not so harsh and daunting in the extreme, there could be no pinnacle of heroism, no self-sacrifice, nor indeed the other virtues we praise. It is, as the RAF's motto goes - 'per ardua ad astra': we achieve only because a hostile nature has thrown down the gauntlet. The ever-sunny epicurean world the Rubaiyat's narrator would make with Fate and his beloved would be quite devoid of this heroism and defiance of horror which we so much admire. There would be no saintly dedication to the poor and suffering if there were none to be succoured; no self-immolation to save another if none were endangered.

Kenneth Clark in 'Civilisation' puts it:

'And yet we recognise that to despise material obstacles, and even to defy the blind forces of fate, is man's supreme achievement...'

Decartes starts off his philosophy with his famous *'cogito ergo sum'* - 'I think therefore I am'. But surely it is suffering (Latin: perfero) that is the only thing none of us can deny and so makes us certain beyond all peradventure that we exist? So shouldn't it rather be: *'patior ergo sum'* - 'I suffer therefore I am'?

The ever painless 'soma'-sucking denizens of Aldous Huxley's *Brave New World* enjoy an interesting diversion: to visit a nature park where there are a few humans living the olden-time life of striving, suffering and fleeting joy. Thus Aldous Huxley suggests that the actual state of Man is in some important sense superior to that of the painless denizens of his *Brave New World.*

Before Man, all of nature behaved in the way it had developed: all was in balance, though a shifting balance through the aeons. Dinosaurs acted like dinosaurs. Then in later ages the birds sang, the flowers bloomed - and the microbes struck, as did the crocodile, the shark. And of course the 'tyger' whose 'fearful symmetry' had emerged from untold ages provoking William Blake's question, 'Did He who made the lamb make thee?'

Then Man emerged, not just with his apparently unique premonition of personal death, but with - however rudimentary at first - a sense of right and wrong. This eventually went beyond what was required as what worked best for his social group. Conscience was born and with it an awareness of both the force of evil and of the sense of good. Though often modified all but unrecognisably by social pressures, conscience orients us towards what is positive - another name for good.

Good, evil, and conscience

And if nevertheless we do a negative (wrong) we feel regret even though we may so insistently over-ride it that regret is dulled. A basic sense of sin - of having betrayed one's own concept of right action, does not require a belief in any religion. Most of us are conscious of our sinfulness - though the word 'sin' is taboo with the 'politically correct' (their idea being that we aren't really responsible for the things we do wrong: 'it was all in our genes' and other such exculpatory excuses). Of course there are many valid excuses for appalling actions - for example criminal insanity. But in most cases we know 'in our hearts' if not our full, then at least our residual guilt. That last word brings me to the concepts of good and evil - terms that the media still uses because their readers can't help using them, but which are out of fashion among the 'politically correct' because they suggest a 'beyond'. (And that's something today's 'politically correct' don't like mentioning unless they absolutely have to!)

Although, even with 'googling', I can't find any poll on the subject, it seems the vast majority of us can't help but recognise the categories 'good' and 'evil'. Rather like numbers these seem to have an imperishable existence somewhere 'out there'.

Here Buddhist philosophy is profound - Nirvana, like the Tao, is beyond our ability to comprehend: a state of nothingness ('blown out like a candle'), yet of indescribable bliss, maybe one could say an overcoming, a surpassing of good and evil - the 'beyond' not only of good and evil but also beyond suffering.

Out of evil, good emerges

The Buddhist flower, the lotus, is profoundly symbolic. It has its root in the mud of the abyss but it grows up right through the surface of the everyday world to flower high above - exalted. Rough and tough, with its roots drawing its life from the mud of 'ahor' (as Jung named archaic horror), the lotus produces a most beautiful and delicate flower. This inspires two thoughts in particular: chaos is cheap - destruction swift and easy. And evolution, from rough and ready (the day to day struggle of humans over the millennia, and the few decades of struggle of each ordinary human) strives towards the furthest excellence of what we term beauty, delicacy, sensitivity, discernment, subtlety. Think of Mozart, Tu Fu, Michelangelo and of so many of great genius. But yet, of course, among the billions that live and have lived: how few are those of supreme genius. And all so wantonly destroyed - Keats at 26 and Pushkin at 38.

The Vietnamese poet asks: 'of all the rosy cheeks throughout the millennia, has cruel time spared even one?'

Yes, we begin to apprehend that in the very heart of darkness, the beautiful and good have their origin. And even, that out of the nadir of our crimes can sometimes be found some nugget of preternatural worth.

Hans Egon Holtusen in his Tabula Rasa composed after the years of horror ending with the collapse of the Nazis, composed these two magnificent stanzas that I cannot read without a catch in my throat:

> Und doch wir leiden. Sprachlos. Aber wer,
> Wer schweigt aus uns, and was wird uns verschwiegen?
> Wer zählt die Trümmer unsrer Welt - und mehr:
> Die Dunkelheiten, die dazwischen liegen?

> Wer ist es, raunend in Verborgenheit,
> Und Wohnt in eines Menschenherzens Enge
> Und keltert einen Tropfen Ewigkeit
> Im dunklen Wirbel unsrer Untergänge?

(And yet we suffer. Speechless. But who, who is silent within us, and what is it that is passed over in silence? Who counts the ruins of our world - and more particularly the darknesses that lie between them?

Who is it, whispering secretly, and dwells within a human heart's confine and distils a drop of eternity in the dark whirlpool of our disasters).

The Vietnamese too, have a profound saying linking the creation of good with evil - 'God must love a little good most deeply, that he tolerates so much evil.'

A thought complemented by two words of the mystic Julian of Norwich - 'Sin behoveth.'

After an anguished contemplation of the abyss but detecting even there a distant glimmer we are led when following it to the very confines of experience, to sense not only a 'numinous beyond', but even at least a hint of a moral imperative within us. So we find that - like today's scientists at the 'cutting edge' of physics - we are asking questions of a religious nature.

And the first question is: are we simply to bury ourselves in the Epicurean life of Omar Khayyam, which so many around us attempt, as we all mutely await death or the next tragedy on life's road, or should we follow that distant gloaming, just detectable even in the abyss, in an effort to find out if there is something else that we should be doing?

The call of the mystical

Edward Browne in his *Year Among the Persians* (1893) found in the great Persian poet Hafiz an imperative to seek the mystical 'which thrilled me to my very soul' :

"They are calling to thee from the pinnacles of the throne of God: I know not what has befallen thee in this dust-heap." (In Chinese poetry too, the material world is often called 'the world's dust'). Browne, a medical student, goes on: 'Even my medical studies, strange as it may appear, favoured the development of this habit of mind; for physiology, when it does not encourage materialism, encourages mysticism; and nothing so much tends to shake one's faith in the reality of the objective world as the examination of certain of the subjective phenomena of mental and nervous disorders.'

He explains: 'if in hospital I saw much that was sad, much that made me wonder at man's clinging to life (since to the vast majority life seemed but a succession of pains, struggles and sorrows), on the other hand I saw much to strengthen my faith in the goodness and nobility of human nature. Never before or since have I realised so clearly the immortality, greatness, and virtue of the spirit of man, or the misery of its earthly environment: it seemed to me like a prince in rags, ignorant alike of his birth and his rights, but to whom is reserved a glorious inheritance.'

FIVE THINGS THAT STRIKE ME ABOUT RELIGION

1. A plethora of superstitions leading to human sacrifice – leading on to religion

The first thing that strikes us when looking at religion and its history is the extraordinary variation of religious and animistic practice throughout prehistory and history, but in every case there is that same close link between religion and superstition. We've seen that, left in a harsh world and with no guidance, humanity turned to all manner of expedients to placate supposed unseen hostile forces. Of course none of these superstitious practices proved reliable in bettering the human condition, so (as our very earliest records show) however diverse these practices, they led, as I've said, to the development of human sacrifice in virtually all parts of the world as a kind of logically ultimate effort to placate these forces or bribe them into beneficent behaviour.

Two cases are notorious. The destructive Hindu mother goddess Kali with her "unquenchable thirst for blood" whose human sacrifices were outlawed by the British governors of Bengal; and the mass sacrifices of the Aztecs ended by the Spanish conquistadores. Particularly interesting according to a Spanish account, is the practice of the Aztec priests of sprinkling the victims' blood on dough which was then distributed to the people who declared that they were unworthy of it. This brings to mind the bloodless sacrifice of the Catholic Mass, when, before consuming the sliver of bread he believes is "body of Christ", the communicant strikes his breast ritually repeating the "Domine non sum dignus... " (Lord I am not worthy...).

Human sacrifice took place in pre-Shang dynasty China, among the Celts and the Norse, among some African tribes, in S.E. Asia and reportedly even among the Aborigines of Australia. It survived into the early days of the Roman Republic being ended by Senatorial Decree in 97 BC when it had long all but died out. As their monotheistic religion developed, the Jews ended the practice. But following on this worldwide concept that human sacrifice is the ultimate gift to the gods, is the striking story of Abraham whose utter belief in Yaveh made him willing to sacrifice Isaac, his only son - being ordered not to do so only when, dagger raised, he had passed this supreme test of belief. This story has Abraham acting "in persona Dei" - in the person of God - a precursor, for the Christian, of God's sacrifice of Himself in the person of Jesus self-described as Son of God.

Do we see in this, and in the Aztec 'communion' an evolution in religious practice from the blood sacrifices of humans, then animals, gradually becoming a non-bloody purely spiritual ritualistic action?

2. Few conversions, much doubt but few search. The appeal of atheism, barbarism

The second thing that strikes us as we survey the religious scene, is that worldwide, the great majority of those who profess a religion do indeed (more or less) accept the religion into which they were born even though they may be at least dimly aware that there are other forms of belief to consider. Almost nowhere are there many conversions to another religion except from tribal animism which survives hardly when faced with a monotheistic religion. And yet nothing, surely can be as important as to discover whether we do indeed live by more than bread alone - and if so, what this "more" is and what it asks of us in our lives. Surprisingly few people though, trouble to ask about other religions or read even a few pages of their scriptures. If vaguely dissatisfied with religion of their birth - or even if convinced of its wrongness - most people simply cease practicing it.

But - as G. K. Chesterton put it: "When a man stops believing in God he doesn't believe in nothing, he believes in anything." As Europe began to lose its Christianity, many embraced Nazi-ism and communism with their fierce denial of the spiritual. And today, as the Christian religion weakens further in the 'West', vast numbers put their faith in astrology (as we have seen) and also in necromancy, Tarot cards... or, and perhaps sometimes more fruitfully, in the more exotic practices of the Orient.

Cruelty and Greed - universal characteristics of humanity

It is quite the fashion today to decry all religions claiming that religions do nothing but harm (the Inquisition is often cited, so is today's extremist Islam) - that is as may be, but one must point out that atheism does at least as much harm. You only need to think of Hitler, Stalin, and Pol Pot - impeccable (if that's the right word!) atheists. And how many millions did they kill between them - maybe more than all religious human sacrifices put together? The problem is with Man, not with religion nor with atheism. Born out of the evolutionary 'survival of the fittest' those two prime characteristics of man are cruelty and greed, both of which he cultivates in a manner unknown to other species (the cat playing with the mouse before killing it is something of an exception).

As for greed - all animals will do almost anything to obtain food, but once they have had enough they seek no more until they hunt again. There are those like squirrels and some insects that put aside for future needs but when they have made their provision they too, seek no more. Man is different. As I have said in Part I about inequality, there is no end to human greed even if it should lead to the extinction of mankind.

3. The prevalence of empathy and compassion among the religious

Thirdly, one cannot but be struck by the way the religious, if not their religions, so often correct the barbarism in man by showing their compassion through 'good works'. For Man has another characteristic rare in nature (porpoises and elephants have been cited) and that is empathy and its relative, compassion, and both of these are found typically among the genuinely religious, but also among many agnostics and atheists.

To take compassion first - that ability to feel the sufferings of others: Lamartine, again in *Le Lac,* has his love, in the midst of a day of great happiness, call out:

> "O temps, suspend ton vol! Et vous, heures propices,
> Suspendez votre cours!
> Laissez-nous savourez les rapides délices
> Des plus beaux de nos jours.
>
> "Assez de maleureux ici-bas vous implorent
> Coulez, coulez pour eux;
> Prenez avec leurs jours leurs soins qui les dévorent;
> Oubliez les heureux."

(O time suspend your flight! And you, propitious hours, suspend your course, let us taste the swift delights of the fairest of our days! Enough unhappy beings pray to you down here on earth: flow on, flow on for them; together with their days take away the cares that consume them; forget those that are happy)

Charles Dickens had that character, Mrs Do-As-You-Would-Be-Done-By, named after the so-called Golden Rule: 'do unto others as you would want them to do unto you.'

It seems all the great religions have a close equivalent in their texts: Hindu, Zoroastrian, Islam, Sikh, Buddhism, and the moralist Confucius, somewhere hold the same. For Christianity Matthew 7:12 (King James Version) has: 'Therefore all things whatsoever ye would that men should do to you, do ye even so to them: for this is the law and the prophets'.

But that brings us to the concept of justice where the civil power endeavours to limit the social disruption caused by endless vendettas. That has to be prevented so the authorities (often the religious authorities) establish a system of retributive justice. For example Exodus 21-25 (KJV): 'And if any mischiefe follow, then thou shalt give life for life, eye for an eye, burning for burning, wound for wound, stripe for stripe'. But that leads to the distasteful spectacle of society enforcing the same damage as had been inflicted: e.g. the blinding of an eye if the sight had been lost through an attack on the plaintiff. Martin Luther King puts it pithily: "the old law of an eye for an eye leaves every one blind."

For Islam this is 'qasas'. Koran II.178 (A. Yusuf Ali's translation often considered the best by British Muslims) upholds the principle of retributive justice, but it mitigates it somewhat: 'if anyone forgoes this [punishment] out of charity, it will serve as an atonement for his bad deeds' - i.e. it is up to the plaintiff to decide if the punishment is to be inflicted. Indeed in Saudi Arabia recently, just before the death sentence was to be carried out, the plaintiff announced her forgiveness and the execution did not go ahead.

Jesus in effect abrogates the old law (Matthew 5.38/39 KJV) with his famous, much discussed, even enigmatic, teaching effectively bypassing the 'Mosaic law' (and of course he does this again in the case of the woman caught in the act of adultery): 'Ye have heard it hath been said, an eye for an eye, and a tooth for a tooth, but I say unto you, that ye resist not evil: but whosoever shall smite thee on thy right cheek, turn to him the other also.'

Empathy and compassion bring us close to the concept of virtue as kindness. As a 'behind the scenes' founder of the original Tibet Society when the Dalai Lama escaped from Lhasa in 1959 - I was much moved by his recent declaration: "My religion is very simple: be kind." Which reminds me of the novelist Henry James' reported remark to his nephew: "There are three things that are important in human life. The first is to be kind. The second is to be kind. The third is to be kind."

And kindness is inseparable from mercy: in Judaism (e.g. Deuteronomy 4.31) 'For the Lord your God is a merciful God.' Christianity several times repeats this attribute of God. And every Surah of the Koran begins 'In the name of God, most gracious, most merciful.'

Going one step further, but back 2,500 or so years, the author of the classic *Tao Te Ching* (*Dao De Jing*) the Chinese sage known only as 'the old one' - Lao Tse - made this, to me sublime, remark: 'The sage has no interest of his own, but takes the interests of the people as his own. He is kind to the kind; he is also kind to the unkind: for Virtue is kind. He is faithful to the faithful; he is also faithful to the unfaithful: for Virtue is faithful.'

And that begs the question what is 'Virtue'? The behaviour of the 'gentleman' (in the best sense of the word) or is the moral code something from a 'beyond'? Is 'Virtue' more than this, is it itself a description of the 'beyond' - one might even say a name for God.

The Sufi mystics, that branch of Shia Islam that so attracted Edward Browne that he went to Persia, have a salutary teaching that compassion should lead to action: 'Past the seeker as he prayed came the crippled and the beggar and the beaten. And seeing them he cried, "Great God, how is it that a loving creator can see such things and yet do nothing about them?"...God said, "I did do something. I made you."'

Is not kindness the cardinal virtue? Certainly it is the occasions when I have not been kind - worse, when I too, have been cruel - that I feel ashamed and contrite for having indelibly besmirched my tiny sliver of time. There may be forgiveness but there is no expunging that. Unkindness and cruelty are for me, as for so many, the worst of sins.

Emily Dickinson puts it:

> 'Remorse is memory awake,
> Remorse is cureless,
> The disease that even God cannot cure.'

4. Religions and the state both suppress freedom of religion

The fourth thing we notice about religion is that we are very far from applying the UN's Universal Declaration of Human Rights (1948) guaranteeing the right of the individual to join the religion of his choice. Partly this is because toleration does not ride easily with religious belief. Many don't want to live together with people who do not believe as they do - their faith challenges your's, and you don't like having your's put in doubt. It is easier to believe your particular faith if everyone else in your society has your religion. In the 15th century *Los Reyes Catolicos,* the Catholic sovereigns Ferdinand and Isabella, took this to the extreme expelling Muslims and Jews from their reunited Spain. Today though, it is a large part of Islam, rather than the extremist Christians that is intolerant towards the Jews - though among them too, the curse of anti-semitism is still very much alive.

Then again you may seriously disapprove of some beliefs in the religions of others and particularly of your own - for example 'mainstream' Christians find in certain sects that claim to be Christian, the idea that God rewards those of their sect, ensuring prosperity in this world - 'Give me your tithe, and you'll flourish here and now'. Many object to Mormonism for this reason. Sunni Muslims have major concerns about some Shia beliefs - even to the extent of calling them blasphemers. (A way of getting rid of your unwanted neighbour, especially Christian, in Pakistan is to accuse him or her of blasphemy - maybe claiming that they threw the Koran on the floor. Then you kill them or have the law do that for you).

It's not just the antipathy to being around those who believe something different casting doubt on your faith. There's a second reason for religious intolerance: the children of interfaith (or inter-sectarian) marriages. For you are likely to want them to be brought up in yours. Before the 'Milosović war' both Christian and Muslim Bosnians, in the cities at least, were surprisingly tolerant, often participating in each other's festivals. Mixed marriages were quite common. But it requires great tolerance for anyone who takes their religion seriously to allow their children to be brought up in another faith - or even in another sect. The Dutch have a saying: 'When two faiths share a pillow, the devil sleeps in between.'

Partly it is because of the strength of religious intolerance that many governments, if not opposed to all religion, want to damp down the problems religions can cause. In the UK where 'political correctness' holds sway (that secular dogma largely espoused by the three main parties), its agnostic tenets are now being increasingly imposed on religious organisations.

In others, like Russia and Greece, the traditional faith (Orthodoxy) is bolstered at the expense of freedom for others. In largely Hindu India there is sometimes lethal discrimination against Christians and Muslims. Then there is, not just the Christian & agnostic versus Islam divide influencing governments, but the sectarian divide between Sunni and Shia that we've seen. Sometimes that mirrors the violence that characterised the Protestant/Catholic divide in the 17th century (and still simmers in Northern Ireland). Other states do to some degree tolerate the major religions, but not 'sects' and those practising aggressive proselytism.

And where does society or the state draw the line? A judge interpreted freedom of religion to uphold the right of a 'Satanist' to serve in the Royal Navy when his commanding officer had sought the man's removal from his ship.

Intolerance in Islam, hadith

Then there is the Muslim world where apostasy is punished, sometimes with death. Indeed, few religions readily accept an individual abandoning the faith, but Islam is notable for providing a swift way in (reciting the one sentence Shahada) and but rarely a way out. In certain countries fear of violent punishment by fellow Muslims prevents many who were born Muslims from 'coming out' as agnostics, atheists, or converts to another faith. A recent poll in Egypt suggests that nearly 84% of Egyptians believe apostasy should be punished by death (if correct almost all the Muslims do, as the Copts alone still account for some 7%). Another poll (Policy Exchange) gives 31% of British Muslims as agreeing.

As quite often in Islam, zealots go much further than the Koran - they stone apostates to death if they can, whereas the Koran says: (A. Yusuf Ali's translation, XLVII, 25) 'Those who turn back as apostates after guidance was clearly shown to them - the Evil One has instigated them and buoyed them up with false hopes. This, because they said to those who hate what God has revealed *"We will obey you in part of (this) matter; but God knows their (inner) secrets. But how will it be when the angels take their souls at death, and smite their faces and their backs?"*

So it is, it seems, the angels who will punish apostates, not men stoning them to death. This interpretation is supported by Mahmoud Shaltut, Grand Immam of the prestigious Al Azhar university in Cairo. (Incidentally, surah XXIV.31 (also per Yusuf Ali) about women's dress says only that women *'should not display their beauty and ornaments except what [must ordinarily] appear thereof; that they should draw their veils over their bosoms and not display their beauty - except to* [certain of those close to them]'. There is no mention of head scarves let alone burkhas - this appears another case of zealots going much further than the Koran requires, often by relying on hadith. Just one other example: the objection to ownership of dogs is also nowhere in the Koran.

Indeed a great problem when studying Muslim beliefs lies with the hadith, which many Muslims consider should be added to what is contained in the Koran. These are the sayings and actions of the Prophet, of which there are hundreds, quite a few of which have led to present day Muslim practices - and also to disputes within the Muslim community as to their interpretation and validity, especially as the hadith were at first not written but remembered by those close to the Prophet. The hadith are not considered 'de fide' for Muslims, but to be worthy of study.

Even a little more than a century after Mohammed's death in 632 many hadith were rejected as spurious so Sahih al Bukhari, after years of travel and study, selected those he believed to be genuine - but many even in his collection are challenged. The uncertainty about the hadith makes it very difficult to determine what should be considered orthodox Sunni Muslim belief and practice. Particularly as Shia Muslims have their own equivalent of orthodoxy and many Sufi (those mystics in Shia Islam) insist that external actions (promoted in many hadith) are far less important than the inward sanctity at their root.

All this uncertainty about hadith leads to past and present disagreements as to whether female genital mutilation (euphemism: 'female circumcision') - or even male circumcision are in anyway required, or even recommended in Islam: which may come as surprise. (Of course, circumcising boys as late as 12 or 13, as in some African cultures as well as Islam, implants through pain an unforgettable consciousness of belonging to that culture. That then gets transmitted to succeeding generations. Indeed women who have been mutilated often feel their daughters should also be mutilated.)

Even Muslim treatment of women as inferior to men is challenged by some pointing to Kadija the prophet's one wife until her death (she was also his employer for several years). For Kadija, according to tradition, was the person who encouraged Mohammed to take seriously his first revelations when he was in doubt as to their reality. They point too, to Aisha who had been his child bride and is later credited with being the woman closest to him until his death. It seems many of the hadith considered particularly reliable, are Aisha's.

The 'Golden Age' of Islam

Which brings me to the great historical question of how so brilliant a civilisation as that of the Islamic Golden Age came to decline, as Ancient Greece did, although it had been on the very threshold of breaking through into the scientific age. This Golden Age is often dated, from near the beginning of the 9th century CE during Europe's Dark Ages, and after a long period of decadence, finally ending abruptly with the sack of Baghdad by the Mongols in 1258.

The previously diverse and often warring tribes of Arabia appear to have been unified by their Prophet's Islam with the political consequence of changing world history. For it so happened that both the great empires on Arabia's borders were in terminal decay. They burst out of Arabia with a previously unknown tactical use of cavalry, exploiting a foolish spat between the Byzantine empire and the Persian empire.

They quickly overran much of the former, occupying Jerusalem (in 637) and Egypt (in 639), destroying much in their way. Almost immediately after, they attacked the Sasanian Persian Empire which finally collapsed in 651. As they had been with the Byzantine Empire, the Arabs of Arabia were in direct touch with the Sasanian Empire which then extended down the coast of the Arabian Gulf as far as Oman. It was indeed commerce with both empires and India and even China that made the caravans passing through Arabia so profitable.

The Arabs went on to conquer the whole of former Roman North Africa which had been greatly weakened by the barbarian invasions some two hundred years before (Rome fell in 410), invading Spain and southern France until turned back at Poitiers. This had two decisive results: the establishment of Islam in Spain still in contact with its 'capital' in Baghdad, and, as needs to be stressed, the exile of Christianity to Europe - severed from its middle Eastern origins.

Indeed, until the 16th century with its great European navigators, Christianity (apart from substantial pockets here and there in the Muslim countries) remained exiled in Europe, developing a European 'flavour' which it then exported throughout the world. This 'flavour' notably included the rediscovery of 'the Glory that was Greece' - thanks to its preservation during Islam's 'Golden Age'.

At first the Arabs destroyed what they found of Greek and Persian civilisation - notably the great library in Alexandria, reputedly the best in the Mediterranean world. Then, turning on the Persians, the Arab invaders also destroyed the Academy of Gundishapur and its perhaps equally great library. It is worth quoting here Dr. Gianpaolo Savola-Vizzini's paper published by SOAS:

> 'Most Sasanian records and literary works were destroyed. A few that escaped this fate were later translated into Arabic and later into Modern Persian. During the Islamic invasion many Iranian cities were destroyed or deserted, palaces and bridges were ruined and many magnificent imperial Persian gardens were burned to the ground. According to Al-Tabari, the Arab Commander Sa'd Ibn Abi-Vaghas wrote to Caliph Umar ibn Al-Khatab about what should be done with the books at Tyspwn (Ctesiphon) in the province of Khvârvarân (today known as Iraq). Umar wrote back: "If the books contradict the Qur'an, they are blasphemous. On the other hand, if they are in agreement, they are not needed." All the books were thrown into the Euphrates.'

But soon the Arab conquerors came to value and rediscover what they had despised - quickly surpassing that and becoming the most brilliant civilisation on earth drawing not only on Greek and Persian but even on Chinese culture, and introducing Indian numerals which we now call Arabic. They introduced paper, algebra, even the beginnings of calculus, and made major advances in astronomy. Indeed, in just about very sphere of endeavour they were No. 1 from architecture to medicine, even introducing a form of 'national health' for the poor.

The Mongol invasion of Mesopotamia and Persia in the 13th century mirrored the 7th century Arab invasions on a far more terrible scale: newly unified tribes, the brilliant use of cavalry against decadent empires. And far more than the Arabs, Man at his most cruel. Baghdad fell in 1258 with the slaughter, it is said, of a million. The 'House of Wisdom' (and its refounded) library was destroyed. This could in itself explain the demise of Arab cultural predominance. But there was another much earlier factor which is of importance today. Even one of the most brilliant

Caliphs, Al-Ma'mūn (d. 833), was dogged by the split within Islam of Persian Shia and Arab Sunni: all over who should have been the rightful successor to the Prophet. Those who claimed Ali Ibn Talib (Mohammed's cousin and son-in-law) should have succeeded - their followers are now Syria's ruling Alawites - were the predecessors of the Shia.

Many believe that the Shia position was adopted by the Persians to assert their independence from their Arab conquerors. The Abassids' new capital was Baghdad in the Persian sphere of influence. Al-Ma'mūn was half Persian and had a Persian vizier. He tried to put an end to this enfeebling division by placating the Shia, but that only put him in conflict with his Sunni supporters. He ended up trying forcibly to impose his own form of Islam on all his subjects, but he failed spectacularly. The Arabs, but not the Shia Persians, fell under the Turks in the 11th century, and under the French and British in 1918. But Persia preserved its independence - so the Shia/Sunni split simmered on until it exploded again today.

Though, of course, my 'take' is only superficial, I think there is much to be said for the view that the continuing theological disputes put the clerics in charge, and thus science and philosophy became subordinated to religion -and that it was largely because of this, that the so-called 'Golden Age of Islam' crawled to a halt. That left it to the clerics, Sunni and Shia, to define Islamic 'orthodoxy' into each of the two rigid uncompromising and intolerant forms we know today. 'Moderate' Muslims may well complain that their religion has been 'hi-jacked' by the extremists, but this began to happen centuries ago.

One is reminded of the Catholic church's suspicion of Copernicus and of the notorious trial of Galileo for daring to prove that this world is a planet and not the centre of the solar system, let alone of the universe. But, in contrast to the Islamic clerics three or four centuries earlier, the Catholic hierarchy soon reversed itself and Jesuit missionaries brought the new learning as well as Christianity even as far as China. Europe went on to burst through into the scientific era with the indispensable help of Islamic sources.

5. Beyond dogma - much similarity in the apprehension of the 'beyond'

The fourth thing we find is a profound similarity in apprehending the 'beyond' despite that pervasive ignorance of religions other than one's own (or of atheism or agnosticism) which includes many people with otherwise excellent general knowledge.

For most religions it is not easy to discover what is orthodox belief. Even when one has stripped away accretions of superstition (which, as I say, religions tend to attract as a boat does barnacles) the underlying consensus may be hard to determine. Taoism (Daoism) for example is based on a short, profound and mystic text from around 500 BCE. But visit a Daoist temple and you find this elusive early message about the nature of the unknowable Ultimate (the Tao) all but submerged. One learns though, of the useful role of ritual and of how it can reflect the depths of belief. And these 'depths' are in many ways common to all profundity in religion.

The Tao Te Ching together with the Analects of Confucius are the twin pillars of Chinese morality - for both the state and for individuals. The former epitomises the Chinese mystical tradition and its approach to the 'beyond'. Of the Tao one of the host of translations (by Gia-Fu Feng and Jane English) puts it:

> The Tao that can be told is not the eternal Tao.
> The name that cannot be named is not the eternal name.
> The nameless is the beginning of heaven and earth.
> The named is the mother of ten thousand things
> Ever desireless one can see the mystery.
> Ever desiring, one can see the manifestations.

> These two spring from the same source but differ in name; this appears as darkness.
> Darkness within darkness.
> The gate to all mystery.

Here there is another dualism - the named and the unnamed: a recognition that Man is unable to comprehend 'the beyond' but that there is an element of it with which he can have some relationship.

The Hindu writings, from even more ancient times, number it is said over one thousand volumes. And of all religions Hinduism may be the hardest to discern the essentials. Again, it is not in the temples that the outsider meets the impressive mystical revelations of union with 'That Which is Eternally', that is to say 'Brahman'. This has been defined as 'the unchanging reality amidst and beyond the world' which 'can never be exactly defined'. So here again is this idea that 'the beyond' is entirely beyond human abilities to know or experience, but that nevertheless Man can still approach what is named 'Brahman'.

Buddhism too, has a vast literature in Pali alone. But here the essentials are easier to grasp through the 'Noble Eightfold Path'. And Buddhism starts from awareness of suffering - just as I have done in this note. It was Gautama's (Sakyamuni's) intense awareness of human suffering which led him to leave give up his princedom and seek enlightenment. The path he took ends with the perception of what some call the extinction of the self: that 'Nirvana' I mentioned. Philologists say the word 'nirvana' means 'blown out' like a candle. But in fact descriptions of nirvana fit well with the words of several Christian and Sufi mystics: 'it is the union with Brahman'; 'in view of all, but difficult to approach: freedom from pain and all life's sufferings'; 'the highest happiness'. The Bhagvad Gita calls it 'perfect peace of mind'. To my mind the most mysterious of all is: 'where there is nothing, where nought is grasped, there is the isle of no Beyond'.

As you see from the Baghavad Gita quote, the word nirvana is common to Hinduism as well as to Buddhism. Ghandi remarked that "to the Buddhist, nirvana is empty, to the Hindu, oneness with Brahman" but evidently that depends on what one means by 'empty' - for in one sense it is, in another sense it is total fullness.

St. Nicholas of Susa - like other mystics - said that for an understanding of religion "one must keep two contradictory thoughts in mind". Robert Buchanan, in *'City of Dream'*, has this thought in a nutshell:

>'Thou art and thou art not,
>And ever shalt be!'

There is this mystery also for the Jews and the Christians: there too, is the unnamed - that which cannot be grasped by Man for lack of capacity, and the named with which Man (at least through the prophets) is capable of having converse. This name, as it is of great sanctity for the Jews, is written only in the 'tetragrammaton', the four letters: YHYH which in full give the ineffable name of God: "I am that am". "I am" is, of course, the name that Jesus gave himself to reveal his claim to divinity: "Verily, verily I say unto you, before Abraham was, I Am." (King James version John 8.58). This is so astounding a statement that I found it worth checking against the Greek codex with a little aid from a Greek dictionary: εἶπεν αὐτοῖς Ἰησοῦς, Ἀμὴν ἀμὴν λέγω ὑμῖν, πρὶν Ἀβραὰμ γενέσθαι ἐγὼ εἰμί - surely an exact a translation as is possible.

The 'leap into faith

We must surpass logic if we are to approach 'beyond' for there's that requirement to hold two contradictory thoughts in mind. We are used to this duality in science in the wave-particle theory of light. There was much argument about whether light was waves or particles - both turned to be true, but it goes deeper than that.

So in 'dealing with' the 'beyond', there is no way of satisfactorily proving anything. In terms of the material world there can be no certainty in any religion: there has always to be a 'leap into faith'. As 'faith' comes from Latin 'fides' = trust, the dictionary correctly defines it as 'a belief that is not based on proof'. Alas, just because there is no certainty, the purveyors of 'faiths' often try to persuade us that there is! And all too often want to kill us if we aren't!

A BRIEF OVERVIEW OF SOME RELIGIONS

Hinduism, Buddhism, Sikhism, Bahai, Mormonism

I have already mentioned my leaning towards Buddhism. I'd just add that in Laos and Cambodia I particularly liked the monastic practice whereby, very young, you can be a 'bonzillon' taking the saffron robe and be introduced to monasticism. You can leave without taking any oaths, and return later in life when you wish. Political and other leaders as well as ordinary people do this for a year or so of contemplation away from the hurly burly of the world. Such a 'sabbatical' might well be beneficial for our politicians and businessmen too!

As we have seen, Hinduism is closely related to Buddhism and there is much of universal interest in Hindu literature. I myself am put off, to say the least, by the caste system in India which continues to be practised although under Artical 15 of the post independence Constitution (1950) any discrimination on caste is illegal, and Article 17 makes any practice of untouchability illegal. Brahmins at the top are said to be 6% of India's population, Dalits - or 'untouchables' - 16%. To me this goes fundamentally against 'kindness' and the idea, common to many religions, that in a real sense we are all equal, or at least born equal and not members of some inferior social group.

Which brings me to Sikhism - a monotheistic religion from India (centred on the Amritsar temple) which is often left out of the list. Begun in the 15th century by Guru Nanak, equality is basic. Following the chanting of Sikh hymns in their Gurdwara the Sikhs consume *Karah Prasad* which is reminiscent of, though theologically quite different from, Christian communion (in this case made of flour, butter and sugar). This is shared by the congregation to demonstrate equality and the rejection of caste. Rather like some other religions, Sikhs struggle against lust, rage, greed, attachment and ego - the five evils. And the five virtues to be practised are truth, compassion, contentment, humility, and love. In its essentials I find it a most attractive belief, but Sikhism does not proselytise.

What I find particularly interesting is that it was born in the Punjab amidst the contention between Islam and Hinduism. It is an attempt to 'defuse' the antagonism - it upholds Islam's oneness of God, but at the same time holds that 'all religions are equally valid and capable of enlightening their followers.' This is very close to the Catholic position following the encyclical Nostra Aetate promulgated in 1965 following Vatican II which accepts that there are valid truths in other religions - including Islam and of course, Judaism.

There is one monotheistic religion which is also generally overlooked: the Bahai Faith (bahai, adjective = glory, splendour in Arabic). Founded in Iran in the 19th century, it is particularly interesting. God is too great for humans to know except through His manifestations and revelations each of which is suited to its time and place. Bahais accept as 'revealers' Abraham, Krishna, Moses, Buddha, Jesus and Mohammed - and most recently the Bab (= the gate) who declared himself to be the Mahdi, the 12th Imam of Shia Islam. (Which understandably alarmed the Shia Ayatollahs of Iran, such that the Bahai faith was, and still is, mercilessly persecuted). The Bab was executed in 1850 and his remains were brought to Israel where he has a shrine in Haifa. This was arranged by Baha'u'llah, the founder of the Bahai faith who caused the Bab to be seen as its forerunner. So for Bahais too, Israel is important as a 'holy land' as it is for Jews, Christians and Muslims.

Bahais are against superstition in religion and against prejudice. They believe humanity is in process of collective evolution and say that what is required is a real move towards peace, justice and unity on a global scale. Particularly interesting is the Bahai concept of religion as progressive, evolving - which evokes Cardinal Newman's 'progressive revelation' meaning that God's revelation to Man is on-going. So the bible should be read as God increasingly revealing himself to the Jews and, by extension, to Christians (this has been recognised by Vatican II).

There is one perplexing monotheistic faith: Mormonism. This claims to be a Christian sect calling itself The Church of Jesus Christ and Latter Day Saints but it is one which a number of 'mainstream' Christian sects do not consider a sect of Christianity but as a separate religion. It has added a scripture of its own which, Mormons believe, was revealed to Joseph Smith (d. 1844) who claimed to have seen in the 1820s scriptures in gold which he copied down as the Book of Mormon, translated into English with the help, he said of, Moroni, the son of Mormon.

After Smith's death Brigham Young became the leader of the small group of Mormons who practised polygamy and for this and theological reasons were persecuted by 'mainstream' protestant Christians. The Mormons trekked West and settled in what is now Utah where they are still based. Their isolation outside the United States in the early days and their influence in Utah ever since has preserved them from the sort of criticism that puts an end to many such sects. They renounced polygamy in 1890 and so settled down into the United States with its religious freedom. By 'tithing', requiring $1/10^{th}$ of the income of believers to be paid to the Mormon Church, they have become rich and able to proselytise and there are now, it is believed, more Mormons outside the US than inside - about 15 million in all.

The candidacy of Mitt Romney, a Mormon, for the presidency again raised the question: how far it does it matter what religion a political leader, nominally at least, believes? No one had raised this so long as the candidate was nominally a protestant of some main-stream church. The issue was raised forcibly when John Kennedy, a Roman Catholic, became a candidate for the presidency in 1960. But Kennedy was just an ordinary member of that church. That made him easier to accept - especially when many much admired politicians in Europe had been Roman Catholics, a 'main-stream' Christian belief in much of the world. Romney, though was a Mormon bishop closely involved with the beliefs and controversial financing of the Church of Latter Day

Saints. Psephologists do not appear to believe that this lost him very many votes even though, for many voters Mormanism is considered to be a bizarre and far from credible a religion. But who is to judge? As I say, all religions are simply 'faiths' and, looked at dispassionately, all make bizarre claims.

Christianity and Islam as originating in Judaism

Which brings us to the three main monotheistic religions, Judaism, Christianity and Islam - all three are linked to each other and the latter two to a greater or a lesser extent originate in Judaism. Abraham and Moses are often seen as the founders of Judaism and in some form it appears to have originated in ancient Egypt. According to Exodus the Jews had already achieved a relationship with God before they escaped servitude in Egypt. It seems though, that very little is known about Judaism before the Exodus. But the other two have founders who appeared in history -Jesus of Nazareth in 1st century Israel, and Mohammed of Mecca in 7th century Arabia. One curious thing about Judaism is that it is not a proselytising religion: having given so much to the world it would seem that it is now up to others to reap its benefits.

'Moderate' Islam and its, and our role in countering 'jihadism'

In Germany there's currently a move to promote 'moderate' Islam in an attempt to counter the appeal of Wahabism, Al Qaeda, and ISIS. But, like mainstream Christianity there's a lot of diversity among 'moderate' Muslims who oppose these versions of Islam. Only 'mainstream' Christians know each other despite their differences and they know too, the 'far right Christian extremists' who endanger world peace. And, in my experience at least, it's the same with 'moderate' Muslims - it's the 'moderates' who know extremism. So any effort to promote 'moderate' Islam can only come from Muslims. I've explained how far more dangerous it is for a Muslim to oppose the extremist versions than for us non-Muslims and our governments which are also afraid of violent 'Islamists' as we call them. However the more atrocious the violence, the more the 'moderates' are likely to feel they must speak out and endeavor to change the present climate where so many young Muslims are attracted by violence.

I believe those of us in positions of influence must ourselves know more about Islam so that we can support them. There is far too much ignorance - too few, even of our intelligentsia, have considered the subject at all. So I dare venture a few - I hope not too controversial - words of my own about Islam as seen from outside, which may possibly help in stemming today's all too frequent, all too unhelpful knee-jerk opposition to even the most beneficent Muslims.

A word about the Koran and other Islamic scriptures

Because of the great importance today of the Islamic scriptures for non-Muslims, I think I should add a bit to what I have said in Part I about the worldwide political effects of Saudi Arabia's Wahabism and the 'jihadism' it spawned, for all parties claim to follow the correct way to act as revealed primarily in the Koran - the foundation of Islam. As I say, I hesitate because the subject is so delicate and my studies so superficial.

As I understand it, according to one Muslim tradition the revelations of Mohammed were collected after the Prophet's death in 632 CE. According to this, the first successor to the Prophet, the Caliph Abu Bakr, ordered a collection to be made of them - some from 'parchments, leaves, stones' etc. and some memorised - and it was from all of this that the Qu'ran was originally compiled. But almost all agree that the Koran derives from the command of Uthman Ibn Affan, the 3rd Caliph (644-658 CE), to determine which reading of the several versions of the Koran then circulating should be adopted. After the exhaustive scholarship that he instigated from 653-656 CE, Uthman selected the version which emerged as being the most authoritative, and so promulgated the Koran we have today. Uthman ordered the destruction of all other versions of the Koran.

The early copies, including Uthman's definitive version were 'scriptio defectiva' - meaning omitting the notations for vowels later used in Semitic languages. This gave rise to controversy, as without the vowels, alternative readings are possible in several places. For this and other reasons several critics insist that we have no 'textus receptus ne varietur' - an agreed text. This is a common defect with the scriptures of other religions, but of far more importance given the 'orthodox' Sunni and Shia belief that the Arabic of the Koran that we now have is the final word of God for an and exactly as it was given from Heaven.

The Koran and 'higher criticism'

The Koran has not been subjected to the same critical attention as the Jewish and Christian scriptures partly because scholarly excellence (German in particular) in 'higher criticism' in the 19th century concentrated on the Jewish and Christian scriptures. So the Koran, hadith, and shariah law did not have the same priority. Moreover Orientalists of the highest quality were in short supply. The German Orientalist Theodor Nöldeke made a promising start with his '*Geschicte des Qorâns,* 1860 (*History of the Qur'an)*, and his attempt to put the Surahs in order of revelation, 1872. In 1934 Nöldeke's work was republished together with the work of his students Berlegstrasser, Schwally, and Pretz. This essential work is now available in English translation from Brill publishers (2013) and on line. (Some pages giving an idea of the work may be read on line). That this readily available work is not far better known is astonishing given the immense importance of Islam in today's world.

Apart from Nöldeke, the only other critic I recall hearing of when I was at LSE just after World War II was the Australian Arthur Jeffery whose work was then quite new, so I 'googled' him as I was writing this and got the first 60 pages of his '*Materials for the History of the Text of the Qur'an',* Brill, Leiden, 1937. Anyone interested in the scientific approach to the origins of the Koran could usefully read on line at least the first page of Jeffery's preface, mentioning as it does Professor Bergsträsser's work and his setting up of the Korankommission in Munich to follow up these studies by him and Professor Pretzl, his successor. The reader will maybe be surprised that Jeffery cites for study a number of pre-Uthmanic codices. Jeffery remarks in his preface just before World War II, 'this is a field which offers almost unbroken ground'. Even today, for example, there is pressing need need for further examination of the Koranic references to Judaism and Christianity for they raise the question: what did the revealer of the Koran know of these religions and their scriptures? This subject is of great potential importance for correct interpretation of the Koran. (This study is similar to work on the much debated question, 'what did Christ know?')

Recently I tried to buy a copy of Jeffery's book but I could not find one. It is out of print despite its obvious importance for Islamic scholarship. Dr. Mohammed Mohar Ali - a Ph.D. from the School of Oriental and African Studies (SOAS) - does though, give it a detailed rebuttal from his Muslim viewpoint, in his *'The Qur'an and the Orientalists', 2002* but this really needs to be read alongside Jeffery's work.

I find that the American John Wansborough, who spent most of his working life at SOAS did break some further ground with his *'Qur'anic Studies: Sources and Methods of Scriptural Interpretation', 1977*. The French Orientalist Roger Arnaldez also did valuable work before his death in 2001, notably discussing the Islamic doctrine of the utter transcendence of God - that He is above reason, and if so minded can change His very nature.

But this kind of higher criticism that has proved of such great value when applied to the Jewish and Christian scriptures, came up against the Muslim self-described 'orthodox' view that the Koran should not be subjected to such criticism. So Nasr Abu Zayd, at Egypt's Al Azhar University, was constrained to leave Egypt when he attempted to follow Wansborough's methodology. At least two Islamic scholars have been obliged to use pseudonyms (Ibn Warraq and Christoph Luxenberg) for fear of violence. And the media reported that the lecturer Suliman Bashear (a Druze) was 'defenestrated' from a second floor window at Nablus University in Palestine for teaching about Christoph Luxemberg's work - his wife though, denied this.

With the rise of Muslim extremist violence that I mentioned in Part I (e.g the Head of State of Iran, Ayatollah Khomenei's 1989 fatwa calling for the assassination of the writer Salman Rushdie and the 2005 violent international reaction to the Danish cartoons, not to speak of today's 'jihadists'), the objective study of the Koran, an exceptionally demanding discipline in itself, has become a life-threatening one.

Mohammed claimed to be the messenger of God to man, receiving God's messages through the medium of the Angel Gabriel (in Christianity, the angel who asked Mary the mother of Jesus if she would agree to bear the child). He never claimed to be other than a man. The collection of 'Hadith' (sayings and actions of Mohammed) put together by Al Bukhari in the 8th century, maybe less than hundred years after the death of the Prophet in 632 CE, is considered one the most reliable though it too, has been much criticised by Muslim scholars. Notably it contains a considerable number of hadith by Aisha (the child bride I mentioned who was the wife present in the Prophet's last days). In one 'Aisha then asked Allah's Apostle about the punishment of the grave. He said, "Yes, (there is) punishment in the grave." Aisha added, "After that I never saw Allah's Apostle but seeking refuge with Allah from the punishment in the grave in every prayer he prayed."' If a genuine hadith, it suggests that Mohammed, like many of us, was aware of sinning and sought the forgiveness of Allah.

Islam's founder was clearly a quite extraordinary man: prophet, ruler, lawgiver, and warrior. His 'quasi-idolisation' as 'the perfect man' developed later, and some Muslim theologians have pointed out that that can come close to deification which would be utterly opposed to the strict monotheist message of the Koran.

The Jewish and Christian Scriptures and the Koran

The four Christian Gospels, in contrast, were written solely as biographies of Jesus of Nazareth and to proclaim that he was "both true man and true God" - an 'incarnation' of the one God. The Koran V.19 condemns as blasphemers those who make that claim. But Jesus is nevertheless declared a 'righteous prophet' and Surah

V. 49 and 50 (again according to A. Yusuf Ali's translation) reads - it is God speaking - [49] "And in their (the Jews') footsteps we sent Jesus the son of Mary, confirming the Law that had come before him: We sent him the Gospel: therein was guidance and light, and confirmation of the Law that had come before him. A guidance and an admonition to those who fear God. [50] Let the people of the Gospel judge by what God hath revealed therein…"

So according to the Koran both the Jewish and the Christian scriptures were sent by God. Unfortunately a great many Muslims (some citing the Koran II.79, - 'woe to those who write the Book with their own hands and then say "this is from God" to traffic with it for a miserable price') believe that these scriptures have in some way been 'corrupted'.

Besides the Koran, the Tawrat (the Torah) is recognised although there is this suspicion of corruption. But here it is hard to make the case for corruption because, although no ancient codex exists, there is the Septuagint translation into Greek from the original Hebrew and Aramaic. The translation began in the 3rd century BCE and was completed by 132 BCE and there are contemporary and near contemporary references to it.

Besides the Tawrat, Islam also recognises the Zabur (the psalms of David). This can taken to mean only those psalms written by David, but no one knows which, if any, were. So many Muslims are put off reading these quite exceptional contributions to the world's religious literature.

As regards the Christian Gospels, Islam recognises the 'Injil' (the teaching of Jesus - but not the Gospels, which are also believed corrupted specifically in their claim of the divinity of Christ). Thus many Muslims are put off reading them. Yet the only early texts which relate the teaching of Jesus are those of the New Testament. The fact that the four Gospels and Paul's epistles were written to announce the divinity of Jesus need not stop anyone seeking to know his teachings from reading them. After all, these writers could perfectly well have been mistaken in their main intent: rejection of Christ's divinity is the position of all other religions and none, and is no reason for failing to use the gospels to discover Christ's teachings - or for stopping anyone else from doing so.

This common reluctance of Muslims to read the Judeo- Christian writings is regrettable because it is a major reason for so few Muslims even dipping into either the Old or the New Testament despite what the Koran says, and despite the Koran's naming of most of the Jewish prophets along with the Prophet Mohammed's claim to be the last of those prophets. This has led to grave misunderstandings and misconceptions which have contributed to our 21st century revival of past religious conflicts, so exacerbating the 'War on Terror' and Islamic extremism.

The Koran is a difficult read for many particularly because, in the Uthman canon, the Suras are not arranged in order of revelation but rather in order of decreasing length. This is which is why Nöldeke and others sought to arrange them in order of revelation. Even with the vowel markings in the modern Koran the meaning of the text is in several ambiguous or hard to understand, let alone interpret without assistance. To my mind (indeed to a number of qualified critics) the tone of the Koran is quite similar to much of the Old Testament - notably containing much about war, law and prescribed punishments (e.g. see Leviticus and Deuteronomy).

Those who don't know classical Arabic miss, Muslim friends tell me, the poetic element and the rhyming scheme of much of the Koran. Chanted in Arabic (the only authentic language - it is regarded as impossible properly to translate) much of the Koran can have an extraordinarily uplifting mystical effect on hearers much beyond the actual words. It is particularly prized by Sufi mystics. And even one of the harshest critics of Islam, the Christian historian, Philip Schaff, has this to say about the Koran: (it has) "many passages of poetic beauty, religious fervor, and wise counsel, but mixed with absurdities, bombast, unmeaning images, low sensuality."

Islam – a religion with political implications

I mentioned that to join Islam is easy (one only has to recite with sincerity the Shahada: "there is no god but God and Mohammed is the prophet of God" in the presence of two Muslims) but to leave is hard especially given that apostasy is indeed punished by death in some Islamic countries. And this although, as seen, the Koran does not require any punishment for it in this world. Most religions gather superstitions but Islam has gathered an accretion of legalism in the form of Sharia law, and the Sunnah ('way of life' of Sunni Muslims) which includes an unspecified number of the 'hadiths' (as mentioned many are dubious).

There are several versions of Shariah law dealing with almost every aspect of life. The imposition of some version of Shariah law on non-Muslims (and indeed on many Muslims) is perhaps the main cause of opposition to Islam. Famously, when Sharia law was imposed in the Sudan after the end of the Anglo-Egyptian Condominion in 1955 (I mentioned this in Part I) it led to such violent opposition, especially in the non-Muslim south, that after decades of war and appalling suffering, the country split in two with the emergence of South Sudan.

As Islam is the only religion that is feared in 'the West' it is 'politically correct' to give Islam a privileged position compared with other religions. A recent example: in the UK an applicant for a visa may be refused entry to the UK 'if the Secretary of State believes that the person would make Islamophobe (sic) statements', even with no intent to cause a breach of the peace. In the UK you can make propaganda against Christianity, or Hinduism etc. with impunity and get a visa for the UK specifically to do so. Given the way extreme Muslims do threaten to kill or actually kill those they consider blasphemers (like Salman Rushdie or the Danish Cartoonists) one can see that it is only prudent for a government to avoid offending such people: freedom of speech famously does not include the right to cry "fire" in a crowded theatre!

But surely the right to choose one's religion, allowed in many countries (and which for many may be seen as the most important 'right' of all) should allow serious people, who are not out to cause a breach of the peace, to visit Britain and give their reasons for criticising Islam? I think Eleanor Roosevelt (wife of the President) and the others who worked so hard for, and ultimately got, that UN Declaration of Human Rights would be much disappointed by the way 'Freedom of Religion' is disregarded even in the advanced democracies today!

It is of course well known that the Koran states (II.256) 'Let there be no compulsion in religion...' (because, A. Ali's gloss has it, 'religion depends on faith and will and these would be meaningless if adduced by force'). Unfortunately religious believers tend to 'cherry pick' and this injunction is not 'picked' by Islamic extremists when they force 'conversions' under pain of death.

So-called 'moderate' Muslims, those opposed to violence, are, as I've said, often blamed for failing to speak out against the extremists who have 'hi-jacked their religion' - forgetting that we in the 'West', even our governments, also dare not speak out for fear of reprisals. How much more vulnerable are Muslims, even those living in the 'West'!

Iranian Shia clerics repeatedly describe the United States, or 'the West' as a whole, as 'the Great Satan' and Shia and Sunni clerics often intemperately criticise Christianity and are often party to, or even instigators of, the persecution of Christians. But when Pope Benedict XVI, during a lecture at Regensberg University in his native Bavaria on 12 September 2006 dared quote a question about Islam asked by an emperor of the Byzantine empire - to which many today would like an answer - 'all hell broke loose' in the Western media condemning him out of hand.

It is worth quoting Benedict XVI in full: 'He [the Emperor Manuel II Palaeologus 1350-1425] addresses his interlocutor with a startling brusqueness, a brusqueness that we find unacceptable, on the central question about the relationship between religion and violence in general, saying: *"Show me just what Mohammed brought that was new, and there you will find things only evil and inhuman, such as his command to spread by the sword the faith he preached"*. The emperor, after having expressed himself so forcefully, goes on to explain in detail the reasons why spreading the faith through violence is something unreasonable. Violence is incompatible with the nature of God and the nature of the soul. "God", he says, "is not pleased by blood - and not acting reasonably is contrary to God's nature"'.

This did lead to some Islamic scholars inviting the Catholic Church to consider more deeply the relation between religion and violence. Here was an opportunity to tell us what Mohammed did bring which was new, but that, it seems went unanswered. Instead many Muslims showed the same violent intolerance that the Byzantine emperor had complained of! Many called for the Turkish government to withdraw an invitation to the pope for his forthcoming visit to Instanbul. As I say he was almost unanimously condemned by the Western media for merely quoting 'so provocative a remark'.

According to some figures there are 2.1bn Christians and 1.6bn Muslims in the world. But all such figures are highly suspect: a great many are counted as Christians or Muslims although they in fact have little to do with their respective religions except perhaps for marriage and burial. In my day in schools and the armed forces you were put down as 'C of E' unless you declared you were something else. Very many have Christian or Muslim names because they were given them - maybe by parents who also merely went along with the culture they themselves inherited. Such people commonly reject the extremist interpretations of their religions and, in the case of Muslims, attempts to make them accept Sharia law.

There are also many believers of both religions who follow high standards of personal conduct based on the best moral injunctions of their faiths while strongly opposing appeals to violence. There are in particular a great many Muslims whose fine morals very often put to shame what pass for ours in this 'Age of the Golden Calf'.

The Jews as a people

Religious violence is certainly not confined to extremist Islam. Take historic Christian persecution of the Jews. As I said, the Jewish Torah is accepted by both Christianity and Islam. In Christianity 'salvation comes from the Jews' and their sacred writings are integral to the religion. Christianity began as a sect of Judaism and so, like Judaism, enjoyed an exceptional protection under the Romans. It was only when it came to be regarded as a separate religion that Roman persecution of Christians began. In the Koran the Jews, with Christians, are 'peoples of the book'. That has not stopped Muslims as well as Christians from persecuting the Jewish people, in some cases mercilessly. It is hard to deny that such prejudice did much to prepare the ground for the 'holocaust'.

There are now believed to be only some 14 million Jews in the world - but their success is outstanding in every field of human endeavor. A poetic wit remarked: 'how odd of God to choose the Jews'. It is not odd at all if He wanted to choose the most exceptional race able to give the world monotheism through a long line of prophets, developing over a thousand odd years before Christ an ever clearer, more sophisticated understanding of the nature of God. This continued, Christians of all denominations agree, with the coming of Christ, his mother a Jew, and his 12 apostles, all Jews. We know about them because (three at least) of the four Gospels were written by Jews.

The derogatory image of 'the Jew' as exceptionally money minded, extortionate, and uncaring is far from the truth. There are of course, some very rich Jews who are no more caring than the average billionaire. But even among the extremely rich there are many who play a major role, even a leading role, in doing good works - the name of George Soros comes to mind (he was a contemporary of mine at the LSE though I never met him).

There are also a quite disproportionate number of Jews who excel in almost every calling. There is Jewish excellence in every field from Einstein in physics to today's Daniel Barenboim in music (with his part Israeli part Palestinian orchestra bringing much needed understanding between the two communities). We are talking of what today is not permitted - racial superiority - when putting Hitler's absurd obsession with 'Aryan' supremacy upside down. In Part I, I mentioned my own indebtedness to Jews and one Jewish charity in particular. And among my eminent Jewish teachers at LSE was, of course, Dr. Himmelweit who did so much to enable me to attempt this Part II!

It is astonishing that, out of over 850 Nobel prizes, 20% of them went to Jews although Jews number less than 0.2% of the world's population. When I was at university a recent study in racial intelligence suggested that there was no significant difference in average intelligence between the 'white', Indian, Chinese, and Japanese races. But that the Jews on an average had a small but statistically significantly higher intelligence. (Today, of course, it is politically incorrect to make such racial observations).

What the world owes to the Jews is a debt beyond measure. So immense that one finds it hard not to wonder whether there is something stemming from the 'Beyond' about all this!

Here we must stop and ask what explains the appalling treatment of the Jews, after they lost Roman protection, by Christianity and then later by Islam. It is fashionable today to suggest that the Jews were well treated under Islam but from the history it is hard to say which religion persecuted them most. A notable book on this is the French *'Juifs et Musulmans'*, (Le Point Références).

Evil and religion

We have seen that 'the man in the street' cannot be separated from the concept of good and evil. Indeed it is extremely difficult to deny the existence of a malign force which we recognise even within ourselves - although the fashion today is to regard anything involving things in any way 'spiritual' as 'unscientific' nonsense. But before our consciences get blunted by persisting in actions we regard as bad, we have an 'inbuilt' feeling that we should not do certain things. Indeed all cultures accept the reality of good and evil although not always agreeing what these terms mean.

If we accept the reality of evil, when then did it come to be? 'Before all ages?' Or at some point in time - with the advent of Man? Or from the beginning of creation? I suggest the latter, for examining evolution we can't help seeing an interaction of both good and evil. It is based on the food chain - a hierarchy of predation from animals to viruses that appears prima facie 'wrong'. But that produces a host of extraordinary, marvelous, and beautiful results - including of course ourselves: a continuation of this good and evil.

There is insistence on the reality of evil both in the Koran and the bible: there are many allusions to Iblis or Satan in the Koran. For example Surah LXXXV.6 (A. Yusuf Ali's translation) 'Verily Satan is an enemy to you: so treat him as an enemy. He only invites his adherents, that they may become Companions of the Blazing Fire'.

Two similar verses from St. John's gospel stand out - the first describes the 'Evil One' as Jesus termed him: 'Ye are of your father the devil, and the lusts of your father ye will do. He was a murderer from the beginning, and abode not in the truth, because there is no truth in him. When he speaketh a lie, he speaketh of his own: for he is a liar, and the father of it'. (KVJ Jn 8.44)

The second has mystical profundity: 'Hereafter I will not talk much with you: for the prince of this world cometh, and hath nothing in me'. (KJV Jn 14.30)

The Evil One, as the 'prince of this world', is thus given as the cause of God's will not being done in this world.

What do the assaults of evil mean for religion?

Once one accepts the reality of good and evil it is hard indeed not to see the Evil One as the mysterious enemy of God (and of Man). Hence his temptations of Christ. Indeed, all those who are leaders in religion must surely be priorities for the Evil One - popes, saints and bishops down to priests and religious, Orthodox patriarchs and their clergy - and equally Ayatollahs, Muslim clergy and Mohammed himself. Neither Dalai Lamas nor Buddhist monks, nor Hindu Holy men are free from his assault, nor theologians - and nor, down at the bottom of the religious ladder, the ordinary believer. Atheists and agnostics are also no exception for they too can be got do the bidding of the Evil One - perhaps the more easily as they don't believe in his existence. In this way religions get subverted and secular organs led astray. The Prince of this World, the murderer and liar, is out to corrupt all that is good. Even Hitler's *Mein Kampf* mentions God - clearly referring to the Evil One.

With this in mind the all-pervading mass of gross evils, whether or not done in the name of God, are hardly a surprise. Today we see international terrorism in the name of Islam and harsh intolerant Islamic theocracies, just as less than a century ago Japan's Shinto, and the atheism of Fascism and Nazism led to the torture and deaths of many millions. We also see 'far right' Christians using Christ's name to promote aggressive wars.

Particularly prevalent today is how religion has been subverted by leaders of supposedly Christian sects promising earthly rewards for their followers - provided the followers fill their coffers. Very many seeking some relief from insecurity and actual suffering, fall for this - and their pastors can then buy a prestige car, or even a private plane. As I say this is the age of the Golden Calf - and religion can be big business! Rather similarly Islamic extremists offer a worldly paradise for their suicide-vest martyrs.

And this is nothing new - for quite early on Christianity began its appalling persecution the Jews although 'salvation comes from the Jews' from Christ down. In its beginnings Christianity owed everything to Judaism which its founder claimed he had come to complete: the coming of the Messiah having long been foretold. During his life, the gospels relate, Jesus had gained many Jewish followers and they were one reason why Christianity was able to spread throughout much of the Roman empire because pockets of Jews were residents in so many of its vast territories. Exceptionally - when the Empire's official religion was polytheism - they were permitted to practice their religion and Christianity began as a recognized Jewish sect. Roman persecutions of Christianity only began when it ceased to be regarded as such.

Despite that, no sooner did Christianity become the established religion than persecution of the Jews began. It is hard to think of any greater perversion of the religion Christ founded than the persecution of the Jews by both Catholics (notably by the Inquisition) and Orthodox (the Russian pogroms). All too many protestants have had a hand in this too. And as I say, many have suggested that if it hadn't been for this 'grooming' over the centuries, Hitler would have had much difficulty in carrying out his genocide, the Shoah.

The idea that the Jews as a people were, or even still are, guilty of deicide is quite extraordinary when one reads the gospels - for over and again there are references to Christ's followers: a striking example is his welcome to Jerusalem. It was the Jewish religious authorities who rejected him and gave him over to the Romans to execute. The crowd crying for the release of Barrabas, not Jesus, more likely appear to have been incited by the those authorities rather than demonstrating overnight fickleness. The phrase 'for fear of the Jews' thrice repeated in St. John's gospel when the author himself was a Jew clearly refers only to the Jewish authorities. Indeed internal evidence suggests that the Jewish writer of the fourth gospel may himself have been a young rabbi.

Isaac Watts (b. 1674) put in verse the teaching that, for the Christian, neither the Jewish authorities nor the Romans are to blame as much as are Christians who sin:-

> In vain I blame the Roman bands,
> And the more spiteful Jews.
> 'Twere you, my sins, my cruel sins,
> His chief tormentors were.

The second, related, evil for which the Catholic church is responsible was, of course, the Inquisition - the policy of enforcing religious belief - utterly contrary to Jesus's way of teaching by persuasion and example, not force. For the same reason the seven (or nine by some counts) Crusades, the results of which are still with us today, surely need to be counted as an evil - as St. Francis understood in his historic attempt at negotiation with the Sultan during the Fifth Crusade.

And then there are the deeply distressing reports of priestly sexual abuse of children - behaviour alas far from confined to Catholic priests: here again the power of evil to undermine the church through its servants is astonishing. But then don't we all know how hard it is to resist evil carefully targeted to our weak points?

When I consider the history of the monotheistic religions I remember the remark attributed to Kaiser Wilhelm II during a visit to the trenches in World War I: "Ich habe es nicht gewünscht!" (I didn't want this!). Looking at much of what is done 'in the name of God' by some of those who claim to be Christians or Muslims, I feel both Jesus and Mohammed might agree with that sentiment! The Jewish scriptures warn: 'Thou shalt not take my name in vain.'

COMING TO A CONCLUSION

I began by observing the extremity of suffering in the world and noting that, were the environment not so harsh and hostile, and had nature not thrown down the gauntlet, there could be nothing of what we admire most: heroism, self-sacrifice, kindness, generosity - and perhaps most importantly the mutation of massive evil into the most sublime good. So in a most profound way evil is at the very heart of creation and 'sin behoveth'. We saw too, that not only can we not deny the reality of good and evil but that there is, to my mind, conclusive evidence of a 'beyond' - a spiritual category that cannot be ignored and which the greatest art takes us to its frontier.

We had a look at the world's principal religions. A quick look, but even so we saw much of great value in them. We saw that all of them are intolerant to some degree and that this is perhaps the main thing that puts many people off religion. But we also saw that atheism can be at least - or even more - devastating.

We started with the dying god - even self-immolating god - which Frazer considered of such significance that he opens his Golden Bough with this myth. And we find ourselves meeting this Jungian 'archetype' in Jesus of Nazareth who offers the 'Way' to God. Perhaps one could say, in our age of information technology, that Jesus is Man's 'interface' (though that's far too cold a word) with God the unknowable. An 'interface' not just for his followers but for all mankind.

He makes that astounding claim: (KJV John 14.9) 'Jesus saith unto him, have I been so long time with you, and yet hast though not known me, Philip? He that that hath seen me hath seen the Father; and how sayest thou then, shew us the Father? This surely must mean that in his personality, in his behaviour we can get closer to the personality and behaviour of God the Father.

So what do we find? That Jesus, and hence the Father, though firm and judgmental, is kind and merciful. We see too, that he is ever ready to correct Man where he has got scripture wrong - thus his revelations about himself to the Jews and to mankind as a whole are progressive, not set in stone.

And, it seems, most importantly, that Jesus accepts extreme suffering as inseparable from the creation in time and that this acceptance is the only way to break through to the 'beyond'. So it seems that God himself accepts all suffering and, mystery of mysteries, accepts too, separation from himself: that cry of Jesus 'with a loud voice saying, "Eloi, Eloi, lama sabachthani?" That is to say, my God, my God, why hast thou forsaken me?' (Matthew 27.46, also Mark 15.34)

Evidently the ultimate desolation of separation from God is known to the ultimately unknowable God whom the poet described as "I am and I am not and ever will be." (Of course Christian theologians often endeavour to soften this by explaining that Jesus was merely quoting the twenty second psalm which ends in an affirmation of God. But this cry, which hardly encourages belief in Christ's divinity and which has been used to claim he is a fraud, is cited in the original Aramaic by two evangelists who wrote their Gospels in koine Greek, the lingua franca in the east of the Roman empire - and indeed among the educated in its west too. So clearly these words were regarded by both evangelists as of outstanding importance.

Peace

All this brings me back to the sombre 'il se pourrait que la Vérité soit triste' - it could be that the Truth itself is sad. In this world one seems obliged to agree that this is so. But perhaps not in the 'Beyond' of what we consider to be the 'beyond'. And there, we are told lies peace. One of the greatest works of art is, of course, Johann Sebastian Bach's Great Mass in B minor - it ends with the haunting 'Dona nobis pacem' - give us peace. ('Dona eis pacem', grant them peace, is the prayer for the dead). Muslims regard peace as the greatest boon that can be conferred on the Prophet: when mentioning his name one interjects "peace be on him" (often shortened when written to PBOH). It does appear that 'Beyond the beyond' lies peace. Nirvana as well as nothingness ('the blown out candle' I cited), is among other things 'perfect peace of mind.'

A couple of quotations of the primacy of peace:

Oscar Wilde, written in his last years:

> Come down, O Christ, and help me…
> Nay, peace I shall behold, before the night,
> The feet of brass, the robe more white than flame,
> The wounded hands, the weary human face.

Sarojini Naidu, the Indian poetess:

'In salutation to the eternal peace:

> O inmost wine of living ecstasy! O intimate essence of eternity!'

Nietzsche instead uses the word 'serenity' in one of the best known of his poems:

> Heiterkeit, güldene, komm!
> du des Todes
> heimlichster, süßester Vorgenuß!

(Serenity, golden, come! Thou, death's most secret, most sweet, foretaste! (Genuß = delight, hence a foretaste of delight.)

And of course, the resurrected Christ's words - his 'legacy' you might say - in John 14.27 (KJV): "Peace I leave with you, my peace I give unto you: not as the world giveth, give I unto you. Let not your heart be troubled, neither let it be afraid".

If Christ does indeed show us the 'Father' in the sense of the 'Beyond of the beyond' then he reconciles us to the difficulty of the commandment in Deuteronomy 6.5 (KJV) - 'And thou shalt love the LORD thy God with all thine heart, and with all thy soul, and with all thy might.' You might say that this is the most difficult of all the commandments for two reasons - the cruel nature of the world and so our readiness to blame its creator, and the fact that love cannot be commanded.

Jesus though, repeats that command saying: 'Thou shalt love the Lord thy God with all thy heart, and with all thy soul, and with all thy mind. This is the first and great commandment. And the second is like unto it, Thou shalt love thy neighbour as thyself. On these two commandments hang all the law and the prophets'. (Matthew 2.37 sequ. KJV)

Now it is different. We are reconciled to the Deuteronomy command if we accept Jesus's divinity and see the Father in Jesus. For then it is hard not to love the Father, so easy is it to love the Gospels' depiction of Jesus. And of equal importance - a kind of bonus, is the second sentence. For it encourages us do what is in short supply in this world, to love - or if that's too hard, at least respect, our fellow men.

Christ's claim to be both 'the son of God' and 'the son of Man' ('true God and true Man') is the most striking affirmation of the brotherhood of man on which many religions insist. For according to the gospels, it is the Spirit of God which fructified his virgin mother's parthenogenesis (the Koran too, affirms this Sura III.45-48) and his mother's humanity which made him also Son of Man. So when he teaches us to pray to 'our Father' he is speaking as 'one of us' - we are his brothers and sisters.

Is this not the nearest glimpse we are likely to get of the 'Beyond of the beyond'?

MY SEARCH ENDS

So my particular search ended in 1948 with the Catholic Church - were I Russian it would be with the Orthodox church - though I subsequently wandered far away for a number of years. For me the phenomenon of Jesus and the astonishing story surrounding him which not even the supreme genius of a Shakespeare could have devised, seemed to fit in so intimately both with the inmost nature of the material world and with the 'Beyond' as I personally had found them. That's despite the sometimes appalling behaviour of those in charge of these institutions. But "follow the light, not the lantern" as the Devon parson said when accused of too much fox-hunting!

I started off as a Stoic - 'grin and bear it' (which I later found can be far from easy!) But I came to consider that 'grin and bear it' as one must, needs to be accompanied by unceasing effort to recognise good on one's own particular path and to encourage it; and to recognise too, the evil on that path and to shun it or attempt to mitigate it. Success is not important: in the merciless Soviet 'archipelago' of prison camps a message was found: 'It does not matter if flowers are not seen, many are those that grow away from the paths to be seen only by God'.

I do believe too, that outward actions are unimportant compared with one's inner intent. For example, I really don't see that it matters whether one's food is Kosher or Halal - far more important, surely, is how you avoid evil and strive to do good. Even without those dietary concerns, I find that far from easy, particularly when besieged as we are with temptations.

Suffering and prayer

As I have explained, to my mind what is essential is to be certain you are praying to the good God and not to the Evil One. This is more difficult than one might suppose! For, in radio terms, the 'frequency' of the Evil One is close to the 'frequency' of God - and the Evil one's message comes out louder than 'the still small voice of God'.

Washing your hands before prayer is fine symbolically, but isn't it far more important to wash your heart! A heart full of anger, jealousy, revenge, and cruelty links straightway to the Evil One! And how many religious leaders, when praying, are in fact addressing that Evil One? Popes are supposedly elected by the Spirit of God - but what if some cardinals are more concerned with political power, who are they praying to? Can that not explain the election of bad popes such as the notorious Borgia pope Alexander VI in 1492? And, in our day, to whom did the fatwa-wielding Ayatollah Khomeini pray? More pertinently: to whom do we pray? To the good God or to the Evil One?

Francis Galton asks whether prayer 'works' in his *'Statistical Enquiries Into the Efficacy of Prayer'* (1872) making, inter alia, the intriguing point that British sovereigns lived less long on average than their subjects despite the host of prayers for their longevity raised in so many churches! But it does not need a statistician to point out that for many years many millions prayed their hearts out begging to be relieved either Hitler or of Stalin - and in many cases, of both: all to no avail. Stalin lived to the ripe old age of 74 and Hitler brought about his own Götterdämmerung - a quietus with a single bullet: a death longed for, but denied so many of his victims. How many millions each of these two atheists managed to kill is still debated.

Of course Galton and those who follow him are only talking of petitionary prayer all of which must be preceded by 'if it is thy will' - a condition making statistics unsuitable, for (as the Vietnamese saying goes) "who can know the will of Heaven?" Indeed the Lord's prayer "thy Will be done on earth as it is in heaven" suggests that all too often it is not.

Many cultures recognise this, and speaking of the future say 'God willing', 'Deo volente' (often written 'D.V.') and of course 'Inchallah'. My favorite is Croatian: 'Ako Bog da' (If God gives it). Russian 'с божьей помощью' is slightly different 'with God's help'. The Chinese is 天意 (tian yi - if Heaven so intends').

But there are other forms of prayer. The efficacy of expiatory prayer in particular can even on occasion be observed, for here the believer humbles himself, recognizes his sins, and begs forgiveness. Indeed frequent prayer to the good, the Holy One, often marks not just the behaviour but the face of the one who prays, appearing to reflect from that 'Beyond the beyond' an unmistakable holiness. I have only seen that twice - once in face of an Anglican monk, and once in the face of a Buddhist who had survived the Khmer Rouge horrors. (A Cambodian friend took me to meet his father as though inviting me to view stigmata - so in awe was he of this manifestation). These are people who don't have 'faith', they 'know'. The question is: is such 'knowing' just a cruel quirk of the human brain or does it come from an apprehension of the Beyond? For me it is the latter.

The Holy

As if the differences between the world's religions isn't enough, even among Catholics there's disagreement between those who regard the Tridentine Mass (promulgated in 1570 by Pope Pius V as correctly embodying historic practice) as par excellence the evocation of Holiness, and those who have become accustomed to the 'new Mass' (promulgated by Pope Paul VI in 1969) which led to a period of ill-disciplined experiment.

That led Pope Benedict XVI to lament: 'Many young people seek holiness but do not find it in the Catholic Church'. He did much (cruelly dubbed God's Rotweiler!) to encourage a rediscovery of the holiness that had inspired so many of the greatest musicians (including the protestant J. S. Bach) to compose Masses which had won world renown for expressing the concept of the Holy far beyond the confines of Roman Catholicism.

When it was known that Paul VI was about to suppress the Tridentine Mass, fifty six of some of the most prominent figures in Britain, many of them non-Catholics, begged him not to. The Pope gave limited permission for the 'old' Mass to be celebrated in England and Wales - this came to be known as the 'Agatha Christie indult' for she was one of the signatories. Benedict XVI widened this to authorise the use of the traditional Mass throughout the world. During his pontificate he did much to restore discipline and revive greater respect for the Holy - that ineffable 'Beyond the beyond' which awakens such overwhelming awe when we sense it. (I well understand that at 86 he resigned, finding the burden too great! He had though prepared the way for the new broom of Pope Francis to take on the burden of reform after a restoration of discipline).

When Paul VI's reforms threatened to end Gregorian chant it was the world's musical community that revived it: the chant rose to the 'top of the pops' and now continues to be performed by enthusiasts in many countries for its unique spiritual depth. It has returned to the Mass in some places.

Some - the privileged - have an awareness of the Holy in their everyday lives. And of course the purpose of the Mass is to bring Holiness to those who attend - and most particularly to those who take communion. But the recipient has of course to prepare him or herself through an attempt at utter humility, utter contrition, and utter forgiveness in order to receive, albeit briefly, that peace of the spirit which is so immensely valued in so many religions.

Envoi

Boris Pasternak puts in one verse what the fortunate few can feel as they look back on their lives - that all that they have experienced and the good and the evil that they have done, fit together like a jigsaw puzzle:

> Кончаясь в больничной постели,
> Я чувствую рук твоих жар.
> Ты держишь меня, как изделье,
> И прячешь, как перстень, в футляр».

(Ending in a hospital bed, I feel the heat of Your hands, You hold me like an artefact, and hide me, like a ring in its case).

But for those who have had to bear atrocious cruelty or unremitting suffering from Man or nature with no sense of purpose we can only hope they will enjoy that 'glorious inheritance' of which Edward Browne speaks.

The great T'ang dynasty poet Li Po (Li Bai) sums up:

> You ask me why I dwell in the green mountain
> I smile and do not reply for my heart is at peace.
> The peach blossom follows the flowing water
> To another world beyond the world of men.

My last word comes from Jonathan Swift (with whom I feel a 'remarkable affinity!'*):

On the death of Dr. Swift –
'His fire is out, his wit decay'd,
His fancy sunk, his muse a jade.
I'll have him throw away his pen;
But there's no talking to some men.

*The Diplomatic Platypus (Patrick Barrington)

I had a duck-billed platypus when I was up at Trinity,
With whom I soon discovered a remarkable affinity.
He used to live in lodgings with myself and Arthur Purvis,
And we all went up together for the Diplomatic Service.

POSTSCRIPT: 15 August 2015 (written after the endorsements)

A year after I finished writing this book in July 2014 I find that events have gone very much as I suggested - or feared – they would: no amendment to the text is needed. But, for this second edition, I believe it useful to look at how the more important themes I dealt with have worked out over the past year.

Climate Destabilisation
For the better certainly, has been a quite remarkable and rapidly growing worldwide awareness of the existential threat of climate destabilisation - or 'global warming'. The 'deniers' (Republicans; the world's billionaire oligarchs; mighty corporations - including coal magnates like the Koch brothers; and rent-a-scientists employed by these) can no longer so easily persuade us that human activity has nothing to do with such 'warming'. Not just in 'the West' now, but in a great many other countries many more quite ordinary people are expressing real fears for the future of their children. Increasingly it is not just the old industrialised countries that are getting the blame for putting humanity at risk, but also developing countries like China and India for blindly following suite.

Only three months away now from the much heralded United Nations Climate Change Conference in Paris (Le Bourget) November 30-11 December, only a very limited step forward towards limiting carbon emissions is expected. It seems unlikely that there will be agreement on substantially increasing government investment in research and development and actual projects to reduce or replace carbon emissions. For example, there is little likelihood of agreement to impose duties on ships proportionate to the amount of pollution they caused in transit, on aviation fuel to reduce aircraft pollution, or on haulage to limit the distance from origin to point of sale.

Nor does it look as if there will be an international agreement to impose 'Tobin' type taxes on financial transactions. Yet such taxes, easy to collect, would substantially reduce pollution and at the same time, some experts calculate, would provide those funds needed for research and development into alternative energy. That would do much to fund the start of a new energy era based on the sun and renewables - even making it possible to dispense with nuclear energy with its unresolved problem of neutralising spent material.

It has become increasingly clear that waste too, needs to be tackled with far more determination, for example appointing waste 'czars' as cabinet ministers. Governments press ahead with damaging 'austerity' when the elimination of waste would go far to cover their deficits. Across the board austerity remains the order of the day, although some items need greatly increased investment while others can be eliminated altogether. Our leaders seem unable to accept the finding of economists that overall austerity is counter-productive in times of recession. It is most fortunate that the US Federal Reserve staved off disaster with qualitative easing (the 'creation of money').

Despite protests, new Trade Agreements are in the pipeline greatly limiting sovereign decisions to ban the import of wasteful and dangerous products - for example cigarettes which are now being foisted on the 'third world' overloading their nascent health services as sales in the 'West' fall. Indeed such trade agreements, by protecting Intellectual Property Rights, can do great harm by denying states the legal right to protect their peoples from noxious or unacceptably expensive imports. For example 'Big Pharma' can more easily maintain high prices limiting the use of far cheaper generic pharmaceuticals now available in the 'Second World'. And the spread of highly controversial scientific 'advances' like Monsanto genetic modifications, becomes all but impossible to combat.

As hoped, China, people and government, have woken up - linking appalling pollution with the threat to climate. But vested Party interests have still to be overcome. The Agreement between President Barack Obama's US and President Xi's Jinping's China to limit pollution is most welcome news, except that Obama will be gone by January 2017 and, if the Republicans have their way, the Agreement risks being nullified. If so, Xi, who has his own opposition to overcome and depends on the US taking action, will be hard put to it to enforce severe anti-pollution measures.

All in all, we are still a long way from that 'Hitler across the channel moment' that I suggest will be needed before truly determined and effective international action is taken on climate.

Over-population
It is good news that Pope Francis has recently come on board in defence of the planet. But, like so many other converts to the urgency of protecting it from its human passengers, he fails to see that climate change (which worries him) and over-population form that 'double helix' - the twin pronged existential threat to the very existence of mankind (and indeed of most other creatures). The scriptural divine exhortation to 'be fruitful and multiply', made over two millennia ago in very different circumstances, still determines much religious teaching - and the practices of half the world. Religious dogma - particularly Catholic (despite the supremacy of 'conscience') and Muslim - still has a stranglehold making it difficult and sometimes

impossible to provide information and ensure contraceptives in the many countries that need it most. Yet reversing population growth in the Indian sub-continent, much of Africa, Indonesia – and the USA, will determine mankind's future.

While much progress has been made in awakening the peoples of the world to Climate Change, in the last year there's been very little progress in awakening them and their governments to over-population and its inescapable link to climate. No international 'Over Population Conference' is envisaged to follow the Climate Conference. It is not just religious sensitivity that militates against one - at least as important is racial sensitivity: 'they (the white race) want fewer of us'. This perception inhibits leaders in these countries from putting across that a couple of well-educated children can far better ensure a sufficiency in your old age than several living in poverty like you.

There is not even a coordinated international programme for the education of women - the one proven way of limiting childbirth voluntarily. Yet even limited funds can have considerable effect: just one example, it has been shown that simply providing free contraceptives can reduce pregnancies by more than a quarter.

The July 2015 UN population report no longer speaks of a possible descending curve, but of a rise to 9.7 billion by 2050 - as foreseen by Professor Stephen Emmott in his book 'Ten Billion', (which was poo-poohed for exaggeration and pessimism).

Despite sterling work by many NGOs (like Population Matters) and the Bill and Melinda Gates Foundation there is still far too little acceptance that over-population and climate change are inseparable. And too many politicians still believe that the greater the population, the more powerful the state. In a word, that 'eureka moment' when drastic action is seen as inescapable is further off with over-population than with Climate Change.

More Climate/Over-population Related Issues

Water shortages, rising sea levels, and mass migration are three more challenges that can be addressed only by drastic action to counter climate change and over-population. Shrinking glaciers in the Himalayas, the Andes and even the Alps, together with the melting of Arctic and Antarctic ice threaten the survival of civilisation as we know it. And we are already experiencing the beginning of mass migration due to both climate and population. All this threatens to reverse the success of the last few decades in freeing tens of millions from abject poverty.

It is though, often hard to distinguish those in search of a more affluent lifestyle from those fleeing wars and civil wars (as in the Middle East) and harsh incompetent governments (as in Central America). Except in the Middle East, much could be done with international cooperation to persuade, even oblige, the worst governments to improve their act, thus reducing the pressure to flee. And in the Middle East, governments - like the US and the UK - which have been responsible for military interventions which have caused, directly or indirectly, large numbers of civilian casualties and economic ruin, could do a great deal more to support migrants and resettle refugees, especially those in the many crowded and under-resourced camps.

There is already unwanted migration to under-populated areas, for example in the Russian Far East bordering China. Migration within economic areas, often overburdening already densely populated areas - for example in the EU, China, and the US - can only be met with incentives to stay put. This often requires an economic plan encouraging investment.

The Threat from Nuclear Weapons
Besides Climate Change and Overpopulation there is that third existential threat to mankind - nuclear weapons. In the last year the emphasis has been on limiting their proliferation. After much bargaining all the members of the Security Council US, China, Russia, and France plus Germany) have negotiated with Iran a Joint Comprehensive Plan Of Action (JCPOA) designed to prevent more states from acquiring nuclear weapons - so discouraging other states (like Saudi Arabia) from obtaining them. Senate Republicans joined by some Democrats strongly oppose this Plan (as does Israel) so it could be that the US, which led the negotiations, will be the one member of the Security Council dropping out. Yet as Mikhael Gorbachev (who with President Reagan did so much to limit nuclear arms) remarked, in an interview in Der Spiegel of 7 August 2015, "If we cannot get rid of them sooner or later they will be used". But there is that link to conventional weapons: no nuclear weapons would leave the world at the mercy of overwhelming American conventional forces. Détente with Russia would lead Congress to start questioning the continued need for such immense expense. Major disarmament would then be largely determined by China's policies.

That the major powers are strongly opposed to the proliferation of nuclear weapons is immensely important, but there is an equal need to prevent their accidental detonation - a matter of great concern given the very large number in existence. Even the US has had some troubling incidents. We do not know about Britain, France, and China. Because of internal lack of security Pakistan's weapons could fall into other hands than the government's. And we know nothing at all about the precautions taken by the Israelis in their very small country, or by inscrutable North Korea - events there in the past year have been alarming as the new 'Supreme Leader' attempts to consolidate power.

EU Russia relations

The greatest obstacle to meeting the challenge of those three existential threats is the lack of international determination to take the drastic actions required. This has to come from the world's leaders because, unlike the case of Climate Change, there is little media and popular pressure to see comparatively petty national concerns in proportion. Indeed the media often finds it expedient to magnify them to gain attention. Throughout Part I of 'A Valedictory Despatch' a leitmotif is the imperative need remove the present unnecessary obstacles to close EU/Russia relations as a prerequisite for moving on from our times of confrontation to an era of cooperation utterly essential for facing up to the existential threats - and much else that needs to be done in the world. With the United States now in decline and presently all but ungovernable it is hard for it to provide the leadership expected of by far the richest and most powerful country. And a rising China is beset with its own grave problems of governance. Europe though - EU and Russia together - has the combined enlightened self-interest and the international weight to start leading the world towards far greater international cooperation.

But in the Ukraine the already deplorable situation I described in May 2014, has, as I feared descended into a disastrous civil war freezing hopes for Ukraine becoming a beneficent hyphen joining the East and West of Europe instead of today's bone of contention. Blame attaches to both the EU and Russia - but even more to the resurgent US neo-conservatives who exploited the crisis in their goal of an American 'unipolar' world at the expense of both the EU and

Russia. As I write both Russia and the EU are re-assessing their Ukraine policies. The House of Lords has produced this year's 10 February scathing report on Foreign Office (and so EU) policies towards the Ukraine and Russia, and, for professionals concerned with the Ukraine, Professor Sakwa of Kent University has produced a monumental work impartially criticising the EU, Russia, and the US.

The need to reassess too, the EU/US relationship

Since World War II and the Cold War, Europe has accepted US leadership - the wealth brought by capitalism and the security provided by NATO. But the collapse of the Soviet Union and the success of the EU as the world's leading trading bloc means that the EU has to find a more equal relationship with the US. This is now urgent because of the dominance of a new uncompromising Republican party linked to those resurrected neo-conservatives, the Murdoch media, and the 'Atlanticists', which is paralysing US policy and preventing the US from continuing to provide the leadership the world needs. These interests are making the United States act as a spoiler - not just in the Ukraine, but over climate, jihadism, the proliferation of nuclear weapons, and much else.

Still scarcely noticed by the 'Western' media, Secretary of State Kerry has met Russian Foreign Minister Lavrov at least five times so far this year discussing 'subjects of mutual concern' - meetings that have the backing not only of President Obama but of President Putin in whose Sochi dacha the first one was held. It is just possible that the two are considering how the Ukraine can become that hyphen between the EU and Russia which is in the national interests of both Russia and the US. So, in the absence of an EU foreign policy of its own, it may be that a US/Russia rapprochement over the Ukraine will remove the road block that severely limits 'Western' cooperation with Russia on all those other subjects of such importance.

As Obama's presidency draws to a close he could yet do much to correct what outstanding diplomat, US Ambassador Chas Freeman Junior, has called the US's 'diplomacy deficit' in a speech entitled 'Too quick on the Draw. Militarism and the malpractice of diplomacy in America'.

But hopes of enlightened leadership of the US are in the balance for, hanging over the world scene, is the possibility of a Republican President with a Republican House, Senate, and Supreme Court, giving him the authority that President Obama never had. EU governments and almost all others (except Israel's) must be rooting for a Democratic President like present front runner Mrs. Clinton despite her deeply flawed tenancy of the State Department. They will all have to work with whoever wins, no matter how unsuitable for the world's top political office - even the contentious Donald Trump (net worth $4 - 9 bn?) who, some claim, is out to buy the presidency. In the US it is easier for a politician with no real experience of government, even in opposition, to win the highest office without the necessary qualifications, than it is in most other advanced countries.

The precedent set by the US
The decline of the US has caused increasing concern because it is no longer seen as a worthy example for aspiring countries to follow. Socially it lags behind other advanced countries in the provision of national health services (although President Obama, despite determined Republican opposition, has done much to improve this), the high proportion of citizens incarcerated, inadequate public education, the prevalence of weapons, the subordination of policy to wealth, and, of course, deep-seated racism. In the past months further revelations of widespread torture by the

CIA during the G. W. Bush presidency show a hypocritical approach to human rights. While much can be excused during the Cold War confrontation with the USSR, US military intervention since in a number of countries accompanied by the neo-conservative drive to create that 'Unipolar' world through political, often clandestine, 'special political action', combine to present the US as the country many others consider the most to be feared. All in all the US, despite its many virtues, can hardly be seen as setting a good precedent for other great powers to follow. We now see Russia reacting with military force to avoid US hegemony and China acting unilaterally to carve out its claim to the pie. Nevertheless there are many indications that these powers and others are open to discussions - so great is today's need for cooperation.

Race in the US
Sadly what I said last year about deeply ingrained, though increasingly covert, racial prejudice in the US has been glaringly revealed by a number of events, notably the riots in Ferguson Missouri. Polls suggest that racial tensions have got worse since the election of President Obama from whom 'blacks' hoped much but whose expectations he could not meet for he too, is hobbled by his race. So 'blacks' have suffered more than others from the 2007 financial fiasco. This deterioration has further diminished Obama's authority and aided the cause of right wing extremists - greatly helping them in gaining control of both House and Senate. Polls in both the North and the South show how widespread is 'white' refusal ever to vote for any 'black'. This prejudice goes far to explain why President Obama did not get the overwhelming mandate widely expected after the, one can even say calamitous, 8 year tenure of G. W. Bush. It is a tragedy for the world that so outstanding a politician, so anxious to promote peace, happened not to be 'white'.

Democracy and Politicians
The US Supreme Court, with its Citizens United decision (2010), has made it possible for the billionaire 'oligarchs' and the great corporations to funnel vast sums into US elections - probably enough to determine the outcome especially when they control the lion's share of the media. The mountainous gap between the very rich and the middle classes, let alone the poor continues to widen not just in the US and the UK but in much of the rest of the world. With such gross inequality distorting democracy, increasing poverty is now more widely seen to be grotesque and unsustainable - a time-bomb threatening the social order in many countries.

In the UK, the failure over the past hundred years to redress Scotland's grievance at being short changed by the Union, led to the referendum in 2014 which gave the Scots, but not the Welsh or the English, a vote on the continued existence of the United Kingdom of all three. The vote was far closer than expected and has been followed by the General Election in May 2015, where the Scottish Nationalists won all but three of Scotland's 59 parliamentary seats. Prime Minister Cameron, in favour of the Union, came all too close to ending it. He has now undertaken to hold by 2017 a further referendum, this time on Britain's membership of the European Union of which, like the UK union, he is in favour. As things are, it is quite likely that this vote will go against him. This would not only lead to an isolationist Britain but to another challenge to the Union should Scotland vote in favour of remaining a member as now seems likely, and England and Wales vote against.

There has been no improvement in finding politicians who really understand the problems they are elected to resolve - leaders who are more than 'pollingticians' and lead, instead of following, the public. But, for the reasons I gave, the truly able rarely choose politics. Few are the politicians we can rely on as much as most other professionals. The already widespread distrust of politicians has increased, largely because it is ever more apparent that they don't properly know their job. The ideology of 'democracy before all else' has recently led to calls for the UK's 'unrepresentative' House of Lords to be abolished in favour of a popularly elected chamber. That would deny us the impressive expertise among members of the House of Lords for examining the legislation of the elected House of Commons where so many members are ignorant of the issues before them.

In the United States there is much talk of the need for reform, particularly of the Senate - but the Republican Majority seeks to keep such institutions as the filibuster because it can stop legislation, however necessary, that it does not like (e.g. the confirmation of Administration appointees and the ratification of treaties even if in the true interests of the United States). It took 167 days for the Senate to confirm Loretta Lynch, an African American, as Attorney General of the US. This exemplifies the Republicans' determination to paralyse the US government in order to hamstring President Obama. But there is no indication that their policies would change under a 'white' - even a Republican - President.

Islam
In the world at large the cause of democracy is being harmed by the growing threat of Muslim extremism and resultant anti-terrorist measures. As I have said, an ideology like that of ISIS, is hard to defeat militarily - it must be understood before it can be effectively countered. But in the past year there were still few attempts to do this, although many studies of the Koran, Hadith etc. are readily available. There is also much useful research showing why in the 'West' young Muslims feel so alienated living in virtual ghettoes -

the more so since the banking crisis - that they become converts to so murderous a regime as ISIS.

Making use of such work is essential when 'mainstream' or 'moderate' Islam has been infiltrated by elements of Wahabism exported worldwide from Saudi Arabia. It would help in countering today's extremism to rediscover the work on the Koran of the Korankomission (Munich 1938). Nothing though, can replace Muslim 'higher criticism' of Islam - but, as I said, Muslim theologians often work at the risk of their lives. A major problem is that adoption by many in 'mainstream' Islam of Wahabist beliefs and practices. For example, many Muslim clerics trained in seminaries funded by Saudi Arabia do not preach tolerance towards those not of their brand of Islam, let alone towards atheists, agnostics, and those of another religion. All too often we hear that Muslim prison chaplains - in France and the UK especially - do nothing to counter, and may even assist, radicalisation. Far too little is being done to promote tolerance and to demonstrate that it is perfectly possible for people of different religions to live together in harmony and mutual respect as it once was in Lebanon, provided only that violence is renounced.

And the long-standing Shia (Iran) and Sunni (Saudi Arabia) divide, exacerbated by US/UK military action, has brought both the faithful and their governments to theological quarrels and armed action similar to the Wars of Religion in 17th century Europe.

<u>Israel and Palestine</u>
Hardly had I 'put down my pen' last year than Israel launched 'Operation Protective Edge' bombing the Hamas controlled Gaza strip in retaliation for Gaza based rockets landing in Israel - an action that many, even in the US, considered disproportionate. The legacy of Adolf Hitler and

his massive genocide of the Jews continues to poison today's international relations with suffering and death - such that the treatment of the Palestinians remains the grievance par excellence not only of Palestinians but of Muslims worldwide. The Netanyahu government's policies of ever more alienating the Palestinians with further encroachments of Israeli settlers in 'Palestinian' territories and in once Arab Jerusalem with no remedial policies designed to mitigate the distress of the occupation, has lost much sympathy for Israel. More seriously it has stoked up the 'jihadi' extremism of ISIS and its murderous 'anti-semitism'.

The 'Quartet' of the UN, the US, the EU, and Russia set up to promote peace between Israel and the Palestinians was again side-lined in 2014 - no progress proved possible given the US's support for Israel no matter how misguided its policies. President G. W. Bush's nomination of former British Prime Minister Tony Blair (who led the UK's invasion of Iraq) as the 'Quartet's' Special Envoy did much to discredit it in the eyes of the Palestinians - and many others: he didn't resign until 27 May 2015.

This total failure once again to address the chronic Israel/Palestine crisis had had the disastrous consequence of reviving 'anti-semitism' because of widespread failure on the part of both individuals and even governments to distinguish between Jews and Israel's government. ISIS has exploited this, and the way Palestinian Israeli relations are left to fester despite worldwide concern at the Gaza bombings. Together with the revelations of US torture and other gross human rights abuses, this has provided a toxic mixture for gaining recruits in much of Europe - even for suicide bombers. Before murdering them, ISIS emphasises the link by dressing up its victims in orange jump suits similar to those worn in US detention in Guantanamo Bay.

Preventive measures to avoid the mounting cost of illness

Governments are slowly responding to the need to limit the rapidly mounting cost of health services - in 'the West' efforts to limit cigarette smoking continue to make an impact, but still next to nothing is being done to counter tobacco companies heartless drive to increase smoking in countries that have no means to treat the victims of their products. Little too, is being done to limit the scourge of obesity which originally afflicted the affluent but which is now spreading worldwide like a pandemic even among the deprived.

The surprising failure of the World Health Organisation - or anyone else for that matter except Médecins Sans Frontières - to act immediately when the ebola epidemic broke out in south eastern Guinea has served to remind the world of the need for instant reaction to deal with epidemics in our new overpopulated and interconnected world.

MY OVERALL CONCLUSION

The world continues to 'sleep-walk' towards the point of no return

I think this 2015 'summer term' report suffices to make the point that the world's leaders are running out of time to cry 'wakey wakey'. Governments lack true leadership - the most able so often go into banking, science, or technology not politics. And, in 'The West' at least, it's a 'celebrity culture', one of 'follow my leader' where celebrities are the role models. We are constantly enjoined to listen to this week's 'top of the pops', see the latest block-buster film, read the last best-seller, go to the currently most fashionable resort - and so on. We hear little of what is new which all too often gets suppressed when it does not fit in not only with the fashion of the day, but also with the political preconceptions of the few who control most of the media. Thinking that does not conform to their agenda all too often simply gets overlooked. We are fobbed off with the ephemera of scandals, sport and celebrities, deliberately leaving little space for in depth coverage of the world scene. In this strictly homogenous environment it is difficult indeed to make the case for the crying need for a fresh approach to relations with Russia, let alone to the world crisis.

In large measure this is due to a persistent failure of those in power and those with influence to practice that number one rule in diplomacy - as in much else in life - to examine every problem from the viewpoint of your adversary.

We need to look anew at our predicament. Then we would get the fresh thinking we need to start resolving the issues that stand in the way of global cooperation. We would see that Ukraine, Israel/Palestine, Syria, and ISIS are just a few of the obstacles requiring cooperation to remove or contain. That would bring us nearer to countries' armed forces becoming the means of policing the world as was the intention when the UN was set up - part of the solution and not part of the problem as they are today.

The challenge for the growing number of us who are aware of the immense dangers we all face, is to win attention for our message, urgent though it is: at present it risks going unheard in the lemming-like rush to 'follow my leader' in everything and in our subservience to what we are fed by governments, who are so often fed by the media.

'Globalisation' despite its glaring faults, has though, brought us a great step forward thanks to the ever growing realisation of governments and peoples that we live in a 'global village' where there's no room for 'street fights' threatening the good of the whole, let alone for 'bullies on the block' making us live in fear. There has now to be a lot more 'give' as well as 'take' if the world is to move in time from a 'default' of confrontation to that era of cooperation indispensable for ensuring a future for all of us.

As regards the 'beyond': the past year has witnessed ever-greater devotion to our worship of the 'Golden Calf' which enables immense wealth to buy almost everything - even decisions which endanger the very existence of Mankind. The most immediate problem of all - and perhaps the most difficult one to resolve - is somehow to ensure that money does not talk so loudly that the world cannot hear itself speak!

Printed in Great Britain
by Amazon